Military Reform

Military Reform
An Uneven History and an Uncertain Future

Winslow T. Wheeler and Lawrence J. Korb

Stanford Security Studies
an Imprint of Stanford University Press
Stanford, California

Stanford University Press
Stanford, California

First published in paperback in 2009.

Military Reform: A Reference Handbook, by Winslow T. Wheeler and Lawrence J. Korb, was originally published in hard cover by Praeger Security International, http://www.greenwood.com/psi/, an imprint of Greenwood Publishing Group, Inc., Westport, CT. Copyright © 2007 by Winslow T. Wheeler and Lawrence J. Korb. This paperback edition by arrangement with Greenwood Publishing Group, Inc. All rights reserved.

Printed and bound by CPI Group (UK) Ltd, Croydon, CR0 4YY

Library of Congress Cataloging-in-Publication Data
Wheeler, Winslow T.
  Military reform : an uneven history and an uncertain future / Winslow T. Wheeler and Lawrence J. Korb.
      p. cm.
  Originally published: Westport, CT : Praeger Security International, 2007.
  Includes bibliographical references and index.
  ISBN 978-0-8047-6163-5 (pbk. : alk. paper)
  ISBN: 978-0-275-99349-8 (cl: alk.paper)
  1. United States—Armed Forces—Reorganization. 2. United States. Dept. of Defense—Reorganization. 3. United States—Military policy. 4. United States—Armed Forces—Appropriations and expenditures. 5. United States. Congress.
  I. Korb, Lawrence J., 1939– II. Title.
  UA23.W4135   2009
  355.6′8670973—dc22   2008051014

Meaningful military reform requires more than mere words; it requires vision, action, and persistence. For that reason this book it dedicated the memory of Philip A. Straus, Sr., and to Philip A. Straus, Jr., the founder of the Straus Military Reform Project of the Center for Defense Information in Washington, DC.

Winslow T. Wheeler
Lawrence J. Korb

Contents

Preface

WHO NEEDS REFORM?

America whipped Saddam Hussein in Operation Desert Storm in 1991 when he was pushed out of Kuwait and again in 2003 when President Bush invaded Iraq and deposed the Iraqi dictator. Members of Congress in the House Armed Services Committee have called America's armed forces the best in the world; some even say the best in history.

What is there to reform? If it's not broken, don't fix it, as the saying goes.

Inspected a little more closely, the facts tell a very different story. America did quickly beat Iraq's armed forces in 1991 and in the early phases of the 2003 invasion, but those victories were both incomplete and against forces best characterized as grossly incompetent—the "most incompetent in the world" according to one authoritative source.[1]

Even those seemingly easy victories revealed serious, fundamental, pervasive problems to those with the expertise to see them. One retired Army colonel, a decorated veteran of Operation Desert Storm in the 1991 Persian Gulf War observed, "In war, military strategy is supposed to reduce the probability of armed conflict, to persuade those who might fight not to fight, and when necessary, to win at the least cost in lives and treasure in the shortest possible time. In Iraq, America's top generals achieved the opposite outcome."[2] As we shall see later in this publication, the victories against Iraq showed American armed forces making serious errors that truncated the first victory in 1991 and made the second campaign in 2003 a necessity. In 2003, the Army's most senior commanders again made fundamental tactical, operational, and strategic errors and in one situation virtually panicked even when faced with an enemy that was virtually immobilized by its own incompetence.

American soldiers, sailors, marines, and airmen and women are rightly honored by the American public for their courage in Iraq and Afghanistan, but the quality at the combat unit level cannot compensate for inadequate senior leadership at the higher levels. At the civilian end of things, in the Pentagon that is supposed to arm and train and otherwise support the military services, the situation is, if anything, worse. By objective measures that we will discuss later, the Pentagon is very probably the worst managed major agency of the U.S. federal government.

To demonstrate, the Department of Defense (DoD) has been shrinking our armed forces, while making their equipment—on average—older and doing so at increasing cost—and doing so for decades. Today, the U.S. defense budget is higher, in real terms, than at any time since the end of World War II, and we have fewer ground combat divisions, tactical and strategic air wings, and naval combatants than at any time since 1946. While some believe this force shrinkage is compensated by the extraordinarily high quality of modern American equipment, others ask why America lost to such crudely equipped forces as the Viet Cong and the underequipped North Vietnamese in the Indochina War and appears to be repeating the experience in Iraq and Afghanistan thirty years later.

As for a symmetrical conventional opponent, such as China (for those who perceive there a military threat that must be thwarted), modern "high tech" American equipment may turn out to be something less than its extraordinarily high cost would seem to imply. For example, in 2006, two aviation experts with decades of practical experience, one of them an internationally recognized combat aviation designer, assessed the Air Force's much vaunted F-22 fighter and deemed it a "war loser, not a war winner."[3]

Today, the Pentagon's leadership is exceedingly bureaucratic, risk averse, professionally ill-trained, and badly unsuited to the complex tasks of directing military forces in war and supporting them with cost-effective equipment, adequate logistics, and properly trained replacement units.

It is difficult, even inconceivable for some to contemplate, that America's armed forces and the Pentagon that purports to support them are in a crisis:

- Our military and civilian national security leadership lacks skill and especially real character, mostly at the very top;
- Both political parties are ignoring the problems, and—mostly but not always—work long hours to make the problems worse.
- If at some point in the future, America encounters a competent foe, the outcome is by no means assured. Indeed, against poorly trained and equipped irrelgulars in Iraq and Afghanistan, American armed forces have manifestly failed to prevail and by some accounts have already lost.

And so, if we need to fix things, should we all pull together and increase the defense budget to provide the equipment our personnel need and to recruit and retain the people and leaders we need? Almost certainly, more money will make the problem worse. Constant increases over the decades have made that clear.

Then what about frugality? Can't we force the Pentagon to make better decisions by culling out the wasteful, ineffective weapons, and by forcing managers to think before they spend. We might save some money, but it will simply mean a smaller defense budget not a better force, and if the cuts are applied with as little thought as the increases, the result will be the worst of both worlds.

Then, surely, it's the people. Throw the rascals out and replaced them with the right people. The right people? We have been churning through different Pentagon leaders both civilian and military for decades. Result? Nothing changes; in fact, the problems deepen.

Indeed, for decades—you might even argue for two centuries—special committees, blue ribbon commissions, and other extraordinarily convocations of specialists have been convened and have made recommendation after recommendation to fix identified problems in the DoD, and before that in the Departments of War and the Navy. With only a few exceptions, that recurring work brought forth no meaningful improvement and sometimes made things worse.

If so much has failed, what will succeed?

That is what this book is about. We will take you, the reader, through an analysis of past and contemporary history to identify the problems in America's defenses, past efforts—both constructive and not—to fix those problems, where we are now, and where we could go if we were to glean the constructive lessons of the past.

Many of those constructive lessons are made available to us from a unique group of individuals, contemporaneously known in the 1970s and 1980s as the "military reformers" who not only thought through the problems and produced a coherent set of recommendations but who also proved the validity of their ideas, both in the bowels of the Pentagon's gigantic and seemingly impenetrable bureaucracy and on the modern battlefield.

Since the emergence of the so-called Military Reform Movement in the Pentagon and Congress in the 1970s and 1980s, many others have emerged dubbing themselves advocates of "military reform." Today, it is a free lance operation. Sadly, however, it is all too commonly not a set of coherent ideas drawn on the lessons of the past and the present, but instead is ideas that may sound theoretically reasonable but which on close inspection are riddled with either loopholes or a misreading of history's empirical lessons, or no reading of them at all. The result is—again—a deepening of our problems.

The two authors of this book have spent decades working in the Congress, the Pentagon, and the Washington, DC, think-tank community. Coauthor Wheeler was a direct participant in military reform movement in the Pentagon and Congress in the 1980s and provides a never-before-published history of the events inside Congress and the Pentagon surrounding that era's military reformers, and subsequent events. These first-hand observations provide an understanding of how the American government operates that is simply not available from academics and national defense "experts" who have observed but not participated in the events they write about. Wheeler previously described other elements of his thirty-one-year career in Congress, working for politicians from both political parties, and in the Government Accountability Office (GAO) in his book, *The Wastrels of Defense* about Congress and national security.

The other coauthor, Lawrence Korb, has been analyzing military issues for some thirty-five years from both inside and outside government and has written extensively about the civilian and military leaders of the Pentagon, national security strategy, and defense budget issues. His most recent work, published in January 2006, is *Restoring Military Power: A Progressive Quadrennial Defense Review*.

This book starts with coauthor Wheeler's brief history, from the Continental Congress forward, of the more salient examples of commissions, blue ribbon panels, and special congressional committees to change, if not "reform," business as usual in the Continental Army, the Departments of War and the Navy, and the Department of Defense. Both high points (the "Truman Commission" of World War II and the Fitzhugh Blue Ribbon Commission of 1971) and low points (the Committee on the Conduct of the War during the Civil War and the "anti-reformist" Packard Blue Ribbon Commission of 1986) are described, demonstrating various reform and antireform behaviors.

In Chapters 2 and 3, Wheeler presents a description of his experiences in government during the rise and fall of the military reform movement of the 1980s. The focus is on Congress and its interaction with the Pentagon and the press. Here we observe the individuals, and their thoughts, who made up the core of the military reform movement. We also encounter, in their public and nonpublic activities, the numerous prominent members of Congress who embraced the thinking of the core military reformers—for at least a short period—and who gave the political impetus to the reform movement, thereby slicing up business as usual in the Pentagon—in the words of one of its top managers—"into itty bitty pieces." The reformers key political allies included such members of Congress as Senators Gary Hart, David Pryor, Nancy Kassebaum, Charles Grassley, and Representatives Newt Gingrich, Barbara Boxer, Tom Ridge, and many more.

Discussion here will illuminate how, after the initial success of the "Congressional Military Reform Caucus," the primary interests of politicians came into fundamental conflict with the principal goals of military reform, illustrating the difficulty of imposing reform on the Pentagon from institutions that are both external and primarily political.

While the congressional aspect of the military reform movement ultimately proved a flop, the discussion of some of the reforms of this period demonstrate how reform need not be a political exercise but can indeed come from inside the Pentagon: accomplishments such as the design and production of several highly successful combat aircraft, a new military doctrine for how to win in combat against any opponent—now partially adopted by the Army and more fully embraced by the Marine Corps—and a set of concepts to redesign the management of the DoD.

In Chapters 4 and 5, coauthor Korb describes the Pentagon's attempts to repair itself in the 1990s to adjust to the end of the cold war. Chapter 4 will discuss the four major reviews by the Pentagon of itself and three independent panels commissioned by the Congress to review the Pentagon. Korb will also discuss the attempts by the Bush administration and Secretary of Defense Donald Rumsfeld to "transform" the military through both information technology and long-range war-fighting capacity—which together have been called a "revolution in military affairs."

In Chapter 6, Wheeler presents a brief analysis of Operations Desert Storm in 1991 and Iraqi Freedom in 2003, and the aftermath conflict, which typifies "4th Generation Warfare" (4GW). The discussion demonstrates the only partial success of the military reforms of the 1970s and 1980s and the absence of meaningful reform in the 1990s. The chapter closes with a summary of three essays, presented as Appendices A, B, and C, that address how elements of the U.S. military services still clearly need reform, how soldiers and officers can be educated to more clearly think and operate under the stress of combat (i.e., where they failed to do so in Operation Iraqi Freedom in 2003) and, finally, why the management of the Pentagon needs fundamental change and how to inculcate the needed reforms— all drawing on the lessons of this and the forgoing chapters.

The book will close with Wheeler's and Korb's conclusions about the status of meaningful military reform in America and an articulation in concise terms of what military reform truly is and is not.

Notes

1. See further discussion in Chapter 6.
2. See "Fire the Generals" in Appendix I of this book, p.1.
3. See Pierre Sprey and James Stevenson, "The F-22, Not What We Were Hoping For," *Janes Defense Weekly*, September 20, 2006, p. 23.

CHAPTER 1

A Mixed History in Congress and the Executive Branch

Winslow T. Wheeler

Understanding military reform, especially distinguishing changes that are either ineffective or counterproductive from meaningful constructive changes, can be assisted by a brief review of history.

There are many lessons, some of them extremely important and instructive, from other nations—especially the extraordinary reforms in Germany in the middle of the nineteenth century and, again, in the 1920s and 1930s; however, the history of the German experience has been described and analyzed at length in other excellent volumes, such as in Trevor N. Dupuy's *A Genius for War: The German Army and the General Staff, 1807–1945*. This volume focuses on the American experience. Furthermore, the spotlight applied in this and the next two chapters shall in large part, but not exclusively, be on Congress. Much has also already been written on the American military reforms stemming from the executive branch in the early twentieth century, many of them interpretations of the German model. There is also no attempt here to retread that well-covered territory. Indeed, some convincingly argue that the time has arrived—if not long passed—to move beyond those early industrial era American reforms that came out of the executive branch. For example, an excellent discussion not only of the importance of the reforms of Elihu Root and Emory Upton but also of their limited utility for the twenty-first century can be found in *The Path to Victory: America's Army and the Revolution in Human Affairs* by Donald Vandergriff. Perceiving and employing personnel as if they were interchangeable cogs in a machine, those turn of the century and subsequent "reforms" impeded the formation of personal bonds between people in military units ("unit cohesion") and can be regarded as an example of a step backward, rather than forward. *Fighting Power* by Martin Van Creveld presents a classic case of how the American industrial mentality toward personnel issues made U.S. ground combat units less effective than their German counterparts in World War II.

But why focus largely on Congress? Presidents, secretaries of defense, generals and admirals, captains of industry, and even some senators and representatives themselves, frequently disparage Congress' interjecting itself into the internal affairs of the Pentagon. Their pique is sometimes inspired by the obvious political biases of congressional inquisitors or by their often clearly evident, very shallow knowledge of the issues. Many congressional interventions have certainly been dominated by political bias, and some have been excellent examples of how *not* to conduct reform. There are even some examples that generated some form of help to an American enemy, perhaps in the form of information, and many certainly did generate friction in the conduct of U.S. national security policy.

As an example of the former, it is notable that hearings of the House and Senate Armed Services and Appropriations Committees are routinely printed and made available to the public. While they do not contain classified information, they are certainly reviewed by America's friends and enemies alike for the information they contain. The author recalls an incident in the 1970s when it was learned that representatives of the embassy of the Soviet Union asked for and received hearing volumes from the Senate Armed Services Committee. Thereafter, the document clerk in that committee was advised not to comply with requests from the Soviet embassy, which presumably continued to receive the unclassified, public volumes through intermediaries. Today, with the Internet, collection of such material is surely inestimably easier.

The criticism of Congress notwithstanding, if it did not interject itself into the inner workings of the Pentagon—including the biased and incompetent activities and even those that somehow unintentionally aided America's enemies— American soldiers would have little worth fighting for. Without the power vested in Congress to conduct "oversight" for itself and citizens to learn the goings on inside the executive branch, American liberties would wither on the vine. The right of the Congress to scrutinize the executive branch and to act on its findings is fundamental to the separation and balance of powers in the American system of government and to our democracy. Because Congress is an essential component of decision making in the American government, and because Congress can undo virtually any reform—for better or for worse—initiated by the executive branch for the American armed forces, military reform in the American context cannot be understood without understanding the congressional experience.

The Congress' interventions have usually emerged from two sources. There have been many investigations emerging from Congress itself, and there have been numerous commissions, usually appointed by presidents, to study and make recommendations on how to address problems in the Department of Defense (DoD), and its predecessors—the Departments of War and the Navy. For either internally or externally initiated exercises, recommendations for specific legislative actions usually result, and it falls to Congress to act on them, however it may choose.

Congress' self-initiated investigations have been the more predominant form; however, during the cold war, presidentially appointed "Blue Ribbon" commissions became a common method for the executive branch to attempt either legitimate efforts at reform or to preempt unwanted congressional initiatives. Even in those cases of executive initiative, however, it has fallen to Congress to study the suggestions before legislative action is taken. Thus, it is the investigatory power, and how well or poorly it is exercised, that is key.

Historian Arthur M. Schlesinger, Jr., observed that "The Founding Fathers supposed that the Legislative branch would play its part in preserving the balance of the Constitution through its possession of three vital powers: the power to authorize war; the power of the purse; and the power of investigation."[1] And again, "While the conventional assumption is that the strength of legislative bodies lies in the power to legislate, a respectable tradition has long argued that it lies as much or more in the power to investigate. The investigative power may indeed be the sharpest legislative weapon against Executive aggrandizement."[2]

In addition, the Constitution charges Congress, not the president, to "raise and support armies," "provide and maintain a navy," and "make rules for the government and regulation of the land and naval forces." Those responsibilities cannot be carried out unless Congress can determine what is actually occurring in the armed forces and if its laws and appropriations have the effect intended.

As we shall see, Congress' involvement in managing the armed forces has sometimes been a real benefit, an effect sometimes achieved over the bitter protests of presidents, secretaries of defense, and generals and admirals, which is discussed in subsequent chapters. At other times, Congress' intrusion into national security has been a real nightmare. The more useful question is not whether Congress has the right, even the responsibility, to interject itself into the internal affairs of the American military establishment. It is better to ask what factors make Congress' self-interjection positive and effective, and under what circumstances does the effect become ineffective or negative?

These are timely questions. American armed forces are struggling to defeat an insurgency in Iraq, and the "global war on terror" (GWOT)—more recently retitled the "Long War"—remains at best undecided. Since September 11, 2001, a transition in the nature of warfare has become apparent. An evolution away from the direct engagement of opposing conventional military units—roughly symmetrical in their fundamental nature—such as in World War II or that was anticipated against the Soviet Union during the cold war toward the insurgency-based type of confrontation today occurring in Iraq and Afghanistan that has been taking place. Such confrontation between uniformed, national military units and opposing ununiformed, irregular units is sometimes called "Fourth Generation Warfare" because the nature of the confrontation has developed new attributes from previous and very frequent examples of "asymmetric" or "guerrilla" warfare.[3]

It is not obvious that the leadership of American armed forces in the Pentagon, the White House, and Congress have acknowledged and responded to the evolving change in the nature of warfare in the twenty-first century in an appropriate manner. Thus, making all too apparent the need for contemporary military reform.

An appraisal of Congress' previous reviews of the Pentagon (and its predecessor organizations) might reveal not just what does and does not constitute military reform, but might give us some useful guidance for how Congress can best conduct its oversight responsibilities to respond to the evolving nature of warfare now and in the future. Put another way, if we forget the past, we are bound to repeat its mistakes. In Congress' case, there is a rich legacy to draw from.

Two Early Bumps in the Road

As early as 1782, the Continental Congress directed its Superintendent of Finance, Robert Morris, to investigate "fraud, negligence or waste of public property" in Revolutionary War purchasing.[4] Morris recommended competitive bidding for contracts to reduce overpayments to war profiteers. This was the first of two centuries of attempts to impose change, in this case the free market system, on U.S. defense purchasing. Morris' own example illustrates one way these reforms can fail: he was not only the first in American government to recommend competition to solve the problem of war profiteering; he was also the first of many to ignore his own or others' recommendations and proceed to award contracts to personal friends without the bother of competing them against others.[5] As one modern advocate of reforms has noted, this has been a recurring pattern. In the case of some reforms, it may be that laws and regulations are fitting and appropriate, but the people charged to enforce or implement them are not doing their job.[6]

The American Civil War spawned Congress' Joint Committee on the Conduct of the War. It was formed on December 9, 1861, after the Union defeat in the first battle of Bull Run (Manassas). Dominated by radical Republicans, the committee lectured President Lincoln, his cabinet, and Union commanders on questions of battle strategy, the loyalty of specific citizens, and—of course—contracting. Like Robert Morris, the Joint Committee had its favorites in the private sector, but it primarily busied itself second guessing Lincoln and attempting to take over the direction of the war effort. Its machinations were so counterproductive that Confederate commander Robert E. Lee commented that "the Committee was worth about two divisions of Confederate troops."[7]

After the Joint Committee and the Civil War were long gone, Congress continued to thrust itself into military affairs, but the nature and depth of the involvement was never again the same. Reviled by historians, the Joint Committee came to be frequently invoked as an example of how Congress should not behave and of subject areas, such as battle strategy, it should stay out of.[8]

Not So Looney Leftists

Another congressional venture historians generally love to hate was the Special Senate Committee Investigating the Munitions Industry formed in 1934 under the leadership of progressive Republican Senator Gerald Prentice Nye of North Dakota. The Nye "munitions committee" investigated the defense industry's role in World War I and its contemporary practices in the 1930s. It and its chairman came up with some lively findings, including:

> I understand the morning after the (appropriation) bill went through, every east coast [ship]yard had its representatives in Washington with their tongues hanging out and all teeth showing ready to fight for their share of the plunder, and the only thing that kept the west coast yards from being here was the fact that they couldn't come bodily by telegraph.

> ... the munitions companies insisted throughout on their pound of flesh in the form of high profits for their production and did not let their patriotism stand in the way of their "duty as trustees" to the stockholders.

> If there was no collusion, there was sympathetic understanding among the big companies of each others' desires. If there were no conversations about bidding among them, there was telepathy.[9]

The Nye committee has been trashed by most historians as conspiratorial, leftist, and isolationist.[10] It concluded World War I was caused by a scheme of arms manufacturers seeking profit; it recommended nationalization of major portions of the arms industry, and its protagonists were highly active in isolationist causes before World War II.[11] Its ultimate reputation was not helped by the identity of one of its legal assistants, Mr. Alger Hiss, the same individual on whom junior Senator Richard Nixon (R, Calif.) cut his anticommunist teeth by exposing as a communist agent in the late 1940s.[12]

And yet the Nye committee articulated findings that today most accept as conventional wisdom—except that the committee's mode of expression was perhaps more lively than the self-consciously elegant Washington, DC, way of saying things in the modern age. It found intimate and unhealthy cooperation between the military services and defense industry. For example,

> ... the Navy League of the United States has solicited and accepted contributions from steamship companies ... on the ground that these would profit from a large navy ... [and] together with various Navy officials have engaged in political activity looking toward the defeat of congressmen unfavorable to Navy League and Navy views.

> ... any close association between munitions and supply companies on the one hand and the service departments on the other hand ... constitutes an unhealthy alliance in that it brings into being a self-interested political power which operates in the name of patriotism and satisfies interests which are, in large part, purely selfish.[13]

And, it found Congress involved, all too closely.

> The committee notes the claims of the Washington representative of United
> Drydocks in 1934 that he could get a bill through Congress for $50,000
> [in bribes], and that 'there is no virtue in being quixotic at this stage.' It
> notes the placing of Congressmen on certain committees at the request of the
> shipbuilders. It notes the claim to have helped the Navy on certain bills and
> to have elected Members to the House Rules Committee.[14]

The Nye committee deserves credit for the insight to identify and criticize what President Eisenhower described three decades later as the "military-industrial complex" and what others later renamed the "military-industrial-congressional complex." Chairman Nye and his committee contributed significantly to an understanding of the American defense industry and its relationship with the military services and Congress; the committee was just a bit ahead of its time for most to accept the characterization.

Solid Citizen

Senator Harry S. Truman (D, Mo.) made himself famous during World War II—before he was elected as President Franklin D. Roosevelt's last vice president. In May 1940, before America's entry into the war, FDR requested an urgent appropriation of $1.2 billion, and then another for $5 billion in June, to pay for America's prewar build up. By December 1, 1940, over $10 billion had been appropriated for new defense contracts.[15] As the money flooded into the War and Navy departments (in 1940, this $10 billion equated to over $180 billion in 2006 dollars),[16] Senator Truman took it upon himself to visit military facilities on the east coast to check on how well the money was being spent.

Unlike today's virtually regal congressional arrivals at military bases and defense production facilities, Truman drove in his personal car (an "old dodge") and was not accompanied by a gaggle of military escorts to arrange his meals and lodging, make pleasant conversation, and otherwise ensure life was comfortable for him. He did not even take along his own staff. He was utterly alone; unless asked, he did not even identify himself as a U.S. senator.[17]

Life for congressional travelers to military facilities today is a little different. In the late 1990s, despite my not being a member of Congress and my working for the only partially relevant Senate Budget Committee, when I traveled to military facilities, I was routinely escorted by a field grade officer who made all hotel and meal reservations, arranged layover's in not so spartan cities like Las Vegas, posted parking spaces on military bases with placards reserving the space for me personally, and generally made sure no unpleasantness occurred. For actual members of Congress, there are order of magnitude upgrades in all respects: military VIP transports (not commercial aircraft), top of the line hotel accommodations, dinner with any and all local military dignitaries, longer and better layovers in cities like Paris, and multiple reserved parking places for the multiple limousines in use. Occasionally wives and almost always staff go along too. All at taxpayer expense.

Truman was horrified at what he found in his lonely travel: huge waste everywhere, corporations making giant profits with no incentive from competition to be more efficient, and military and government officials doing nothing about any of it. He met privately with President Roosevelt to seek action, but finding no interest in the White House to do so, he delivered a speech in the Senate chamber. He proposed a special committee to look into the issues further.[18]

The Senate voted in March 1941 to establish a Special Committee to Investigate the National Defense, with Truman as chairman.[19] The committee's mandate was broad: to study defense contracts, how they were awarded, their geographic distribution, their effects on labor and migration, the performance of and benefits to contractors, and "such other matters as the committee deems appropriate."[20]

Once the committee was established, Truman time and again invested his own time and energy to understand the issues. He studied the history of predecessor committees, especially the Civil War's Joint Committee and the Nye committee. Understanding some of the lessons of the past and committing himself to hard work, performed by both himself and an independent staff, he put himself on a path to expose corruption, inefficiency, and waste, and to make appropriate recommendations to Congress and the President.

The Truman commission ultimately held 432 public and 300 executive (closed door) hearings, conducted hundreds of field trips, and wrote 51 reports. The coverage of the work included aluminum shortages; military construction waste; inefficient production of rubber, aircraft, landing barges, farm machinery, and ships; corporate war profiteering; fake inspections of steel plate; the comparative merits of rayon or cotton tire cord; the financing of one U.S. Senator's swimming pool and payments to another from defense contractors; and—remarkably for a Democratic-controlled committee—inefficiency induced by labor unions.[21]

Truman, his committee, and its staff earned a reputation for independence, professionalism, and fairness. The chairman did not badger witnesses, and he eschewed topics beyond what he regarded as his proper reach, such as military strategy and tactics; he even kept the committee out of the politically sensitive domain of the location of defense facilities.

However, where it did investigate, the committee pulled few punches. Its reports were full of Trumanesque barbs; for example

> ... most American pursuit planes were inferior to the best British and the best German pursuit planes ... Scarcely a week now goes by without some prominent flyer returning to this country and asking why we can't give the boys better pursuit planes ... the Army should ... give less attention to concocting publicity blurbs intended to emphasize that poor planes are better than none at all.[22]

So called competitive bidding has often been used as a cover for collusive bidding on Government contracts.[23]

... we should not attempt mass production of an entirely new model incorporating a whole series of major improvements until after it has been tested and proved.[24]

The committee particularly condemns advertising such as the Curtis Helldiver advertising which was intended to give the public the erroneous impression that the Curtis Helldiver was the world's finest dive-bomber and was making a substantial contribution to the war effort when the fact is that no usable plane has yet been produced. ... The fact that such advertising was approved by the Navy and was based upon a speech of a Navy Admiral does not justify it.[25]

The overall impact of these and many more bare knuckle assertions was not to undermine public confidence in the war effort but to raise it: citizens gained the impression that their interests were being protected and the selfish and the inept were being rooted out. There were also material results. One source estimated the committee was responsible for $15 billion in savings, or in modern dollars $270 billion.[26] Others assert that figure is exaggerated, but the savings were "enormous and unprecedented" nonetheless.[27] Truman also helped to write legislation to reorganize the nation's war production from a confused hodge-podge of overlapping agencies to a more efficient War Production Board that was an element in the hugely prolific American war production effort of World War II.

On the other hand, Senator Truman's work was not without some compromises. He did not look into racial discrimination in hiring at defense plants and segregation in the military services. As president, he would later work for civil rights, and he did desegregate the armed forces, but during the war he backed off. In addition, although many have given him credit for keeping necessary military secrets, he actually did spill the beans about the ultrasensitive Manhattan (atomic bomb) Project in a letter to a former senator.[28] For this indiscretion, he was lucky; word about the Manhattan Project never leaked out beyond his senate pal.

Truman nonetheless deserves much credit. Perhaps the greatest compliment is from the other politicians who followed trying to imitate him.

Cheap Imitator

Lyndon Johnson came to the Senate from Texas in 1948. One of his biographers, Robert Caro, tells in his remarkable volume describing Johnson's Senate career (*Master of the Senate*) of the junior senator's very conscious effort to imitate Truman.[29]

Using his mentor, the powerful Senator Richard Russell (D, Ga.), Johnson managed an appointment to chair a Special Preparedness Investigating Subcommittee of the Senate Armed Services Committee. He promised the full committee Chairman, Democrat Millard Tydings of Maryland, that he would report only to the chairman, and he promised then President Truman that he would not criticize the administration. However, once he had the job, Johnson rushed to leak his reports to the press before any other member had a chance to read them, and he criticized as lax and wasteful the administration he improperly promised to treat with kid gloves.

Over two years, Johnson issued forty-three reports on subjects reminiscent of the Truman Committee on rubber, nickel, tin, and wool defense production and many other subjects. Johnson's and his subcommittee's reports, however, were frequently junk. His first report, released just three weeks after the subcommittee was formed, was a recycling of a report already completed by another subcommittee Johnson controlled. It contained nothing new or noteworthy, but by virtue of the high octane verbiage applied to the report by Johnson and his press staff and thanks to journalists eager for easy headlines, it reached the front pages of newspapers all over the country.[30]

Author Robert Caro portrays the second report on industrial commodities as "scant on specifics; [but] … long on phraseology that was grist for a reporter's typewriter or for a headline writer."[31] Other reports were rewritten papers from the staff of the Library of Congress or others.[32] In fact, as Caro describes it, virtually all of the reports from Johnson's Special Preparedness Subcommittee were either overhyped nonentities or simply stolen from other sources, sometimes both.

Johnson made it clear he cared little about the substance of the issues but greatly about acquiring recognition for himself.[33] Unlike Truman, he was rarely if ever involved in any research or travel, if any was actually done, for reports. Public hearings, where witnesses were tricky to control and where other senators might attract some attention, were scarce. Draft reports and closed door hearing transcripts, even classified ones, were frequently leaked to favored reporters for major newspapers to gain their willingness to report subcommittee findings.[34] When final reports were circulated for the approval of other subcommittee members, Johnson would make any change in the text any member requested—whether merited by the facts or not—just as long as the member would cosign the report, thereby permitting Johnson to sell it as broadly supported and bipartisan, "just like" Truman.[35] In the words of one of Johnson's own staff, "The whole thing was to get Johnson's name in the papers."[36]

Johnson was able to get away with this charade because of a nonvigilant press. None of Johnson's own staff and none of the authors of the stolen reports apparently tipped the press off to the game being played, and the press failed to uncover and report anything except what Johnson was selling. No journalist of the time appears to have done the legwork and research to determine just how weak Johnson's reports were. It was an important lesson on the distinction between hard work and serious research like Truman's and a purely public relations exercise like Johnson's, and it is especially notable that the press was unable or unwilling to discern the difference.

Defense Reform Becomes a Fad

After the Truman and Johnson exercises, many committees, subcommittees, commissions, and blue ribbon panels followed. Some consisted of only members of Congress; some were executive branch creations comprising retired generals and admirals, government officials, and businessmen; some were a mix of all types. They included

- The Hoover Commission of 1949, which studied the newly created Department of Defense, was established by the National Security Act of 1947. This commission recommended further centralization of authority around the Secretary of Defense to reduce "costly duplication in procurement and waste in utilization among the three services."[37]
- The Rockefeller Committee of 1953 sought to enable DoD to "operate more effectively to attain broad objectives ... to provide the Nation with maximum security at minimum cost."[38] This committee recommended still more authority for the Secretary of Defense and urged that the Joint Chiefs of Staff be downgraded because they were found to fail to "rise above the particular views of their respective services."
- The Second Hoover Commission of 1958 found need for further streamlining and consolidation of clear lines of authority for the Secretary of Defense.[39]
- In 1970, the Permanent Subcommittee on Investigations of the Government Operations Committee of the Senate reported on the acquisition of the new "TFX" fighter-bomber that had become the F-111. Despite the design being competed between Boeing and General Dynamics, the aircraft was a joke as a fighter and a maintenance nightmare as a bomber. It was also overpriced, overweight, and delivered late. The Government Operations Committee found that Secretary of Defense Robert S. McNamara ignored a selection board's unanimous recommendation that Boeing's design be selected and chose General Dynamics, which happened to be located in then Vice President Lyndon Johnson's state of Texas.[40] The Government Operations Committee that performed the investigation asked whether the previous reforms that gave more power to the Secretary of Defense should be reconsidered.
- In 1971, the Fitzhugh Commission, a "Blue Ribbon Defense Panel," was appointed by President Nixon to make recommendations to fix all the problems the previous commissions and committees found but failed to solve.

The Fitzhugh panel was particularly interesting. After twenty years of reform panels, it found

> There are too many layers of both military and civilian staffs, and the staffs are too large. ... The results are excessive paper work and coordination, delay, duplication and unnecessary expense.

> The present arrangement for staffing the military operations activities for the President and the Secretary of Defense through the Joint Chiefs of Staff and the Military Departments is awkward and unresponsive; it provides a forum for interservice conflicts to be injected into the decision making process for military operations; and it inhibits the flow of information between the combatant commands and the President and the Secretary of Defense, often in crisis situations.

> The policies of the Department on development and acquisition of weapons and other hardware have contributed to serious cost overruns, schedule slippages and performance deficiencies. The difficulties ... require many interrelated changes in organization and procedures.[41]

In sum, the Fitzhugh panel found the previous two decades of efforts had solved nothing and perhaps had made things worse. It offered 113 separate recommendations. President Nixon declared himself impressed and instructed the Deputy Secretary of Defense at the time, former businessman David Packard, to implement the recommendations and get the problems fixed for once and for all.

Packard oversaw much activity, including helping to push the weapons testing reforms the Fitzhugh panel advocated by promoting the practice to "fly before you buy." This concept—originally advocated by Truman—was a simple but highly successful idea when it was properly employed. The idea was that weapons systems should be realistically and fully tested before they were put into full production. The concept permitted identifying whether the weapon was a winner or a loser and what elements, if any, needed modification before billions were spent on full production. It also obviated wasted time and money to retrofit modifications to prematurely produced units. Its greatest strength was to rely on the empirical demonstration of actual performance, rather than a contractor's or a military advocates hope or promise. In its best form it especially eschews computer simulations, which are often nothing more than advocates hopes expressed in a different format.

Advocates of weapon systems have often attempted to avoid such early and complete empirical testing on the claim that time and money would be wasted. Instead, such "concurrent" acquisition programs that are rushed to production and are tested late very often end up costing extra billions and incurring huge delays as problems are discovered late in the process.

Packard even established an office to oversee weapons testing, and later in 1978 a different framework was tried to improve testing and to observe the "fly before you buy" concept. However, both efforts failed as weapon system advocates in the research and development community retained real control and continued to permit, and in some cases insist on, compromised tests.

Ten years after the Fitzhugh panel, there was a Grace Commission in 1981 that found the same continuing mess. At this point the private sector think tanks got involved in earnest. The Democratic-oriented Center for Strategic International

Studies (CSIS) asked a panel of academics to address inefficiency and bureaucratic chaos in the Pentagon. The conservative Heritage Foundation offered a volume of findings and recommendations. The liberal Boston Study Group came up with its own ideas.

There were also others, but apparently, none of them solved the problems. By the mid-1980s, things had reached a new low. Ronald Reagan's Secretary of Defense, Casper Weinberger, presided over a Pentagon so riddled with waste and foolishness that the *Washington Post's* cartoonist, Herblock, regularly depicted Weinberger with a $600 Air Force toilet seat draped around his neck.

In 1985, the same David Packard who was instructed in 1971 to fix the mess found by the Fitzhugh Commission was appointed head of his own "Blue Ribbon" panel to address precisely the same things. At the end of this work, Packard told Congress "Frankly, gentlemen, ... we have a real mess on our hands"; it is "in worse shape now than it was 15 years ago."[42]

Packard's "new" discoveries were nothing new:

> With notable exceptions, weapon systems take too long and cost too much to produce. Too often they do not perform as promised or expected.
>
> As law and regulation have proliferated, defense acquisition has become ever more bureaucratic and encumbered by unproductive layers of management and overstaffing.
>
> There is great need for improvement in the way we think through and tie together our security objectives, what we spend to achieve them, and what we decide to buy.[43]

Congress held major hearings; the Senate Armed Services Committee wrote a 645-page report, "Defense Organization: The Need for Change," just to catalogue the problems.[44] Major legislation was enacted. Labeled the "Goldwater-Nichols Department of Defense Reorganization Act of 1986," the new statute effected many changes, most of them centered on a new round of reorganization and centralization. The Secretary of Defense was given more authority to control the department. Procurement was centralized under a new "acquisition czar," and the Chairman of the Joint Chiefs of Staff was restored to the military chain of command and given new authority to dominate the Chiefs of Staff of the military services.

Strangely, one of the major thrusts of the Packard Commission was to undo one of the reforms of the Fitzhugh Commission that had become associated with Packard himself: the new commission sought to undo the "fly before you buy" concept by undermining the authority of a new office set up—by Congress—to ensure more realistic tests of weapons by the Pentagon. This was one of the very few recommendations of the Packard Commission that many in

Congress opposed and that was not implemented. The effort to undermine the new testing office was spearheaded by a member of the Packard Commission, who had worked as a senior weapons development manager in DoD and who was subsequently to become President William J. Clinton's second Secretary of Defense, Dr. William Perry.

The members of the Senate Armed Services Committee exuded confidence they finally had the solution to decades old problems. However, after the Packard/Goldwater/Nichols changes became law, the problems in the Defense Department churned on, unperturbed. A year after the bill's enactment, DoD was again involved in a major procurement scandal. This one involved multiple senior officials in a Justice Department investigation, known and "Operation Ill Wind." Both new and old regulations were simply being ignored as defense department officials colluded with industry to award contracts based not on merit but on want.

This author saw a harbinger of the continuing problems when the Senate debated a design for reform different from the Goldwater-Nichols-Packard model. The alternative was in the form of a multipart amendment offered by Senator David Pryor (D, Ark.) who employed the author at the time. The Pryor legislation required all major defense contracts to be offered only as "sealed bid" competitions; it prohibited Defense Department officials to take jobs in industry to work on issues they handled as government employees, and it did much more, all of it opposed by DoD, industry, and most of the Senate Armed Services Committee, whose reforms Senator Pryor labeled as "cosmetic."

Shortly before the Senate vote on Pryor's amendment, the senator told the author that Senator Claiborne Pell (D, R.I.) had earlier said to him he would like to support the amendment but couldn't. The Electric Boat shipyard that built submarines in nearby Connecticut and that employed many Rhode Islanders had called; the Pryor amendment could mean competition for the yard that could cost Rhode Island jobs, and Senator Pell didn't want to lose those jobs, did he?

Pell voted against the amendment; it is impossible to know how many other senators had been put under similar pressure by defense contractors in their states. Hard-nosed competition was not the kind of business the defense contractors had in mind for themselves, and during the Reagan Administration, business was good. The contractors that the Nye committee characterized in the 1930s as having their tongues hanging out, baring their teeth for their share of the plunder, were alive and well—and still snarling—after more than fifty years of military reform.

There were hardly twenty votes in the Senate for the Pryor amendment. The majority had accepted the argument of the Armed Services Committee that it and the Packard Commission had the problems well in hand, and the more strenuous ideas of the Pryor amendment were uncalled for.

Shortly after the Senate preferred Goldwater/Nichols/Packard alternative became law, the Senate Armed Services Committee held more hearings, this time on "National Security Strategy."[45] This resulted in the recommendation that each president and Secretary of Defense should report every four years to Congress on what is their national strategy and what are the plans to manage the Defense Department in accordance with that strategy. The periodic DoD report later acquired the title "Quadrennial Defense Review," the most recent of which was delivered in February 2006.

A long series of Pentagon self-studies resulted; President George H. W. Bush's defense secretary, Richard Cheney, held a "Defense Management Review." Then came President Bill Clinton's first secretary of defense, retired congressman Les Aspin (D, Wisc.), a well-known Hill "defense reformer." Aspin ran his own in-house "Bottom Up Review" (BUR), which some wags characterized as the "bottoms up review." Thereafter, Clinton's second and third secretaries of defense, William Perry and William Cohen, conducted their own "Quadrennial Defense Review" (QDR). The self-review program continued in the George W. Bush Administration; Secretary of Defense Donald Rumsfeld received his own draft QDR on September 10, 2001—the day before the terrorist attacks. That report, as originally drafted, had selected the threat of missile attack on the United States as the penultimate problem to be addressed, and the report prescribed massive investment in national missile defense. When it was revealed as the real threat on September 11, terrorism was patched into the text, but the budget emphasis on national missile defense remained unperturbed. Upon release of the superficially modified report, the consensus response in Washington was to be unimpressed. This reaction was encapsulated by a headline in the widely read *Defense News*, which read "Pentagon Delays Hard Choices; Study makes No Suggestions on Major Programs."[46] Secretary of Defense Rumsfeld's second QDR, released in February 2006 produced much the same reaction. One widely respected analyst characterized it to the author as an "air burger with nothing on it."

None of these efforts over more than five decades of post–World War II activity seem to have brought meaningful change. Despite mixed results on various battlefields in the form of a draw in Korea, defeat in Vietnam, victory against very weak conventional forces in Iraq and an unknown—at best—result against irregular opponents there, these decades of "reform" have produced unmixed results on basic defense issues, such as equipment acquisition, and personnel and financial management. Indeed, a December 2005 government-wide review by the Office of Management and Budget found the Pentagon to be one of the more poorly managed federal agencies.[47] Similarly, the Government Accountability Office (GAO) reported in January 2005 that DoD demonstrated more "high risk" areas of misperformance than any other federal agency.[48]

To explain the Pentagon's successful resistance to reform, a case study should help. We shall examine an effort that involved as supporters civilians inside the Pentagon, officers from each of the military services, members of Congress from both political parties and all ideological stripes, the press, and others. If any effort was to have a chance, surely this one would. It began in the late 1970s and lasted for about a decade. It was called, quite appropriately, "the military reform movement." Its most visible manifestation was the "Congressional Military Reform

Caucus" consisting of over 100 members of the Senate and the House of Representatives. The experience explains much about how the Pentagon resists change and how to both succeed and fail at overcoming that resistance. At the end of that analysis, it should be possible to apply some of lessons from past and contemporary history and to discern what does and does not constitute meaningful military reform and what is required to implement it.

Notes

1. Arthur M. Schlesinger, Jr., "Introduction," in *Congress Investigates 1792–1974*, Arthur M. Schlesinger, Jr. and Roger Burns, eds., Chelsea House Publishers, New York, 1975, p. xi.
2. Ibid., p. xii.
3. For a concise discussion of the new elements of asymmetric warfare that occur today in Fourth Generation Warfare, see William S. Lind, Col. Keith Nightengale, Capt. John F. Schmitt, Col. Joseph Sutton, and LtC. Gary I. Wilson, "The Changing Face of War: Into the Fourth Generation," *Marine Corps Gazette*, October 1989, 22–26.
4. David C. Morrison, "The Defense Reform Merry-Go-Round," *National Journal*, March 22, 1986, 718.
5. Ibid.,p. 718
6. See Thomas Christie, "What Has 35 Years of Acquisition Reform Accomplished?" US Naval Institute Proceedings, February 2006, p. 30.
7. David McCullough, *Truman*, Simon & Schuster, New York, 1992, p. 258; also see Schlesinger and Roger Burns, *Congress Investigates 1792–1974*.
8. McCullough, *Truman*, p. 258.
9. *Congressional Record*, June 26, 1936, pp. 10134–10137.
10. McCullough, *Truman*, p. 258.
11. "Want Government to Make Munitions," Special to the New York Times, *The New York Times*, April 21, 1936, p. 16.
12. Schlesinger and Roger Burns, *Congress Investigates*, p. 249.
13. *Congressional Record*, June 26, 1936, pp. 10134–10137.
14. Ibid.
15. Schlesinger and Roger Burns, *Congress Investigates*, p. 330.
16. Inflation adjustment is calculated from *National Defense Budget Estimates for FY 2002*, Office of the Under Secretary of Defense (Comptroller), March 2002 and from discussion with staff of Congressional Budget Office.
17. McCullough, *Truman*, p. 256.
18. Ibid., p. 256.
19. Ibid., pp. 257–259.
20. Schlesinger and Roger Burns, *Congress Investigates*, p. 337.
21. Ibid., pp. 335–338.
22. *Congressional Record*, January 15, 1942.
23. *Congressional Record*, March 4, 1944.
24. *Congressional Record*, July 10, 1943.
25. *Congressional Record*, July 10, 1943.
26. Schlesinger and Roger Burns, *Congress Investigates*, p. 338.

27. McCullough, *Truman*, p. 288.

28. Ibid., p. 290.

29. Material that follows is a summary of Caro's presentation in Robert A. Caro, *The Years of Lyndon Johnson: Master of the Senate*, Alfred A. Knopf, New York, 2002, pp. 309–341.

30. Caro, *Master of the Senate*, p. 317.

31. Ibid., p. 317.

32. Ibid., p. 323.

33. Ibid., p. 339.

34. Ibid., p. 326.

35. Ibid., p. 339.

36. Ibid., p. 329.

37. Author's notes on Hoover Commission and 1949 amendments to the National Security Act of 1947.

38. Author's notes on Rockefeller Committee, also identified as Reorganization Plan # 6 of 1953.

39. Author's notes.

40. "TFX Contract Investigation," Hearings before the Permanent Subcommittee on Investigations, Committee on Government Operations, U.S. Senate, March 24, 1970, Part 1, pp. 12, 16, 28.

41. *Report to the President and the Secretary of Defense on the Department of Defense*, The Blue Ribbon Defense Panel, July 1, 1970, U.S. Government Printing Office, Washington, DC, pp. 1–2.

42. Morrison, "The Defense Reform Merry-Go-Round," p. 718.

43. "A Quest for Excellence," Final Report to the President, by the President's Blue Ribbon Commission on Defense Management, June 1986, Washington, DC, pp. xvii–xxiii.

44. "Defense Organization: The Need for Change," Staff Report to the Committee on Armed Services, United States Senate, October 16, 1985, 645 pages.

45. See "National Security Strategy," Hearings before the Committee on Armed Services, United States Senate, January, February, March, April, 1987, 1112 pages.

46. "Pentagon Delays Hard Choices: Study Makes No Suggestions on Major Programs," *Defense News*, October 1–7, 2001, p. 1.

47. See Executive Management Scorecard, Current Status as of December 31, 2005, http://www.whitehouse.gov/results/agenda/scorecard.html.

48. See "High Risk Series: An Update," January 2005, GAO-05-207, http://www.gao.gov/new.items/d05207.pdf.

CHAPTER 2

Some Lessons from the Dustbin of History

Winslow T. Wheeler

In the early 1980s a bipartisan group of senators and representatives organized themselves into what they called the Congressional Military Reform Caucus. While its official membership eventually exceeded 150, its truly active members were never more than 10. Despite these tiny numbers, this group enacted into law numerous major changes in Pentagon management over the strenuous objections of the civilian and military leadership of the Department of Defense (DoD) and many in the House and Senate Armed Services Committees, both Republicans and Democrats. By the late 1980s, this congressional reform exercise had run its course, and many of its legislative accomplishments were rewritten. It was quite literally a flash in the pan.

So why write about it? Except for some very occasional references to former Congressman Newt Gingrich and his "Cheap Hawks" and to former Senator Gary Hart and his ideas about warfare, the Congressional Military Reform Caucus has been in the dustbin of history for quite some time. Moreover, the performance of U.S. armed forces in two conventional wars in Iraq, which so many described as brilliant but which—as will be discussed in Chapter 6—actually left very much to be desired, makes learning lessons from previous congressional interventions quite superfluous in the minds of the great majority.

Perhaps not. Notwithstanding its passing effervescence on Capitol Hill, the Congressional Military Reform Caucus was an adjunct of a larger, more profound reform movement in the middle ranks of the military services and in a few other places that has had a more lasting impact. As an integral part of this extracongressional group, the caucus on Capitol Hill comprised a part of one of history's more significant, and in some respects lasting, impacts on the Pentagon.

Moreover, for a period of time, even the congressional element of the military reform movement was having real impact: not appreciating what precisely was happening, and certainly not understanding how or why, a senior Pentagon executive commented publicly in 1984 that the "[Congressional Military Reform]

Caucus is slicing [the] Pentagon into itty bitty pieces," and DoD was "getting no place" preventing what the Caucus was doing to it.[1] It was an impact that many in the Pentagon found extremely troubling and devoutly sought to resist. The interventions were being resisted just as were the findings and recommendations of the countless "blue ribbon" commissions convened in the 1950s, 1960s, and 1970s, but because some real impacts were occurring, the advocates of business as usual were more than a little perturbed. Many in the Pentagon with the institutional memory to recall the failure of the endless commissions to change anything fundamental surely expected the building to squash this meddling bunch of senators and representatives, but this time it would not be so easy, and while the public battles were fought, a more subtle, and important, process was occurring.

What was the real source of this unwanted meddling from Capitol Hill, and how did the politicians become so effective at imposing their will where so many had failed before? The lessons are important both for what is and is not military reform and for understanding how Pentagon outsiders from Congress or elsewhere can overcome resistance to change in the Pentagon, when change is needed but DoD is unwilling to engage in it.

To draw these lessons, the history of this military reform group must first be understood. Having been a participant in it, this author is aware of some of the details.

Modest Beginnings

In January 1981, Democratic Senator Gary Hart (Colo.) wrote a commentary for the *Wall Street Journal*, "The Case for Military Reform."[2] The piece argued that the defense budget was too small; too many U.S. weapons were ineffective, and the way U.S. armed forces planned to fight was predictable and clumsy—a recipe for defeat against the Soviet Union. It was a major departure from the defense budget cutting rhetoric most Americans would expect from George McGovern's 1972 presidential campaign manager.

Conservative Republican Congressman, William Whitehurst of Virginia read the *Wall Street Journal* piece and phoned Hart to ask for a meeting. The discussion that followed in Hart's office resulted in agreement to start an informal bipartisan congressional group, a caucus, to invite members of Congress to meetings to educate them about the nation's defense problems and some proposed solutions.[3]

The first meeting occurred on Tuesday, May 12, 1981, in Whitehurst's office with Hart and two other Republican members, an up and coming congressmen from Georgia, Newt Gingrich, and a senator not heard of before or since, Paul Trible of Virginia. The newly announced Congressional Military Reform Caucus met again the following week and expanded its membership to include three future "heavy duty" members from the Senate Armed Services Committee: Sam Nunn of Georgia (who was making a reputation for himself as a serious defense thinker), Bill Cohen of Maine (who became secretary of defense in 1996), and

John Warner of Virginia (who became chairman of the Armed Services Committee in 1999).[4]

At the first caucus meetings, the discussions were carried by Hart's cerebral, innovative, and outspoken staffer, William S. Lind, and by defense experts invited at Lind's instigation. One of those was an articulate talker, Pierre M. Sprey. These speakers rocked the politicians' defense world—the U.S. Navy was building the wrong ships to defeat the Soviet navy, most Air Force fighters were dogs, and the Army had no clue how to form and operate an effective tank force. Moreover, each military service planned to wage plodding, frontal attrition warfare, which would exterminate its own personnel and waste its own equipment. It was a style of warfare that played to the traditional strength of the Soviet army and would increase the resolve of any other enemy America decided to take on by virtue of its indiscriminant use of firepower and its painfully obvious predictability, as was shown to be the case in Vietnam. The *coup de grace* was that more money wouldn't help and would probably make things worse.

The discussions were spirited and stimulating, but they failed to engage Senators Nunn and Cohen, who according to Whitehurst, said almost nothing at the first meetings.[5] Their behavior in later years would explain why.

High Flown Objectives

As the caucus continued to meet over the next months, its members decided they needed a coherent description of what it stood for. They put together a slide presentation with a prepared script to explain "military reform," a term that was beginning to take on a specific meaning. The presentation was shown to interested or new congressional members of the growing caucus and their staff. Some caucus members presented it to constituents and meetings of defense related groups in their political districts and in Washington.

The presentation recounted the poor state of American military competence, as demonstrated by defeat in Vietnam and the embarrassing failure to rescue the diplomatic hostages in Tehran, Iran, in 1980. Specific note was made of shrinking U.S. land, naval, and air forces and deepening morale problems in all U.S. military services in the 1970s. Then, the presentation stated what was important to build an effective defense: Number one, and most important, was "people." That was "because wars are fought by people, not by machines." It was not pay and retirement benefits, and other tangibles that were important; it was "attracting, promoting, and empowering people who have character, skill, and initiative ... [not just high] scores on a standardized test or a diploma."[6] The briefing stressed developing initiative and imagination among both officers and troops, and it urged building personal bonds and mutual understanding between them— at all levels—to enhance cohesion and initiative (thereby permitting the decentralization of command and fluidity of action). It was these characteristics, not just discipline, pay, or patriotism that enabled human beings to perform under the terrible stress of combat, the briefing argued. Programs that enhanced these characteristics, such as rigorous training under "free play" (unscripted) conditions (as opposed to highly controlled exercises) and organizational schemes that kept units of people together by rotating units rather than individuals were central to the reform agenda. Typical ideas from Congress merely to pander to people in the armed forces with more generous pay and retirement programs were not only irrelevant but degraded the more important attributes because the former appealed only to the baser instincts and attracted and reinforced the wrong kind of people.

Second in importance came strategy and tactics "because wars fought without innovative ideas become pointless bloodbaths." The emphasis was on thinking cleverly about how to operate in war, striking the adversary's weaknesses, in a manner he least expected, and at a tempo his decision cycle could not cope with. "Attrition warfare" strategies, or trying to overwhelm the enemy with firepower where and how he expected it—later to become popularized by the phrase "hi diddle-diddle straight up the middle"—was to be replaced with "maneuver warfare" strategies that emphasized outthinking the enemy by focusing destructive effects on his moral, mental, and physical weaknesses rather than his strengths. Tactics and strategies like the bloodbaths of World War I were discarded in favor of a more agile, dynamic form of conflict that focused on the adversaries mind. A classic example was the German "Blitzkrieg" which neutralized France's Maginot Line in 1940 by infiltrating around its northeastern hinge (in the Ardennes, where it was least expected) and enveloping the French and British armies from the rear as they marched to what they wrongly though was the decisive encounter in Belgium—in an effort to extend their linear (and predictable) defensive barrier to the English Channel.

Hardware was third, "because weapons that don't work or can't be bought in adequate quantity will bring down even the best people and the best ideas."[7] The presentation argued that "we must accept the idea that there can be no [military effectiveness] if we start with hardware and try to force tactics and strategy as well as people to fit the vagaries of hardware changes. . . . Without starting with people there can be no tactical and strategic themes for winning."[8]

The presentation then urged dramatic budget increases in selected areas like training, a new organizational framework for military manpower to hold people in units together, rather than constantly break them up, and finally and most important, to change to a paradigm where individuals are promoted based on their moral and intellectual characteristics and demonstrated tactical prowess, rather than the careerism that built up during the decades following World War II, before its incompetent and morally destructive head revealed itself in Vietnam.

The presentation also urged the acquisition of highly effective but affordable military equipment that remained effective when subjected to the "stress, chaos, insufficient training and hasty maintenance that inevitably accompanies war."[9] Noteworthy on equipment issues was the very conscious disconnect between weapons effectiveness and high cost. In fact, high cost was usually a sign of complexity (cost/complexity advocates preferred the buzz words "high tech"), and complexity was a sure sign that a weapon would be difficult to use, unreliable, and usually unavailable, even if it were effective, which was all too often not the case. Finally, the best way to ensure weapons were effective, the briefing argued, was to submit candidates to combat realistic field testing, known as "operational" testing, and to honestly and completely report the test results to decision makers.

The members of Congress in the Reform Caucus who said they embraced this thinking were not the people who wrote the briefing. With the exception of Bill Lind in Senator Hart's office, not even staffers on Capitol Hill made any significant contributions. Instead, the presentation and the thinking behind it were the product of a small number of extraordinary individuals.

The Core of Military Reform, Congressional and Otherwise

The military reform movement did not begin when Senator Hart and Congressman Whitehurst met in May 1981. It began in the spring of 1967, fourteen years earlier, when an Air Force colonel sought to solve a bureaucratic problem. He was looking for someone to refute the vexing arguments of a systems analysis "whiz kid" Secretary of Defense Robert McNamara had hired to reassess military effectiveness. The "whiz kid" had written an analysis that the Air Force was wasting huge sums of money building heavy, complex, poorly performing aircraft to carry out irrelevant missions. The problem-civilian was the same Pierre Sprey who helped talk up a storm in Congressman Whitehurst's office in 1981.

Eager to counter Sprey's arguments with a sure fire killer, the Air Force colonel brought in a hot shot major who had made a reputation for himself for taking no prisoners in his brilliant analysis of fighter aircraft and how to use them. This major was a self-taught genius with a gigantic streak of independence and self-assurance; he had already told his superior officers of their design for the Air Force's newest fighter, "I could fuck up and do better than that" and proceeded to help guide the Air Force to one of its most successful fighter designs since the Korean War, the F-15.[10] Surely this major had the intellectual afterburners to fry the upstart civilian analyst, Sprey.

The major's name was John Boyd. The colonel's decision to introduce him to Sprey might have been the Pentagon's biggest peacetime bureaucratic mistake of the post-World War II era. Boyd and Sprey quickly became lifetime friends, and the cabal they formed around themselves brought forth many things in the next few decades the regular bureaucracy would fight tooth and nail, but that soldiers, Marines, and Air Force pilots would use in actual combat to the great advantage of both themselves and the United States.

Boyd's and Sprey's work products included some of the most successful combat aircraft the Air Force and Navy developed at least since the F-86 (the highly successful Korean War fighter): the F-15 in the form that ultimately emerged, the F-16, and (indirectly) the F-18 fighter, and the ground attack A-10, none of which the Air Force or Navy wanted when their design concepts were initially proposed. More importantly, the results from Boyd included an approach to aircraft tactics and design, known as "energy-maneuverability." "E-M" enables a pilot to understand his own aircraft's strengths and weaknesses compared to his adversary's; it also gives aircraft designers a tool to devise aircraft that excel at the tasks assigned to them, and perhaps most importantly, it provides a common medium through which pilots and design engineers can communicate their needs, goals, and ideas.

Further, Boyd researched and wrote an analysis of war in the form of a briefing, "Patterns of Conflict." That became the launching point for more work on command and control, technology, and strategy. This body of work had a profound impact on many of the thousands who heard Boyd's presentations. His ideas were incorporated in a rewriting of the war fighting doctrines of the Marine Corps and, to a lesser extent, the Army, which were—superficially—manifest in the ground campaign against Iraq in Operation Desert Storm in 1991 and the initial conventional ground operations in "Operation Iraqi Freedom" in 2003. The results also included ideas to reform how the Pentagon conceived, developed, tested, contracted for, budgeted for, and produced weapons.

Despite being prolific at putting together briefings, Boyd never wrote about his theories and approaches to hardware and warfare in book form. His briefings can be found at a Web site largely devoted to his thinking and others who think similarly; see www.d-n-i.net and more specifically http://www.d-n-i.net/second_level/boyd_military.htm at that website. Much of his work is best described in two biographies: *Boyd: The Fighter Pilot Who Changed the Art of War* by Robert Coram and *The Mind of War: John Boyd and American Security* by Grant T. Hammond.

The members of Congressional Military Reform Caucus who listened were bowled over by the reformers' thinking; some embraced the ideas enthusiastically. Newt Gingrich and another youngish Republican Congressman from Wyoming, Richard Cheney, both spent hours with Boyd in their offices and even their homes, listening attentively to the military reform ideas of Boyd and Sprey.

With the latter two at the core, the group of individuals grew—informally and unstructured, and with little public notice. By the time the members of Congress heard from them in 1981, both the major personalities and the fundamental thinking of the reformers had jelled. The group of individuals included the following:

"Pentagon Maverick"

In 1973, Boyd, now a Air Force colonel was reassigned to the Pentagon. He met Franklin C., "Chuck," Spinney, who was assigned to Boyd's office in the Pentagon. Spinney possessed an aggressive, sharp mind that pursued the objects of his analysis to their bare, naked bottoms. An inexhaustible worker, he performed his work without caring about, but fully understanding, the negative personal career consequences for himself.

After leaving the Air Force as a captain, Spinney accepted a civil service appointment to the Office of Program Analysis and Evaluation (PA&E). It was in this new capacity that he was to become one of the most public of the reformers. His becoming so was pure Boyd: don't groom a slick, media friendly poster-boy; instead, give the press an abrasive, but scrupulously ethical, analyst who has no inhibition against telling his superiors when their decisions are awful, and doing so with inch thick, excessively documented memoranda and multihour briefing presentations. Any in the press with the juice to absorb it all would absolutely eat it up. Spinney would end up on the cover of *Time* magazine in 1983, frequently quoted in every major newspaper in the country on defense issues in the subsequent twenty years, and ended his career as the focus of an hour long, Emmy-award winning Public Broadcasting System TV show in 2003. His road to that prominence was based on his data and analysis and little judo applied to the Pentagon's attempts to suppress his work.

As an analyst in the Pentagon's Office of PA&E, with much encouragement from Sprey and especially Boyd, Spinney produced a long white paper, "Defense Facts of Life," and in 1983, a follow-on study, "The Plans/Reality Mismatch."[11] These unlocked the secrets of the Defense Department's weapons procurement: weapons complexity, unrealistic budget plans, and poor discipline in decision made costs grow faster than budgets, thereby causing weapons inventories shrink and age; it also caused "readiness," which characterizes forces trained and equipped to fight, to decline.

More specifically, Spinney argued that politically driven management in the Pentagon—to say nothing of the same in Congress—produced a system that kept itself in the dark about the medium and long-term consequences of decisions in order to protect the short term objective of initiating and propelling weapons procurement programs through the budget review process. Spinney documented a "repetitive bias to grossly underestimate future costs of [weapons] programs in the early stages of their acquisition life cycles."[12] This he called "front loading"; its purpose being to help a program get started by downplaying its future financial consequences and overestimating its benefits. Once a program is initially approved, the "political engineering" would start, namely the securing of as many subcontractors in as many congressional districts as possible in order to subvert any desire for real congressional oversight and to extort support out of elections-conscious senators and representatives. "The goal is to raise the political stakes before the true costs of the front-loaded program become apparent."[13]

Once the system reaches production, its true costs begin to emerge; as costs climb, the production rate falls; the lower production rate means the existing inventory cannot be replaced at the rate needed to prevent aging. An aging inventory becomes more expensive to maintain and operate, thereby driving up the costs of the operating budget as the acquisition budget also climbs. Pressure grows to transfer money to the operating budget, but simultaneously the more politically powerful acquisition budget seeks to raid money from all possible sources, including the operating budget. Ultimately, readiness—equipment maintenance, training, and other operating expenses—is raided to support an inadequate amount of weapons modernization. Thus, a "death spiral" of "shrinking combat forces, decreasing rates of modernization, aging weapons inventories, with the rising cost of operations creating continual pressure to reduce readiness."[14]

The only solution the politicians in the Pentagon (many of them in uniform) and Congress can identify that helps them avoid painful, but needed, decisions is to increase the defense budget to attempt to buy themselves out of the problem. Without altering the nature of the decision making process, they pile one politically driven decision on top of another and only succeed in exacerbating the lethal spiral, even when budgets increase rapidly, as they did in the early years of the Reagan administration. More money spent the same way literally makes the situation worse and only accelerates the increasing cost of a shrinking, aging, less ready military force.

Two additional attributes make the situation even more intractable. First, the Pentagon's books cannot be audited. The Government Accountability Office and the DoD Inspector General have tried, literally for decades, only to declare the task impossible. Note that it is not that the Pentagon cannot pass an audit; it is un-audit-able; it literally has not risen to the level of financial management competence that it can be audited and fail. Thus, it is quite easy for civilian and military managers to misrepresent—front-load—the future consequences of contemporary decisions. This, in turn, makes it impossible for any conscientious decision maker "to assemble the information needed to synthesize a coherent defense plan that is ... accountable."[15] As a result, the Pentagon's long-range planning system uses a "database [that] cannot pass an audit and the data used in its planning projections are unreliable, arbitrary and, in important cases, systematically biased to grossly understate the future consequences of current decisions."[16]

Thus is also created the "underfunding" problem: the Pentagon's entire program possessing an actual cost well in excess of the predicted cost—an actual cost the Congressional Budget Office estimated in 2005 to be from $50 billion to $100 billion in excess of the stated cost—per year and for the foreseeable future.[17]

Finally, Spinney supplemented the arguments of Sprey and Boyd about the nature of complex and expensive military equipment—equipment the advocates sold as "high tech." New generations of combat aircraft, for example, were progressively more complicated and, consequently, more expensive. The added complexity continually means higher maintenance costs and longer downtimes of unavailability—despite persistent promises to the contrary (just like the front-loading of the finances). The newer systems were therefore not only more expensive at the purchase point but also throughout the life cycle, during which they were also less available for combat. Finally, Spinney pointed out, the original promise of a high level of performance was rarely kept as the performance requirements for the new, more complex systems were persistently compromised as the program encountered technical problems—the inevitable consequence of unrealistic performance aspirations articulated to assist the front-loading of cost promises. In all too many cases, this "rubber baseline" of declining performance requirements resulted in systems that were not just more expensive and less reliable than their predecessors, but also less capable, such as the B-1B bomber and the F-111 fighter-bomber.

There is a notable difference between so-called "high tech" equipment in the military and civilian words. In the former, the equipment is usually more complex and, therefore, more expensive than what it replaces. In the latter, it is often simpler and cheaper, and in those cases where it is not, it often becomes simpler—and cheaper—very rapidly. In the civilian world, consider the replacement of complicated mechanical adding machines with simpler, cheaper handheld calculators, which were also more capable and more convenient and portable. Consider also how generations of technology for the home have become cheaper over time, for example, the continual decline of the cost of color televisions from the 1950s to the 1990s, and the rapid decline of the cost of "more capable" wide-screen plasma and other technology televisions when they started to replace older cathode ray tube TV technology after the millennium. In the military world, cases of the new technology being simultaneously cheaper, simpler, and more capable are extremely rare.

Spinney's first study, "Defense Facts of Life," caught the attention of Sam Nunn, one of the quiet senators in the early meetings in Congressman Whitehurst's office. Nunn asked President Carter's secretary of defense, Harold Brown, to permit Spinney to brief the senator on it. Very probably knowing the consequences of this kind of analysis getting to Congress, Brown refused. Nunn threatened a subpoena. Perhaps perceiving even worse consequences, Brown caved. Nunn listened to the briefing and advised Spinney to write an unclassified version. Later, at a Senate Armed Services Committee hearing to confirm Casper Weinberger as President Reagan's secretary of defense, Nunn asked the nominee if he had heard Spinney's briefing and whether he knew it was being suppressed by his predecessor. Weinberger knew nothing about it, but the public exchange sparked the press. Journalists asked for copies of the study, and the Pentagon was maneuvered into making them available.

"Defense Facts of Life" won a reputation as a solid and stunning analysis. By 1982, it had become internationally known to the extent that it was described in a best-selling novel by a British author, *The Third World War*, where the "Spinney Report" became a—mythical—reason why NATO woke up and spent the necessary resources to adequately support its weapons with spare parts and maintenance to defeat a postulated Soviet attack on Western Europe.[18]

When he was working on his second major study in 1983, "The Plans/Reality Mismatch," Casper Weinberger's Pentagon became so upset about the developing findings on the actual costs of the Reagan defense plan that Spinney's top boss in PA&E, David Chu, told to the press that the study did not exist, an assertion some in the press, who had been privately briefed on the contents, knew to be completely false. Informed of the existence of the study and of Chu's disingenuous denial—indirectly by Boyd—Senator Charles Grassley (R, Iowa) drove himself, alone (like Truman), to the Pentagon to speak to Spinney and listen to his analysis. Grassley was not permitted to see Spinney; so he drove back to Capitol Hill and demanded a public hearing in the Senate Budget Committee, where he was a member, to hear the analysis.

To Senator John Tower (R, Tex.), the chairman of the Senate Armed Services Committee and a major Pentagon-ally, it was obvious the jig was up on pretending the Spinney study did not exist. Tower took a different tact: he claimed jurisdiction over any hearing on the study at the Armed Services Committee, displacing the hearing Grassley wanted at the Budget Committee. Tower also laid plans to make the hearing a nonevent. He scheduled it for a Friday afternoon, when most press were unlikely to attend, and he arranged for a small, out-of-the-way hearing room that had no space for much of an audience, journalists, or the bulky film and TV cameras of the time.

After Grassley and other senators protested, Tower consented to making the hearing a joint event with the Budget Committee. Meanwhile, others made sure the press knew Tower was trying to exclude them, which, of course, made them more interested. Journalists called Tower's staff to demand a larger hearing room to accommodate their now growing number and the multiple film and TV cameras they now wanted to bring. Facing disapprobation from the press, Tower caved. In fact, to accommodate all the journalists and the expanding public audience, the hearing was moved to the large "Caucus Room" in the Russell Senate Office Building, the most prestigious hearing room on Capitol Hill.

As this was going on, John Boyd kept *Time* magazine fully informed of the details of Tower's maneuvers. He also brought in Spinney to brief the magazine's reporters on the content of the briefing. The drama of the hearing, mostly manufactured by Tower's inept maneuvers, and the content of Spinney's study convinced *Time* to put Spinney on its cover, proclaiming him a "Pentagon Maverick" and asking "Are Billions Being Wasted?." Inside was a long article about military reform.[19]

Spinney had written an important study explaining Pentagon pathologies, but it was long and detailed, hardly the usual fodder for *Time* magazine articles. With a little help from Pentagon managers who told fibs about the existence of the study and from clumsy congressional attempts to avoid press attention, what was otherwise complex and boring to most became the basis of a national news story. It was an interesting lesson in leveraging the underhanded opposition to produce precisely what it sought to avoid.

Goddamn Preppy

In 1979, a former speech writer for President Carter, James Fallows, was researching an article for his new employer, *Atlantic Monthly*. He was looking into defense and the additional spending presidential candidate Ronald Reagan would promote if he were elected. Fallows found his way to Bill Lind, who put him onto John Boyd.[20]

Boyd agreed to talk, but only on the condition that Fallows listen to Boyd's complete (four hour) "Patterns of Conflict" briefing. When they first met, neither was impressed; Boyd told Spinney Fallows was a "goddamn preppy;" Fallows saw a disheveled, eccentric, loud, egotistical man and thought "Is this guy nuts?"[21] Nevertheless, Fallows listened to the whole "Patterns" briefing. He was impressed; now, he wanted to hear Spinney's—also—four-hour presentation of "Defense Facts of Life." Then, he had a long sit down with Sprey. Then, he talked with all of them, again and again. He got the "fire hose" treatment.

Using this mother-load of reformist insights and information, Fallows wrote an article for *Atlantic*, "Muscle Bound Superpower." As a Boyd biographer puts it, "While newspaper reporters had written a few articles about Boyd and the reformers and the issues they espoused, Fallows was the first writer for a major national publication to tie it all together, to question the way the Pentagon spent billions of taxpayer dollars and to wonder if America's military was so burdened with high technology that it might fail in warfare."[22] Then Fallows wrote another article, "America's High-Tech Weaponry," about the downside to complex technology. Then, he wrote a book.

National Defense was a more thorough download of the fire hose treatment Fallows had received from the reformers. Fallows also added material based on his own research, but more importantly he included a dimension the reformers were never able to provide for themselves: he made the material digestible for normal human beings, and he presented it without the stentorian tenor the core reformers often applied to their presentations—to say nothing of the requirement that to get any briefing from most of them, one had to be willing to devote four rather grueling hours to hear the presentation. It was "the whole brief, or no brief" an unlikely way to disseminate of one's thinking to potential, but uncommitted, allies in the outside world.

To neutral individuals, uncommitted to the reform movement, Boyd, Spinney, and Sprey often came across strong, often very strong. Each had a different tenor to his presentations, but each also frequently struck new listeners as if he were implying "if you don't understand and accept what I am telling you, there is something wrong with you, not me." It would take a listener new to the reformers with thicker than normal skin, or perhaps an entering bias favorable to the reformers, to absorb the content of these presentations without feeling either defensive or offended. The reformers' presentations did win over many allies, but it is impossible to tell how many potential allies were alienated by the insistent—uncompromising—tone.

The reformers didn't particularly care; they regarded people who were more concerned about style than content as part of the problem. However, in the political environment in the Pentagon and Washington, DC, that's a lot of people, and not all of them are vapid immoralities and few of them are stupid.

Eschewing the "take it or leave it" attitude, Fallows' *National Defense* became a hot seller; it delivered the military reform message to untold thousands, and it made the reformers a part of the national scene.

Inquisitive Staffer

Charlie Murphy was a new staffer for Congressman Jack Edwards (R, Ala.), the ranking Republican on the Defense Appropriations Subcommittee of the House Appropriations Committee. In 1979, Murphy heard about problems the Air Force was having with its F-100 engines in the F-15 fighter. The Air Force told him there wasn't really any problem: the program and all its spare parts were "fully funded." Nonetheless, Murphy decided to travel to some Air Force bases to see for himself. Of course, the Air Force would have to send an officer to escort him; that's how the trouble began.

This officer, a lieutenant colonel, had been hearing about the problems as well and was genuinely concerned. He took Murphy to a Pentagon office he knew had been looking into the issue. That office was the same PA&E where Boyd, Spinney, and Sprey worked and had made into a hotbed of military reform. There, the lieutenant colonel introduced Murphy to Boyd. Boyd and another employee showed Murphy sheaths of data on readiness problems and shortages of spare parts. The data was abstract; Murphy wanted to see things for himself. As planned, he visited several Air Force bases.

Murphy found Boyd was wrong; he had understated the problem. Everywhere he went Murphy found brand new F-15s unable to fly because their engines were being stripped of spare parts to keep other aircraft in the air: "hangar queens." At Cannon Air Force Base (AFB), a base for the notoriously unreliable F-111 bomber, Murphy found worse. Where electronics and engines should have been—even on new aircraft—Murphy found empty holes. Some aircraft were even raised up on jacks to permit maintenance crews to use landing gear parts to keep other aircraft operating. There, and at Nellis AFB, new spare parts were so difficult to obtain mechanics went to Radio Shack to buy surrogates at their own expense.[23] Later, he found the problems were not just in the Air Force; naval air stations and aircraft carriers showed the same problems. Murphy took pictures of it all.

At hearings in 1979 and 1980 in the House Defense Appropriations Subcommittee, Murphy's boss, Congressman Edwards, showed Murphy's photographs to an embarrassed Secretary of Defense Harold Brown. President Jimmy Carter's reputation for taking poor care of the armed forces had already been weak, and now it became weaker. It was another straw on the overstrained back of President Carter's 1980 reelection campaign.

When the new "pro-defense" Reagan administration came to office in 1981, it sought major increases in the defense budget. Thanks to Murphy's work, Congress directed part of that increase to spare parts spending, which went from about $1 billion to over $4 billion in just a year.[24]

But, more money made the problem worse.

Whistleblower

In 1968, A. Ernest Fitzgerald never heard of John Boyd or Pierre Sprey, but he too was giving the Pentagon fits. He was a civilian financial analyst for the

Air Force and had publicly testified to Congress that the Air Force's huge C-5A transport aircraft was having major cost overruns. The Nixon administration leapt into action; on President Nixon's personal order to "get rid of that sonofabitch," Fitzgerald was ultimately fired.[25]

Three effects followed: (1) given the ultimate blank check endorsement by the president, the C-5A's cost powered through Fitzgerald's relatively modest cost growth projection (while it's performance remained below expectations); (2) Fitzgerald became an instant hero and martyr among those dismayed with Pentagon waste; and (3) given his elevated status, Fitzgerald found it easy to acquire the pro-bono legal horsepower to first regain his job in 1973 and then take the case all the way up to the U.S. Supreme Court. In 1982, he won that court's order guaranteeing he keep his job.

When Fitzgerald went back on the Air Force's payroll, he noticed the dramatic increase in spending for spare parts that Charlie Murphy had helped provoke in the early years of the Reagan administration. Fitzgerald wanted to establish what prices DoD was paying for the items. He focused not on sophisticated electronics, or highly machined, alloy parts but on what the military services were paying for mundane things.

He found a stool leg cap in the B-52 bomber; the Air Force paid $1000.00 for it; it was neither gold, nor platinum, it was nylon-plastic. He identified the cost the Navy was paying for a household hammer, $436.00, $600 for a pair of bent nose pliers, and $7,500.00 for a coffee maker. Learning from Fitzgerald, others found the ultimate symbol of defense scandals of the 1980s, the $600 toilet seat, which *Washington Post* cartoonist Herblock slung around Cap Weinberger's neck every time he depicted the secretary of defense.[26] The press loved it. Story after story about these and other spare parts horror stories appeared in newspapers all over the country.

Fitzgerald used the outrageous prices paid for household items to explain what most reporters and members of Congress did not comprehend. When told a fighter aircraft's radar or navigation system costs millions of dollars, normal people have no way to understand if the price is reasonable. But show them something they do understand, a stool leg cap, a hammer, or a toilet seat, and document the heart stopping cost the Pentagon was paying for them; then, people could understand something was wrong. Fitzgerald's *coup de grace* was to explain that a modern, sophisticated military aircraft should be understood— in cost terms—as nothing more than these overpriced parts "flying in close formation."

The Pentagon's response was to try again to get rid of Fitzgerald.[27] One of the many new attempts occurred in 1985; his superior gave him a poor job performance rating, setting him up for a demotion. Congressman John Dingell (D, Mich.) called for a hearing before his Oversight and Investigations Subcommittee in the House Commerce Committee, with the responsible Air Force officials as witnesses. Senator Grassley called for a DoD Inspector General investigation.[28] The press had lots of fun with the David versus Goliath story line. The *New York Times* even devoted a lead editorial to it.[29] Embarrassed yet again, the Pentagon relented. Ernie Fitzgerald retained his job until he retired in 2006.

For any thinking the president and the Pentagon were too powerful to resist, it was an important lesson.

Media Maven

Dina Rasor was a junior radio and TV journalist, but she was not particularly impressed with the people she worked for. Looking for something else, in 1979 she went to work for the National Taxpayers Union, a public interest group in Washington. They asked her to write a piece on government waste. She decided to look into Lockheed's C-5A aircraft and inevitably came upon Ernie Fitzgerald.

Like the Boyd-Sprey encounter, it was a meeting the Pentagon would regret. Educating Rasor in the ways of Pentagon overpricing, Fitzgerald was impressed with her brains and toughness. He decided to help put her in the permanent business of reporting on Pentagon misbehavior by finding financial backing for Rasor from various public interest groups in Washington. They set up something called the Project on Military Procurement.[30] The success Rasor would enjoy was probably beyond her wildest dreams.

Almost immediately after starting the Project on Military Procurement, Rasor met Pierre Sprey (through an intermediary she no longer remembers). That meeting formed the final link that forged the military reform movement of the 1980s and brought it up to "full mission capability." Now there was contact between the Boyd-Sprey-Spinney nexus focused on weapons system design, military effectiveness, and budget planning with the Fitzgerald nexus on cost, waste, and whistleblower harassment and both of those entities with what was to become a daily link to the press and public through Rasor. It was a critical mass.

Rasor started out by using the Project on Military Procurement as a clearinghouse for documents the Pentagon did not want the public to see. The building was full of potential whistleblowers (Rasor called them "closet patriots") who wanted to bring some sort of undisclosed (and unclassified) information about problems in DoD to the public eye. The "closet patriots" had lived with the issues in their professional existence and had grown frustrated when no one tried seriously to address them. From examples like Fitzgerald's, these people also knew there were penalties for "committing truth" to Congress and the public, and they were unwilling to sacrifice their own jobs as Fitzgerald had when he went public with the C-5A cost overruns. These "closet patriots" were also unfamiliar with how to work with the press, or were simply unwilling to risk being revealed by contacting the press themselves. Rasor became their "middleman"; she wasn't interested in opinions, she wanted documents.

Rasor was smart in how she presented her material to the press. She hired a Vietnam War Army helicopter pilot as an assistant; he gave her work the male gender, combat veteran credibility any woman in that era would lack with many in the defense analysis game. She also quickly came to realize the advantages of unlikely political combinations. One such combination was Senator Grassley and a junior member of the House of Representatives, Barbara Boxer (D, Calif.). It was match made in journalism heaven. Boxer was youngish, short, smart, aggressive, liberal, and a quintessential "Jewish American Princess." Grassley was a tall, middle aged, rock ribbed Republican from Iowa, a pig farmer, a slow, gee-whiz talker, and as much a conservative knuckle dragger as Boxer was a liberal screamer. Rasor brought them together for joint press conferences and cooperative action on several issues. Grassley would offer straight faced criticism of fellow Republican Cap Weinberger's Pentagon, and Democrat Boxer would pick fights with her own party's leadership on the House Armed Services Committee. The press devoured the material. In Rasor's words, "I couldn't hold the reporters back."[31]

Rasor started out with the Army's new M1 tank; it was—as they say—a target rich environment. The documents she received in 1981 showed the following.

- The tank had a jet engine with an ultra hot exhaust that made the tank easy—for the enemy—to find on the battlefield using thermal sensors.
- The jet engine also had a voracious appetite for fuel: its three gallons to the mile on the road and eight gallons in heavy terrain became a play-toy for the press, especially given the fuel mileage consciousness of the American public in the early 1980s. Less obvious for ballyhooing but more significant was the operational limitation this fuel inefficiency imposed on the tank. The jet engine gave the tank quick acceleration and a high road speed, but its operational range was very short. Sprey quipped, "The M1 is the world's fastest strategically immobile tank."
- Turret movement and other equipment relied on hydraulics that used a volatile fluid that would incinerate the crew whenever the interior areas of the tank were lit off by an antitank round penetration. So dangerous to crew were American Army hydraulics that in the 1973 Middle East war, Israeli tank crewmen renamed their US M60 "Patton" tanks, the M-1's predecessor, after American cigarette lighters.
- Piles of electronics gave the tank accuracy and other capabilities, when the complex "black boxes" worked, but they also made the tank extremely heavy: it was not the weight of the components, it was their volume that expanded the interior size of the tank; this in turn expanded the exterior size of the tank and hence the weight of the armor needed to protect everything and everybody inside. Moreover, the technical complexity and low reliability required a huge maintenance tail to keep the system running.
- Depending on the nature of the engagement, the most important weapon on a tank is sometimes the commander's machine gun. The gun for the M1's commander was the very effective M2 .50 caliber Browning machine gun, but the gun's mount made it unaimable and almost unusable.

These were not just someone's criticisms; they were revealed by Pentagon documents. Journalists flocked to the information, and the M1 became a major controversy. After the Army's spokesmen reacted, the articles addressed not just the tank but also the Army's denials that its own documents refuted.

Then came the deluge. Articles on the M1 mentioned Rasor's name and the Project on Military Procurement. The phone started ringing off the hook, and the mail box was stuffed to overflowing. Whistleblowers and their documents flooded into the Project on all kinds of military programs. Rasor and her staff of three had more business than they knew what to do with. The Project on Military Procurement became a relief valve for military and civilian personnel who were frustrated with Pentagon managers who refused to address problems. Now the "closet patriots" had a way to force management to pay attention to the problems via public exposure. And they could do so without losing their jobs.

Rasor upped the ante. She wrote a long article in *Reason* magazine. It addressed not just the flaws in the M1 tank and other systems but one of the central reasons the flaws existed: the tank was never tested rigorously and the results were never honestly reported, even inside the Pentagon.[32]

After the article came out, Rasor started running into Senator David Pryor (D, Ark.) at some cocktail parties. He invited her to the Senator's dining room in the Capitol building (where the décor is elaborate and the food is mediocre). They talked about defense problems; he said he wanted to help, but he didn't know where to start. She gave him a copy of her *Reason* article. Pryor read the article and directed his staff to work with Rasor to write a bill.

Pryor's staff met with Rasor, Sprey, and others and with their help wrote legislation to reform DoD's weapons' testing. It isolated combat-like, field testing of weapons, known as "operational" testing, from corrupting influences. If the bill were to become law and take hold, no longer would laboratory tests under cooperative conditions be substituted for combat realistic tests in dirt, mud, and confusion, and using regular soldiers as operators. No longer would the manufacturer be able to design or score the tests. No longer could the weapon system's advocates write the reports on the tests of the weapon they sought to protect. As Senator Pryor said, it didn't "prevent the students from grading their own exams; it prevented the students from writing their own exam, monitoring the exam, and then grading it themselves." The bill also allowed decision makers in DoD and Congress to find out just how well or poorly the system performed in those tests, and it brought this information to their attention before, not after, the weapon went to full production. Put another way, the bill would implement major reforms the Fitzhugh Commission of 1971, discussed in Chapter 1, had recommended, and it would redress the complaints of the Truman Commission of World War II about untested aircraft and armor plate. The need for the legislation was a long time in forming.

The Pentagon's leadership and its allies in Congress hated Pryor's bill. What transpired after it was introduced is another useful lesson in how the Pentagon fights ideas it doesn't like and how that resistance can be overcome.

How to Pass Legislation the Pentagon Hates

In the Congressional Military Reform Caucus' first two years, Senator Hart and Congressman Whitehurst sought to alter how members of Congress thought about defense issues. Some members, especially Newt Gingrich, enthusiastically embraced the reformers' ideas and articulated them loudly and enthusiastically to the press and public. However, by 1983, Lind had become convinced that the Caucus had become too much talk and not enough action. Senator Hart agreed and decided he should step down as Caucus chairman.[33] Lind telephoned the author when I worked for Senator Nancy L. Kassebaum (R, Kan.) to ask if she was interested to be the new Senate Chair of the caucus. She had not even been a member but had caught Lind's and Hart's attention with an alternative defense budget proposal she had sponsored using reform principles. Her amendment increased purchases of major equipment while reducing the procurement budget. It had missed passing the Senate by a hair, but it represented just the kind of legislative action Lind and Hart were looking for.

Kassebaum accepted the invitation, and the new caucus commenced a search for legislation that advanced military reform. The caucus rejected bills that would divide members by party or ideology, such as pro- or anti-arms control issues. They even rejected being for or against specific weapon systems, no matter how well or poorly conceived. Most systems tended to divide members by party or ideology. For example, conservatives and Republicans were almost universally for the MX strategic-nuclear missile; liberals and Democrats were opposed. It was the same for the new B-1B bomber and other likely candidates.

They settled on Senator Pryor's testing bill. The fact that the Pentagon hated the bill was no bar; in fact, it was an advantage. DoD's arguments against the bill brought it more attention and, inadvertently, more support. The Pentagon asserted realistic tests would add time and cost to the weapons acquisition process. The reformers retorted the existing process took huge amounts of time and money, and the costs to fix the problems late in the process were far higher than to fix things early, before tooling and production were already set up. The Pentagon argued that a new office that reported directly to the secretary of defense and Congress would only add a new layer of bureaucracy to Pentagon. Senator Pryor countered that was, in fact, correct, but if a new layer of bureaucracy would actually be noticed in the labyrinthine Pentagon, it also meant that the secretary of defense and Congress would be getting important new information the bureaucracy had previously denied to them. The Pentagon complained that Congress' receiving information on a weapon's flaws only meant it would kill the program; Pryor and the reformers responded that any weapon performing well had nothing to fear; only the dogs would be threatened with delay or worse. The Pentagon's arguments gave fodder to political cartoonists and commentators to mock, and the arguments that Congress should not receive weapons test information only made it easy to win over broader congressional support.

The Pentagon mobilized under Richard DeLauer, who ran weapons development and procurement as the Undersecretary for Research and Engineering. As the Senate prepared to debate the Pryor bill in the spring of 1983, DeLauer directed his staff to write arguments against the bill and feed them to the Pentagon's allies on Capitol Hill. A colonel was assigned to write a letter making the best arguments the building could come up with. Senator Tower was again asked to carry the Pentagon's water by distributing the Pentagon's letter to all other senators.

In addition, Senator Robert Dole (R, Kan.) helped out by introducing legislation different from Pryor's; it changed nothing and simply urged the existing testing infrastructure to try to do a little better. It was pure eyewash, but it gave fence sitters and Tower/Dole allies something they could tell the press and constituents they favored to "improve" testing.

That should be all they needed, they surely thought. The Armed Services Committee rarely lost votes in the Senate on defense issues using these tactics. They never had a chance. For starters, those of us working to help Senator Pryor and his amendment knew what Under Secretary DeLauer and Senators Tower and Dole were up to at every turn. The Air Force colonel whom DeLauer had directed to write up the Pentagon's opposition to the Pryor bill was a protégé of Boyd. Col. James Burton was deeply concerned about the Pentagon's failure to test weapons properly and report the results honestly. What Burton did not or would not—for reasons of integrity—tell the reformers, especially the ones on Capitol Hill, about the opposition's maneuvers was, instead, learned from other allies on the staff of the Armed Services Committee who were also convinced the Pryor legislation was needed.

We also knew what ace in the hole our opponents thought they had. He was none other than the new chairman of the Congressional Military Reform Caucus in the House, Congressman James Courter (R, NJ). Courter had enthusiastically volunteered to chair the House side of the Reform Caucus in 1982 when the first House Chairmen, Congressman Whitehurst, stepped down along with Senator Hart. An ambitious congressman with visions of the governorship of New Jersey dancing in his head, Courter came on strong as an advocate of military reform and had convinced many he was for real.

Courter had spoken enthusiastically about Senator Pryor's bill, but just before the House was scheduled to debate the measure, Courter's staff called me to say they wanted to make just a few changes to their version. In a nutshell, Courter's revisions would have gutted the bill, thoroughly; they could only have been suggested by the Pentagon. I and others met with Courter's staff and managed to talk them out of most, but not all, of their changes. They insisted on just a few; it was very probably essential to their plan. As long as there was any difference in the text of the House and Senate versions of the bill, the House-Senate conference committee appointed to resolve differences would be free to make just about any changes it wanted. Had the House and Senate texts been identical, the provision would have been "non-conference-able," and Courter and Tower would have been out of the test reform undoing business.

While these subterranean exercises were proceeding, the reformers were busy promoting the legislation in the Senate. As Senator Kassebaum's staffer, I worked with Senator Pryor's staff, and the staff of Senator William Roth (R, Del.) to counter Tower's letter, lobby other staff, and sponsor meetings to explain the bill. But these efforts were not the important action.

Almost every day, a major newspaper was printing an article about weapons that flunked tests, weapons that were poorly tested, and testers who fudged the process and their reports. Some of these stories were appearing in the newspapers that every senator and their staff read, such as the *Washington Post*, the *New York Times*, and the *Wall Street Journal*.[34] In the weeks immediately before the Senate's debate on the issue, political cartoonists were mocking the Pentagon on the issue, [35] and the *New York Times* ran not one editorial but two.[36]

The appearance and timing of the media deluge were no coincidence. Dina Rasor, her staff, and others were working full time to give reporters and editorial writers all the information they needed. For example, Pierre Sprey visited me in Senator Kassebaum's office a week or so before the Senate debate on the Pryor bill. He asked me how well I thought the amendment would do. I told him I didn't know, but all the news articles and editorials were surely helping. He asked if another *New York Times* editorial would help, especially if it came right before the vote. Puzzled but enthusiastic, I said something like, "Sure!" He asked me where could he use a phone where others would not overhear. I took him out of the crowded staff room where I worked to an empty conference room with a phone; he looked up a number in a "little black book" and dialed, motioning for me not to leave. He started telling the person on the other end of the phone about the excessive complexity, weight, and size of the Navy's new F-18 and how it failed in tests to match the performance of the older aircraft it was to replace for bombing missions, the A-7. He also discussed the Senate's likely schedule for debating the Pryor testing amendment.

The following week, immediately before the Senate debate, the *New York Times* printed an editorial roasting the Navy and its F-18 for the plane's complexity, size, weight (and cost), and how it underperformed the A-7 as a bomber.[37] It had been written by *New York Times* editorial writer Nicholas Wade, whom Pierre knew had given the moniker "The Hammer of God" for his scorching commentaries. Wade had listened to Pierre's arguments and found a GAO report and other information to confirm them—plus the added dimension of the F-18's cost growth. Wade wrote up the editorial and the *Times* printed it just in time for senators to read it as they decided how to vote on the Pryor legislation.

Once it was clear precisely when the Senate debate would occur and I knew senators and their staff were making up their minds on what to do about the Pryor amendment, I started calling around to senators' defense staffers asking how their bosses would vote. I found roughly 40 senators whom their staff said would probably vote for the amendment and about 20 who said they would likely oppose; the rest were unknown or undecided. I considered this informal head count to be encouraging but not definitive news; the winning margin was among the question marks, and anything could still happen.

The day before the actual debate, I was in the Senate chamber, sitting in the staff seats in the rear, talking with a staffer for the Armed Services Committee. He asked me how well did I think the Pryor testing amendment would do. I told him I didn't know, but I was encouraged by my informal head count. He became very inquisitive; I showed him my notes. He seemed to think it was important and asked to make his own notes from my own. The staffer worked for Senator Nunn, whose reputation as an intellect on defense issues had become solid and who was known as a good bell weather of what makes sense on defense issues. Although his staff was sympathetic to the Pryor amendment, Nunn had been opposed.

Later that day, Nunn's staffer called me; Senator Nunn had changed his mind about the amendment; in fact, he wanted to be listed as a cosponsor of it! My head count convinced Nunn the Pryor amendment was going to pass in the Senate, and Nunn had decided to place himself at the front of the herd, rather than be run over by it.

It was bad news for Senator Tower. With bell-weather Nunn on our side, Tower realized he was fighting a losing battle. He asked to meet with Senator Kassebaum. She and I did so the next morning in the Republican Cloak Room just off the Senate floor. Kassebaum was nervous, but she knew she had the upper hand, and despite her trepidation of Senator Tower, who had a reputation as a bully, she was determined not to let him take her to the cleaners. He told her he would accept the Pryor amendment, implying that he wanted to do so with only a "voice" vote that did not record how each senator voted. Kassebaum responded with something like, "No, John, we want a recorded, roll call vote, and we're going to watch very closely what happens to this amendment when you take it to conference (with the House)." I was impressed; she stood up to Tower, and with a roll call vote, hopefully with a big tally on our side, it would be hard—but not impossible—for Tower to gut the amendment in conference.

We had our formal vote. It was ninety-one yeas to only five nays.[38] Even Tower had joined the herd: that way he could tell his constituents in Texas he was for testing reform. Twelve days later, on July 26, the House passed the Courter version of the amendment, but probably afraid that he would get a strong tally like ours that would impede gutting both versions, Courter agreed to a voice vote.

None of the primary authors of the Pryor amendment (Pryor himself, Senator Roth, and Senator Kassebaum) was a member of the House-Senate conference appointed to resolve the differences between the Pryor and Courter versions of the amendment and the rest of the Department of Defense Authorization bill to which both amendments had been attached. Tower and his allies probably thought they were now "in the clear;" behind closed doors they could now gut the amendment any way they wanted.

We did, however, have staff allies in the conference meetings, and they reported to the Hill reformers every revolting detail. Congressman Courter, who was a conferee for the House, offered to trash the Pryor version and adopt his, with modifications to make it even weaker. When the Hill reformers learned this, we called the *New York Times* informing a writer of Courter's duplicity. The next day the *Times* included in its "Washington Talk; Briefing" a description of what Courter was up to.[39] After the *New York Times* article, Courter said little in the conference, and nothing that we had any serious objection to.

But we still had Tower's opposition to deal with. At Bill Lind's urging, Senator Hart, who was a member of the Armed Services Committee, made an appeal to

Senator Nunn, who was both a member of the committee and of the House-Senate conference. While a late comer to testing reform, Senator Nunn saved the Pryor amendment. He argued forcefully in favor of it; Tower realized he was again isolated and capitulated. The Pryor amendment was adopted generally in tact. The Pryor test reform legislation became law as a part of the fiscal year 1984 Department of Defense Authorization Act.

"Instant" Success

Despite the years, even decades of work behind the Pryor testing reform bill, it was deemed an instant success, and it made the Congressional Military Reform Caucus an even bigger success on Capitol Hill and with the press. There had arrived on the political scene a new dimension to the debate over the defense budget and weapon systems. It was no longer the "pro-defense" (i.e., more spending) senators versus the "anti-defense" (less spending) senators. There was a new "pro-defense" category; those who were critics of the Pentagon but who had convincing, not just rhetorical, arguments that they wanted a stronger U.S. military. Senator Kassebaum was a good example.

As a Republican critic of a Republican president's defense program she immediately stepped out of the usual mold. In addition to digressing from the usual partisan profile of a senator from one party only being critical of the Pentagon when it was controlled by the other party, she was neither a "knee jerk" liberal opponent to defense spending and not an automatic conservative proponent of more and more—the two points of view that had dominated the debate in Congress. Kassebaum was a "cheap hawk" trying to make U.S. defense more effective at less expense.

The Kansas press began to routinely cover her actions and statements,[40] and it gave her highly favorable editorial commentary.[41] She knew she hit the big time when the *New York Times* started boosting her political profile in feature stories with titles like "From 'Nice Little Nancy' to 'Effective'", and "New Breed of Military Reformer."[42] The more coverage she and the other reformers received, the more other members of Congress started to support her initiatives, and that in turn got her more coverage. Politicians like that.

In the aftermath of the success of the testing bill, the news stories evolved to show that she was not just thinking and doing interesting things but was also accumulating a base of power in defense affairs. The Pentagon and the defense-business-as-usual crowd in Congress increasingly had to pay attention to her and fellow reformers. Stories with titles like "Pentagon Worried: Military caucus' mission causing stir"[43] and "Caucus Is Slicing Pentagon into Itty Bitty Pieces," mentioned above, began to occur.

The quote, "Caucus is slicing Pentagon into itty bitty pieces," was from the same Undersecretary of Defense for Research and Development, Richard DeLauer, who had sought to undo the Pryor testing bill. In an associated article, DeLauer stated of Kassebaum, "I can't talk to Nancy Kassebaum. I talk right by her. Her eyes glass over when I talk about trade-offs between survivability and capability and sophistication."[44] As a cogent example of the ethical level at which defense debates can occur, when undersecretary DeLauer made that statement, he and Senator Kassebaum had never met. They did shortly after; at Kassebaum's invitation.

Politically, it was all "manna from heaven." Even if some never came to the Military Reform Caucus' monthly meetings and were in some cases even hostile to Kassebaum's legislative initiatives, over one-hundred members of the House and Senate (Democrats, Republicans, liberals, moderates, and conservatives) asked to join the Reform Caucus and loudly broadcast their membership—and self-described enthusiasm—to the folks back home.

Some were particularly disingenuous. One example, Senator William Cohen (R, Maine) later became secretary of defense. He asked to join the Reform Caucus, listed himself as a member of the Caucus on his press releases, and broadcast to the voters in Maine statements about his support for military reform. However, I never observed him attending a meeting of the Caucus in its later years, and his staff ardently opposed what the Caucus was trying to achieve; Cohen himself often opposed legislation the Caucus sponsored.

Superficial commitment to reform was a problem that the reformers would encounter in the future, but in the glow of success after the passage of the testing legislation it seemed like only a minor concern. It was not, and it would spell the end of military reform on Capitol Hill for decades to come. But that is a story to be told in the next chapter.

Conclusion

It was more than a little remarkable that a caucus of a minority of the members of the House and Senate could overcome strenuous opposition from both the established "experts" on Capitol Hill, the House and Senate Armed Services Committees, and the Pentagon. There are some useful lessons to be drawn from the experience, as follows:

Necessary but Insufficient Condition for Change: External Realities

Probably the most important reason for the congressional reform caucus' success was the existence of external conditions that mandated change. The failure of American armed forces in Vietnam and Iran and the management problems in the Pentagon made the need for change painfully obvious. In Vietnam, American did not just lose, we lost to an enemy vastly inferior in physical resources and technology. In Iran in 1980, the rescue mission did not miss by a hair, it failed to even reach the city where the American hostages were held. In the early 1980s, the Soviet Union appeared to many to have the upper military hand, and American military letdowns gave people immediate, understandable concerns. Later, the flood of information made available by reformers and others, all documented by the Pentagon's own data, made it clear the in-house response to the external realities was flawed.

Sufficient Condition #1: Admission of a Problem

There also had to be a popular perception that the problems were real, not just the creations of partisan critics of whatever party happened not to control the White House and the Pentagon. The obvious nature of the defeat in Vietnam, the collapse of the Iran rescue mission, and the procurement horror stories of the early 1980s were insufficient to convince some the problems existed. Some blamed the antiwar demonstrators and members of Congress for the strategic and tactical failures in Vietnam. Others tried to dismiss the Desert One failure as an isolated equipment failure. Some tried to invent reasons, such as strange distributions of overhead costs to minor items, as the only thing behind the outrageous prices the Pentagon was paying for things. The general population needed an obtrusive indicator that the problems were for real, not political creations.

Those indicators came when Ronald Reagan and Casper Weinberger came to office and it was Republicans (e.g., Senators Grassley, Kassebaum, Roth, Slade Gorton (R, Wash.), Mark Andrews (R, Neb.) and others who led the charge for military reform. Many Democrats, some of whom were informed and sincere—some of whom were not—were happy to come along for the ride and to gain whatever partisan advantage they might; it was, however, the Republican members of Congress that gave the criticisms a note of reality and importance. Of course, even some Republicans were happy to advance their own political careers by criticizing Ronald Reagan's Pentagon, but there were enough of the more apparently sincere members to give the reform effort—along with the documentation of the problems—an element that the press and the public could not ignore or dismiss as partisan or self-serving babble.

Sufficient Condition #2: Coherent and Appropriate Response

Both the Congressional Military Reform Caucus generally and Senator Pryor's operational testing legislation specifically were appropriate to the external realities. The reformers provided coherent explanations of the problems and a unifying theme for solutions. They were laid out in the caucus' briefing for public audiences, Fallow's articles and book, and numerous other articles and speeches. The reformers provided a material, mental, and moral framework to understand the situation. Moreover, they proposed a series of reforms consistent with their diagnosis of the problem.

The reformers' analysis of the problems and their solutions were not cooked up in an ivory tower or, worse, a Washington, DC, think tank. Boyd, Sprey, and others proved they were more than academic kibitzers by devising weapons, like the F-15, F-16, and A-10, which excelled in performance (and later in combat) and which were generally models of the right way to develop, test, and buy equipment. Boyd's and others' work outside the scope of the caucus' activities, such as their contribution to war fighting doctrine as adopted by the Army and later, and more fundamentally, by the Marines, gave the overall reform movement—and the caucus by association—an aura of nonpolitical seriousness and sincerity it otherwise might lack.

Also, the data Spinney analyzed in his work was the Pentagon's own; the costs Fitzgerald revealed were from contractor's own billings. They were not explaining things based on a theory or dogma; the comments about airplanes, fighting, and acquisition were empirically based, proven in the real world. Their work was directly linked to reality, not some individual or group's agenda or based just on theoretical, academic analysis.

Sufficient Condition #3: Unfiltered, Independent Information

There is nothing new or special about members of Congress having access to internal Pentagon information. Today, the House and Senate Armed services Committees get internal Pentagon information everyday. It comes directly from the Pentagon, and it comes through staffers. Some of those staffers are active duty officers who know they must return to their service and are wary of the consequences of providing information or advice their or other services do not want Congress to have. Some are retired officers anxious to "help" their service achieve whatever goals it has laid out for itself. Some are people with no military career, but who are anxious to grow their civilian one by securing a significant Pentagon job when they leave Capitol Hill. What was unique about the information the non-Hill reformers made available to Capitol Hill was not that it came from inside the Pentagon, but that it was information the Pentagon did not want the Hill to have.

This reformist information had a second important quality, beyond independence. Members of Congress and their staff do not know how to design combat aircraft, how to fight, even plan, a competent military campaign, or even how to audit a defense program. Sadly, there is all too much evidence that many in the Pentagon don't know how to do these things either. But, these tasks and more were literally everyday work for Boyd, Sprey, Spinney, and Fitzgerald. By making themselves available to members of Congress, the reformers gave them a functional level of knowledge that is rarely even matched in the Pentagon. Thanks to the reformers, members of Congress and their staff knew why Air Force aircraft were performing poorly and knew which programs were having cost overruns before most people in the Pentagon knew. They also had a basis to identify the bogus Pentagon explanations when they were offered, which was not infrequent.

Sufficient Condition # 4: Powerful Media Conduits

Jim Fallows and Dina Rasor provided an opening to the American people to generate leverage on both Congress and DoD. Fallows did not just explain the reformers, he gave them initial respectability. Rasor's operation went further; she gave them power.

Her documented revelations did not just embarrass the Pentagon, they embarrassed any member of Congress who tried to defend the Pentagon's practices or who chose not to do something about them. For the members who chose to act in concert with the reformers, she provided a link to journalists, whom she gave not just data as grist for an article but also political conflict. This was irresistible to many journalists. In short, Rasor gave members of Congress what they crave: continuing favorable coverage in both national and local newspapers. This sustained the interest of a few relatively serious reformers in Congress, and it brought to their side flocks of opportunists eager to enjoy the ride by voting with them and supporting their ideas.

Sufficient Condition #5: Smart Tactics

The Pentagon-based reformers and their closest allies on Capitol Hill learned to use a highly effective tactic against the Pentagon. Boyd called it the "M&M strategy." Examples of it occurred with the Pentagon's lies about the existence of Spinney's "Plans/Reality Mismatch" study and Senator Tower's attempt to suppress the hearing.

The "M&M" title of the strategy had nothing to do with candy. It had everything to do with the mismatch between motherhood and what some people were actually doing. It was policy-making tactics, guerrilla style. It was not just that the Pentagon's lying about the Spinney study made it more interesting to the press; the lying gave the advocates of the study a powerful lever. It became a story about good and evil. Again and again, Boyd and his counterparts pointed out the Pentagon's ill-behavior, and again and again the Pentagon and its allies would compound their error, as if to prove right what the reformers were saying. The mismatch between motherhood and policy-making Pentagon-style made the press and Congress irresistibly tempted to learn about Spinney's study and to tell the nation about it.

The study was a long, detailed exposition full of complicated charts on why weapon systems cost so much and why the Pentagon budget was out of control. It was a study the press and Congress very probably would otherwise never have the patience to listen to. Drawing attention not initially to the study but the unethical tactics used against it made the study, and its content, the focus of compelling interest.

The object of it all was not just to influence the media, but to alter policy. The subsequent downward trend of defense spending starting in 1985 was a remarkable turn of events for an administration that came to office in large part based on its plans for the Pentagon. And it was a reversal imposed not by the Soviet Union, the black hand of economics, or any new national political philosophy. Instead, it was imposed on the Pentagon by less than twenty people.

As they gritted their teeth, the opponents to reform made plans. They were many things, but not stupid. They would have their day, and military reform would evaporate from Capitol Hill just as fast as it emerged. That story is explained by what happened after the Pryor test reform legislation became law. It also provides some more lessons.

Notes

1. "DeLauer: Caucus Is Slicing Pentagon into Itty Bitty Pieces," *Defense Week*, April 30, 1984, p. 7.

2. "The Case for Military Reform," *The Wall Street Journal*, January 21, 1981.

3. Transcript, comments of William S. Lind at a seminar on the history of the Congressional Military Reform Caucus, sponsored by the U.S. National Archives, Center for Legislative Activities, June 27, 1992, p. MRC-I-14.

4. G. William Whitehurst, *Diary of a Congressman: ABSCAM and Beyond*, The Donning Company, Norfolk/Virginia Beach, pp. 277–279.

5. Ibid., p. 279.

6. Prepared text to "Reforming the Military: Military Reform—A Winning Military at an affordable Price," slide show presentation prepared by J. Boyd, P. Sprey, & W. Lind, in author's files.

7. Ibid.

8. Ibid.

9. Ibid.

10. Robert Coram, *Boyd: The Fighter Pilot Who Changed the Art of War*, Little Brown and Company, 2002, p. 195.

11. Franklin C. Spinney, edited and with commentary by James Clay Thompson, *Defense Facts of Life; The Plans/Reality Mismatch*, Westview Press, 1985, Boulder, CO.

12. Statement by Franklin C. Spinney before the Subcommittee on National Seurity, Veterans Affairs and International Relations of the Committee on Government Reform and Oversight, House of Representatives, June 4, 2002, p. 10.

13. Ibid., p. 10.

14. Ibid., p. 11.

15. Ibid., p. 1.

16. Ibid., p. 13.

17. "The Long Tem Implications of Current Defense Plans and Alternatives; Detailed Update for Fiscal Year 2006," List of Briefing Slides, Congressional Budget Office, January 2006.

18. General Sir John Hackett, *The Third World War: The Untold Story*, MacMillan Publishing Co., New York, pp. 59–60, 65.

19. *Time*, March 7, 1983; see also interior story: "The Winds of Reform," pp. 12–30.

20. The details of this encounter are from Coram, *Boyd*, pp. 350–352.

21. Ibid., p. 351.

22. Ibid., pp. 351–352.

23. As related by Murphy to the author. Also see "Col. John Boyd: Requiem for a Warrior," *Defense Week*, March 24, 1997, p. 20.

24. Approximate data are as recalled by Murphy, who as a staffer for the House Appropriations Committee was in a position to know.

25. Nixon was overheard on the White House tapes in the Library of Congress as a result of the Watergate scandal. See "Defense Procurement Information Papers; Campaign '84," Prepared by Donna Martin, Project on Military Procurement, August, 1984, in author's files, p. 46.

26. For more examples and data, see "Defense Procurement Information Papers; Campaign '84," and other similar publications of the Project on Military Procurement.

27. See details of Fitzgerald's career in his books: A. Ernest Fitzgerald, *The Pentagonists: An Insider's View of Waste, Mismanagement, and Fraud in Defense Spending,* Houghton Mifflin, 1989, 344 pages; and *The High Priests of Waste,* Norton, 1972, 396 pages.

28. "'Whistle Blower' at pentagon Is Given Failing Report Card," Special to the New York Times, *The New York Times,* August 1, 1985, p. 15.

29. "Whistle Blower; Horn-Blower," *The New York Times,* August 13, 1985, p. A-22, lead editorial.

30. Based on author's discussion with Dina Rasor in July, 2003.

31. Ibid.

32. See "Fighting with Failures," *Reason,* April 1982, pp. 19–28.

33. Discussions of Bill Lind with author in 1983 as recounted in memoranda from the author to Senator Kassebaum.

34. See Fred Hiatt, "Pentagon Is Accused of Buying Untried Arms," *The Washington Post,* June 24, 1983, p. A3; Walter S. Mossberg, "Tougher US Arms Tests Are Goal of Senators Pushing for New Office," *The Wall Street Journal,* June 13, 1983.

35. A June 1983 *Washington Post* cartoon by Herblock shows airplanes crashing while one Pentagon bureaucrat says to another "You see, actual weapon-testing would slow up the spending programs."

36. See "Duds and Lemons, American-Style," *The New York Times,* July 5, 1983; and "When Weapons Flunk," *The New York Times,* July 13, 1983.

37. "When Weapons Flunk," Editorial, *The New York Times,* July 13, 1983.

38. *Congressional Record,* July 14, 1983, p. S9947.

39. "Second Look," Washington Talk Briefing, *The New York Times,* August 19, 1983, p. A12.

40. For example, see "Kassebaum to propose cuts in defense budget," *Kansas City Times,* April 8, 1981; "Kassebaum asks major defense cuts," *Topeka-Journal,* April 9, 1981; and "Kassebaum Wants to Cut 'Absurd' Defense Request," *Kansas City Star,* April 9, 1981.

41. For example, see "Getting our money's worth," *Topeka Capital-Journal,* undated xerox.

42. See *New York Times,* July 11, 1983 and October 12, 1983.

43. See *Houston Post,* December 28, 1983

44. AP writer Jim Drinkard, "Military Caucus Turns Pentagon's Head," December 27, 1983, the identity of the specific newspaper is not included on the Xerox copy in the author's files.

CHAPTER 3

Falling Off the Mountain: Congress and the Press Quit Military Reform

Winslow T. Wheeler

When Senator Pryor's test reform bill became law, those of us involved in the effort thought the Congressional Military Reform Caucus was pretty hot stuff. The press was calling Senator Kassebaum's office constantly, asking for comments on one thing or another and what the reform caucus would do next. The Pentagon's lobbyists made frequent visits trying to change my, and more importantly, Senator Kassebaum's, mind. The membership of the caucus grew past 130 House and Senate members from both parties and all ideological persuasions.

Delusions of grandeur notwithstanding, the Congressional Military Reform Caucus was soon to fall apart, no more to have the slightest impact on the Pentagon. The history of that precipitous decline provides additional lessons on what it takes to have a real impact on the Defense Department and what reformers inside and outside the Pentagon today need to understand if they want to have any real effect.

Lousy and Inconstant Bureaucratic Infighters

Basking in the glory of our trouncing of Senator Tower and Undersecretary DeLauer with the enactment of the Pryor testing legislation, many congressional military reformers failed to appreciate that the fight had barely begun. First to make that apparent were the regulations the Pentagon's chief administrator, a former staffer to Lyndon Johnson known as "Doc" Cook, "the mayor of the Pentagon," wrote to implement the new law. It ignored or circumvented every major reform the testing legislation articulated.

Doc Cook's draft regulation was leaked to Senator Roth's office. Senators Pryor and Kassebaum joined with Roth in sending a blistering letter to Secretary of Defense Casper Weinberger insisting on regulations consistent with the law and asking, rhetorically, if Weinberger thought the time had come for the reformers on Capitol Hill to write more explicit legislation. Doc Cook rewrote his wayward directive; the new one simply quoted the law verbatim, thereby leaving the complaining senators no excuse to grouse further but also leaving unwritten the bureaucratic details of how the office was to be run.

Meanwhile, Secretary Weinberger was taking his time to find someone to run the new office. He professed he couldn't find anybody both qualified and willing. At one point he grew frustrated and told his staff to tell Senator Kassebaum to give him a candidate.[1] Kassebaum felt strongly that she should comply with the request and, after a search, accepted a recommendation from John Boyd, who had met with the senator and who had been working with her through the author, to put forward the name of an active duty Air Force colonel, James Burton, the same person who had quietly helped the passage of the test reform legislation. He had been running various weapons tests, insisting that they be realistic and that the results be accurately reported, which—to put it mildly—did not make him popular with many civilian and military weapons advocates in DoD. Kassebaum felt, however, that he was—in her word—"ideal."[2]

Burton had not sought the new job for himself. To help protect him from likely retaliation from the weapons advocates he had alienated, Boyd asked Kassebaum for a favor before she put forward Burton's name as her candidate: that Weinberger be asked to ensure that if Burton were not to be selected for the position, he would be allowed to complete his assignment involving the testing of the Army's Bradley Infantry Fighting Vehicle. As Boyd explained, there was concern that Burton's recommendation by the reformist Kassebaum might ensure his being singled out by the DoD bureaucracy and transferred or otherwise targeted. Kassebaum agreed.

On April 24, 1984, she sent a letter on her personal stationery to Weinberger and followed it up with a personal phone call to him. Although Weinberger's staff failed to give him the letter and tried to discourage Kassebaum from talking to Weinberger about Burton, they did eventually connect after Kassebaum persisted. She asked for the assurance Boyd requested, but got no promise from Weinberger whatsoever. Weinberger did interview Burton for the job, but then things quickly went downhill. A different candidate was offered the job, and, as feared, the Pentagon bureaucracy went after Burton.

Burton was driving the Army crazy with his efforts to test rigorously the Bradley M-2 armored personnel carrier, which was one of the Army's premier new ground combat systems. The Army had promised Congress that the Bradley could fight on the European battlefield and effectively protect the crew and infantry squad it carried inside. Burton was trying to find out if the vehicle was truly capable of doing so. He wanted the vehicle realistically loaded with fuel and ammunition to determine how vulnerable it was to hostile fire and explosion; the Army wanted any combustibles removed. He wanted to use Soviet RPG-7 antitank rockets (which were then and remain today the world's most prevalent antitank weapon); the Army wanted to use a much less common, and weaker, Romanian weapon. He wanted soldier dummies inside the vehicle; the Army wanted them watered down with a hose first. And so on. Burton fought their efforts to phony up the tests at every turn, and the vehicle was tested as he insisted. The results were disastrous. The Bradley proved to be extremely vulnerable to the RPG-7 and other weapons, as well.

As the fights over the Bradley tests progressed, the Army decided to solve its problem creatively—by getting rid of Burton. Senior Army generals spoke with Burton's superiors in the Air Force. Together, they found a convenient solution. Congress had passed legislation to require DoD to reduce overhead staff by 5 percent. Five percent in the office where Burton worked meant one position had to be eliminated. Even though one slot was already vacant and Burton was the only Air Force representative there (the Army had three), Burton was selected. As a senior Air Force general explained to him, none of it was personal, but if he didn't want to be pushed out of the office and reassigned, he could always retire from the Air Force.

All the gory details were explained to Kassebaum. To my very great surprise, she felt no compunction to help Burton. While Burton himself steadfastly refused to ask her to intervene, Boyd met with her to do so, and I, as her staff, urged her to. It was a question of honor to protect someone whose name she had put forward to a hostile Pentagon and who was obviously being punished for the "crime" of realistically testing military equipment—an issue Kassebaum had used to make a name for herself.

Senator Kassebaum chose to parse the situation legalistically: Burton was not being punished because she had nominated him for the testing job; he was being punished for insisting so forcefully that the Bradley be tested realistically, she argued. Therefore, she wasn't responsible for his being attacked, and she had no obligation, moral or otherwise, to help him.

Burton made himself available to her when she had asked. He was being victimized for trying to do his job in a manner consistent with what she said was her agenda for the Defense Department. It was her own nominee and ally getting trampled by the unrepentant DoD bureaucracy. The people who had helped her become a national figure on defense issues were asking for help. None of it seemed to matter.

This author was never able to discern if there was another—unarticulated—reason for Kassebaum's inaction: whether others were offering some compelling argument not to help; whether she had tired of the military reformers as too uncompromising, or anything else.

Luckily, however, things turned out better for Burton, temporarily at least. Although they had not, like Kassebaum, taken the lead in advocating Burton to Weinberger, other members of Congress—Senators Pryor and Charles Grassley (R, Iowa), and Representatives Denny Smith (R, Ore.) and Mel Levine (D, Calif.)—were incensed at the Pentagon's behavior. They wrote to Weinberger and caused enough of a public stink that DoD was embarrassed into relenting. Burton continued to insist on realistic Bradley testing, and major modifications to improve survivability for the crew were implemented. Indeed, when the Army was preparing for Operation Desert Storm in 1991, the U.S. regional commander,

Gen. Norman Schwarzkopf, learned that the Bradleys being sent to him in Saudi Arabia were not the models that were modified after Burton's tests. He had them all sent back to be replaced by models that were.[3]

By then, however, Burton had left the Air Force. By insisting on the realistic tests and accurate reports on them, Burton made many too many enemies in high places in the Army. Discussions were again held with the Air Force, and Burton was forced to retire. Despite the Pentagon's reputation for noncooperation between the military services, when there are issues that one service thinks are really important—like getting rid of someone who does not assiduously advocate for a premier weapon system—one service can be willing to go hat in hand to convince its erstwhile rival to see things cooperatively.

When politicians deal with defense issues, ensuring effective weapons may not always be the most important thing. There was no argument in Kassebaum's office whether Burton was trying to improve the Bradley through better testing. But it was more important to Kassebaum for some other reason to do nothing. Coming from one of the top advocates of testing in Congress, her message was loud and clear: when push comes to shove, the "military reformers" on Capitol Hill can be cowed and do not hold their own self-professed principles above other considerations. No wonder so many in the Pentagon refuse to take the politicians in Congress seriously.

Antireform Wins Some Big Ones

After the Burton imbroglio, Weinberger found the right man for the testing job. He had been the in-house aircraft tester for the McDonnell-Douglas Corporation, a major military aircraft producer at the time. His background was in developmental—that is, laboratory—not operational testing. Also being a product of the corporate, weapons system advocacy community, he was precisely the kind of person that advocates of testing reform did not want. Obviously, he was perfect.

In setting up the office, this new Director of Operational Test and Evaluation (DOT&E) did many things the test reformers wanted to avoid. Perhaps most importantly, he appointed active duty military officers to oversee the testing of weapons sponsored by their own military services. This practice made it especially easy for test supervision personnel and report writers to be intimidated if they sought tough tests and complete and accurate reports on performance for systems the parent service wanted to be treated with kid gloves. The new DOT&E also continued and helped to perpetuate highly inappropriate practices by inviting corporate representatives to participate in operational tests and in at least one case score the results. These and other practices had real impact. When I was an evaluator with the General Accounting Office (GAO) in 1988 studying the work of this DOT&E, I and the other members of the GAO team found serious and uncalled for compromises in the rigor of tests or in the completeness and accuracy of reports for all six of the weapons programs we evaluated.[4]

The Congressional Military Reform Caucus had won a major battle in Congress by enacting operational test reform, but it just as clearly lost the war inside the DoD to see the law carried out as the reformers intended.

The same pattern occurred on other subjects. In 1986 and 1987, Congress passed new laws to protect whistleblowers, who exposed government waste and against whom their bureaucratic superiors lashed out. In 1985, 1986, and 1987, Congress passed successively stronger legislation to shut down the "revolving door" between industry and DoD permitting corporations to hire DoD managers who as government employees controlled the fate of the same corporation's weapons programs. However, these bills never became law in the form their authors intended. The Pentagon and its congressional allies assiduously watered down the provisions of the bills after they passed the House and the Senate and reached House-Senate conference committees appointed to resolve differences in the bodies' different versions of the same bill. Moreover, similar to the experiences of the testing bill, after any provisions with teeth remaining became law, the sharp edges were ground off by writing regulations that preserved the status quo and/or by appointing managers who were anything but aggressive about reforms.

The back-door maneuvering that the testing bill encountered both on Capitol Hill and in the Pentagon was not exceptional behavior by the opponents of reform, it was standard. The congressional authors of other reform legislation were not as vigilant as the authors of the testing bill to uphold the bill's provisions in law and regulation, but even when the legislative reformers were at their best as with the testing bill, they were not up to the task of frustrating at every turn an unrepentant and unrelenting Pentagon bureaucracy and its allies on Capitol Hill.

Ultimately, the Congressional Military Reform Caucus lost almost every battle it fought. Today, while an apparatus exists to protect government whistleblowers, they are still routinely harassed—to the point where organizations, such as the Project on Government Oversight, which is an outgrowth of Dina Rasor's Project on Military Procurement, have plenty of business. Moreover, individuals seeking to help "whistleblowers," such as Dina Rasor (who works at her own investigative firm that specializes in defending whistleblowers), have more clients than they know what to do with. The revolving door also continues to spin at warp speed: senior Pentagon decision makers, in and out of uniform, routinely go to work for the very same corporations that their government decisions had major impacts on.

In short, to have a real impact on the Pentagon, advocates of ideas it opposes need to expect to get down into the dirt of bureaucratic details and to fight sustained, nasty fights against an opposition that is deeply entrenched and that gives up only when it finds itself in dire circumstances, such as harsh press scrutiny. As an institution, Congress has neither the apparatus nor the inclination to fight those battles as persistently and at the imbedded working level of the bureaucracy as is usually necessary.

The Press Turns Away

In the late 1980s, the press was writing fewer and fewer articles about bad Pentagon management. After the umpteenth article about $436 hammers, $600 pliers, and the like, journalists and their editors seemed to think readers required something more. Dina Rasor described it like a cocaine addiction: for the press to think a new story was worth printing, it had to be worse than the one before. For the journalists to think the readers would get a "hit," there always had to be a bigger jolt. That was impossible to sustain; the Pentagon was not interested in making the spare parts horror stories even worse; it was happy to stand pat. What had been the cutting edge of reform in the public's eye, the horror stories about spare parts prices may have been becoming "old hat."

In hindsight, a different perspective argues that the problem may have been a bit different. Many, but not all, of the reformers failed to move the agenda to new subject matters. Rather than even worse horror stories, it was also possible that the press was ready to move to new subjects, and the reformers—at least the more vocal ones on Capitol Hill—failed to address that need. Not appreciating that what was needed was a different perspective on the fundamental problems, rather than still more examples of high costs for common items, some reformers may have failed to appreciate a change in the external environment and adapt to it.

As a result, some of the reformers simply upped the rhetoric without upgrading the data, let alone introducing new subject areas. By the late 1980s, someone came up with the idea during the holiday season to decorate a Christmas tree with DoD spare parts as a device to advertise cost abuses. Senator Roth and Congresswoman Boxer eagerly showed off the new press device, but there were no big new spare parts "horror stories," just a more dramatic trick to advertise the prices. It began to appear to some in the press and even among some reformers that spare parts "horror stories" were the beginning and ending of military reform, rather than a means to an end.

The reformers were also failing to convince the press of the deeper meaning of the horror stories. The outrageous spare parts prices were seen as isolated exceptions—albeit frequent—to the rule, not as examples of a systemic problem or a link to other issues. As news, the horror stories seemed to be a road leading just to repetition, not to a deeper insight into a systemic problem. Transparent press tricks—like the Christmas tree—were almost an admission that the press worthiness of the issue was at an end, that some were overusing a theme that gained them entry to the press without appreciating the need to expand their own and the press' horizons.

The spare parts horror stories were a part of a culture where frugality, ethics, and advocating effective weapons could be career inhibiting characteristics. People who exhibited those characteristics were often seen in DoD as problems, not assets. Such people threatened the weapons advocates, exposed flaws in senior Pentagon managers' decisions, and threatened the careers of what Bill Lind called "milicrats" who made names for themselves pushing weapons programs through production and themselves up the career ladder. In the final analysis, the reformers failed to effectively make the link between these types of behaviors and the "isolated examples" in spare parts price abuse.

The failure to establish the link wasn't for lack of trying by the reformers. They provided examples of the broader, deeper failures, but the examples they used often had a flaw: They involved the reformers themselves. The examples included the poor job performance rating Chuck Spinney's superiors tried to pin on him; the Army's efforts to have Col. Burton reassigned, in one case to Alaska; the almost annual attempts by Ernie Fitzgerald's bosses to fire or transfer him and his persistent efforts to bring the latest attempt (in infinite detail) to the attention of anyone who would listen. The efforts at retaliation and what the reformers were trying to impose on the Pentagon in terms of cost reform, better weapons, and tests and analysis of them were specific, concrete, and documented. However, the examples also seemed self-serving to some, both in the press and on Capitol Hill, especially those who were not already committed—or at least friendly—to the reform movement.

The experience left the impression on some that the reformers were using the press to fight their own internal bureaucratic wars, if not to advertise themselves. These examples did, of course, have such an element to them, embarrassing the Pentagon into ceasing its harassment was one of the intended effects of the revelations to the press. But, that was not the entire story. Why was the Pentagon trying to punish and expel people who were warning it of growing costs, programs that would cost soldiers their lives, and weapons that were likely to fail in combat? The personal elements to the stories may have become an impediment to journalists appreciating the substantive story and to write about the latter for the public.

From time to time I would hear some form of grumbling from journalists about yet another alert that a reformer was being punished by the Pentagon. Some in the press grew reluctant to go down this road more than just a few times; some became more than reluctant. After a while, both the substantive horror stories and the bureaucratic harassment were no longer handled as significant news. The articles slipped to the back pages of newspapers or out of the public's sight altogether.

On the other hand, in the 1990s and after the millennium, some of the reformers continued to have excellent access to the press, including Chuck Spinney. As with his earlier experiences, there was no obvious attempt to attract press attention. Instead, he wrote typically long and data filled analyses (sometimes with, sometimes without his personal commentary) and simply made them available. He published articles in multiple journals and established himself as someone who understood defense issues in excruciating detail. As a result he was quoted in news articles—frequently in national newspapers like the *New York Times* and *Wall Street Journal*—on an almost weekly basis. By the late 1990s he adopted the technique to publish an electronic newsletter—he called them "blasters"—containing his examination of a variety if issues, ranging from the Navy's flawed design of the wing for its new "E" model of the F-18 to water rights on the West bank in the Middle East to the possibility of sectarian conflict in Iraq should the United States ever attempt to invade and occupy that country. He distributed his blasters to hundreds of people many of them journalists.

What was missing, however, was a direct link to legislative action on Capitol Hill or managers in the Pentagon who saw no option but to incorporate his analysis into decision making. Instead, the Hill wandered off into other, mostly nondefense, issues, and Pentagon managers learned that if they simply ignored Spinney, no one on Capitol Hill or elsewhere would make their disregarding him painful to them. The pain would come later when their poorly informed or politically driven decisions fell apart.

The reformers, especially those of us most closely associated with Capitol Hill, essentially ran out the string with the press without being able to convince journalists that we had a broader, deeper story to be told and without, in fact, trying particularly hard to tell any different story.

A few in the press did, indeed, move on to new coverage of the reformers, but not to where some hoped.

The Press Gets Surly

As the articles on Pentagon scandals waned, the *Washington Times* started a periodic column, "Soldiering," by a military affairs writer, Fred Reed. Initially, he seemed highly enthusiastic about the reformers, and he visited Dina Rasor's office to talk to some of her staff. The initial eagerness wore off, and the ultimate result was columns characterizing Rasor as an empty headed dupe who could never get her facts straight. However, no one paid much attention; it was, after all, the *Washington Times*, that few in Washington paid much serious attention, especially then.

Then, in October 1987, the *Washington Post* printed a Fred Reed column in its Sunday "Outlook" section.[5] The piece was not only in the most widely read opinion page in Washington, it was also a personal attack on not just Dina Rasor, but also Pierre Sprey and Bill Lind. Reed focused on what he said was unprofessional, unethical behavior, including "lack of adherence to high school standards of research." He charged the reformers failed to understand technical issues; for example, he alleged the reformers wrongly asserted aluminum armor on U.S. armored personnel carriers burns and helps to incinerate American crewmen.[6]

Rasor wrote a long and detailed rebuttal to Reed's accusations, including the technically wrong conclusion he asserted about aluminum armor, and John Boyd and Pierre Sprey met with the congressmen who in 1987 were the House Chairmen of the military reform caucus, Congressmen Charles Bennett (D, Fla) and Tom Ridge (R, Pa.). After clearing the air about the facts of the matter, Boyd and Sprey reminded the congressmen that a central tenet of military reform, and of the briefing that caucus members and their staff frequently gave to others, was the emphasis on people, especially treating them ethically. Boyd made it clear he believed the congressmen should step up to the plate and defend the reformers. After all, Rasor, Sprey, Lind, and others had done much to help the congressmen with lots of good press and hot revelations about Pentagon misbehavior. Now they were being attacked, and it was time to show that the reformers stuck together and valued their own core principles. It was also another case of the reformers seeking help when they, themselves, were the issue.

Like Senator Kassebaum before them, Congressmen Bennett and Ridge demurred. They said they did not think it wise to respond to Reed's allegations; that would just circulate them to an even wider readership, and in politics that's not smart. Boyd insisted; voices grew louder; tempers flared.

Perhaps Bennett's and Ridge's hesitancy was based on what they thought was smart; perhaps they didn't buy the rebuttal; perhaps they didn't like Boyd's insistent tone and wanted to show who was a congressman and who wasn't. Whatever their real reason, they were declining to come to the public defense of people who had done much to help them. Members of Congress who had drunk deeply of military reform when the press coverage was spectacular were no longer thirsty when the press was being less than idolatrous.

Ultimately, Congressman Mel Levine (D, Calif.) and Congresswoman Barbara Boxer (D, Calif.) did write responses defending the reformers to the *Post* (which the *Post* did not print), and even Bennett and Ridge would write a tepid piece in favor of the reformers six months later in a weekly defense journal.[7] However, the Congressional Military Reform Caucus was never the same again. The links between Congress and the reformers in the Pentagon were permanently broken. In addition, the once hot press operation in Rasor's Project on Military Procurement wasn't getting so many calls any more. The caucus would hobble on until 1992 when Congresswoman Boxer announced its official end with the superficial contention (assessed in Chapter 6) that reform had brilliantly succeeded as demonstrated by the easy American defeat of Iraq's armed forces in Operation Desert Storm, the first Gulf war, in 1991.

The members of Congress were not having fun any more being military reformers. The other side had fought back, and the congressional reformers could no longer just roll over the Pentagon and the rest of Congress with their universally favorable press coverage and novel sounding ideas. When the easy part of the ride came to an end, so did the Congressional Military Reform Caucus.

Reformer Opts for Rhetorical Fluff

Congresswoman Barbara Boxer fought to maneuver the House into passing legislation on whistle-blower and other reform issues in the mid to late 1980s. She worked closely with Dina Rasor, who handed Boxer many newsy items to reveal to the press. These included a $7,600 coffee maker/beverage warmer and several spare parts horror stories. In doing so, Boxer also worked closely with a woman on Rasor's staff, Donna Martin. Ultimately, Boxer hired Martin for her own office, and together they wrote and passed bills the Pentagon worked hard to undo.

Those bills helped Boxer make a name for herself as a no nonsense, highly effective legislator. Without Rasor and Martin, Boxer would have been pretty much nowhere in finding the newsy Pentagon problems and informed ideas for solving them. Time and time again, the combination of Boxer's political toughness and parliamentary acumen and Rasor's and Martin's contacts, documents, and information generated a legislative dynamo in the House of Representatives. Boxer made herself into a national figure.

In 1992, based in significant part on the name she made for herself with Rasor's and Martin's help, Boxer ran successfully in California for the U.S. Senate. Within a week after her election, Boxer had some bad news to pass on to Donna Martin; she told one of her legislative aides to fire Martin. Refusing to meet Martin herself, Boxer had it explained there was no longer any place for Martin on Boxer's new, expanded senate staff.

Since then, Boxer has continued to be vocal about defense issues but has accomplished nothing of note. She gives speeches on defense spending, and she took some pains to talk against the acquisition of Gulfstream VIP transports, which are not made in California. In 2003, Dina Rasor attempted to contact Senator Boxer to see if she wanted to reestablish contact. Rasor was not allowed to speak to the senator and was fobbed off onto a staff member, who was disinterested in anything Rasor had to say and whom Rasor later characterized to me as "an arrogant jerk."

Boxer's discarding both Martin and Rasor as associates gave them all the appearance of being expendable, having served their purpose as stepping stones for the elevation of the politician's career. It was hardly an exceptional experience in politics, but it is remarkable how casually Boxer discarded support integral to her success and adopted a new posture that was voluble but also ineffectual.

It was another clear example that to the politicians on Capitol Hill the primary role the reformers served was to help propel the career of the politicians, not military reform.

Subtle but Powerful Weapons

As many senators will say privately and as I learned over my three decades of working there, the Senate is a club, an exclusive club. Even members who like to parade as iconoclasts like to maintain their good standing in the club.

In 1984, Senator Kassebaum offered an amendment in the Senate chamber to improve the engines of the Air National Guard's F-4 fighter-bombers: they smoked badly, leaving a distinct exhaust trail. This made it easy for the enemy in the air and on the ground to detect the F-4s and judge their speed and direction to attack them. Kassebaum's amendment funded kits to fix the engines by "de-smoking" them. She gave her explanation and justification in the Senate chamber from memoranda I had given her, put her papers on her desk, and left the chamber for other business.

Senator Barry Goldwater (R, Ariz.) had been arguing for the Armed Services Committee against Kassebaum's amendment. After she left the chamber, Goldwater walked over to her desk, sat down in her chair, picked up her papers, and started reading. Sitting in the staff seats in the back of the chamber, I was amazed at Goldwater's brazen behavior. Reading another Senator's notes and memoranda without permission was way, way beyond accepted Senate "club" rules.

I warily got up, walked up behind Goldwater, and said, "Senator, those are Senator Kassebaum's papers you are reading; shall I tell her you found them interesting?" A wide-eyed Goldwater turned around to look at me and said in a surprised tone, "Oh, I used to fly these things." He put down the papers he had filched and returned to his own desk. In Senate terms, Goldwater had displayed for all senators and staff in the chamber to see a crude and open contempt for Kassebaum. He was not willing to grant her even the rudimentary senatorial courtesy of respecting the privacy of her personal papers. That the staffers in the rear of the chamber had received his message was clear to me from their snickering when I returned to my seat. When she returned to the chamber, I told Kassebaum what had transpired. She looked at me in disbelief and said, "Oh, Barry wouldn't do that!" She was not even willing to admit Goldwater had behaved so brazenly insulting.

The point was an important one. The establishment in the Senate on defense issues, the Armed Services Committee, was not going to give the reformers even minimal respect. The message was conveyed not just to the reformers, such as Senator Kassebaum and myself, but most importantly to the fence sitters and sunshine reformers: "if you side with those people, we will treat you with the same disrespect; you will be beyond normal respect; you will be out of the club." In the Senate, this was a powerful message.

While another senator might have upbraided Goldwater for his crude behavior, Kassebaum chose not to. Her confronting Goldwater could have reversed the tables and made him the one defining himself as in not good standing in the club, but that would have raised the stakes of the fight to a level Kassebaum did not seek.

To engage the Pentagon and its allies in a fight over control of America's defenses, as the reformers clearly intended, is to enter a battle that will be fought at many levels. In a political setting like the Senate where the boundaries of what is allowed in a fight are wide indeed, Goldwater evidenced that he was willing to go to great lengths, and finding no opponent in the fight, he won it by default.

The Enemy of My Pork Is My Enemy

There were other ways politicians in Congress fight and which the reformers chose not to engage in.

Even though he never came to meetings in later years, Senator Cohen remained an official member of the Reform Caucus. This meant his staff was invited to all caucus briefings and other events. One Cohen staffer was a retired Navy officer who was particularly protective of his former service's newest air defense technology, the Aegis radar and missile system. Aegis was installed on the new Ticonderoga class cruisers that just happened to be built in Cohen's state of Maine, at the Bath Iron Works, the state's largest employer.

The retired Navy captain on Cohen's staff came to a caucus briefing on the Aegis system on February 23, 1984. There, Pierre Sprey, Bill Lind, a radar expert (Dr. Thomas Amlie), and Congressman Denny Smith (R, Wash.) presented data and other reasons why this high cost radar system was poorly suited to defend against very low altitude, "sea skimming," antiship missiles. These had become immensely popular in most navies, especially the Soviets'. The presenters argued that the Aegis system needed to be much more thoroughly tested against "sea skimmers" before the Aegis/Ticonderoga ship system went into full production.

Cohen's retired Navy staffer took nine single-spaced, typewritten pages of notes on everything said at the briefing and delivered them to the Navy. The notes were detailed and mostly accurate, but also contained various asides to indicate the author's sympathy for the Navy's side of the controversy.[8] The notes were in our own hands the day after the Navy got them—from an ally who also warned us of their source, saying something like, "You have a spy in your midst."

Our source also warned us that the Navy had "loaded Senator Cohen for bear" to aggressively take on Congressman Smith, who was to testify to Cohen's Sea Power and Force Projection Subcommittee of the Armed Services Committee the following March.[9] Smith wanted the Ticonderoga class cruiser and its Aegis air defense system to be better tested before it went into full production.

Cohen's hearings were a stacked deck. As congressional courtesy requires, Congressman Smith testified first. Senator Cohen questioned him in detail on many points, tersely and without the elaborate courtesies members of Congress usually extend to each other. Then followed a procession of pro-Aegis witnesses, a civilian naval historian whose mind was clearly made up in favor of Aegis, the Admiral responsible for surface warfare (i.e., Aegis cruisers), and a captain who was the project manager of the Aegis system. With Cohen leading them through the issues, the civilian and the Navy witnesses aggressively advocated the program and went to lengths to refute Congressman Smith's arguments and obviate any delay in Aegis ship production: Aegis was already thoroughly tested; the system was flawless; Smith didn't know what he was talking about, they argued.

Cohen seemed to be operating from the premise that more rigorous, more realistic tests would harm the Aegis program.

A few years later in 1988, I would participate in a GAO study of Aegis testing: in highly unrealistic, cooperative tests, Aegis performed on average with great mediocrity. In a small number of more stressful tests against a certain (classified) category of targets, the system had a record unblemished by a single success.[10]

The Navy classified these and more details and continued to crow about how effective the system was.

The reformers also threatened other programs: the B-1B bomber, the DIVAD antiaircraft gun, the Viper antitank missile, and the Copperhead guided artillery round, among others. Most of these ultimately proved to be obvious technical failures and were cancelled (however, the Air Force continues to struggle with the B-1B). However, each had its stout defenders on Capitol Hill, many of whom just happened to be from the state or congressional district where major parts of them were produced.

Then, almost as much as now, members of Congress had a knee jerk reaction to what they saw as threats to corporate spending and employment in their states. That the "threat" might make for a better tested, better understood, more effective defense program that saves U.S. lives was immaterial. It was more important to keep the corporation's existing contract and the employment it brought on track than to explore, and if necessary fix, the program.

The threat was not just to the program's schedule, it was also to the politician. If he or she did not protect the program, he/she was not protecting voters' jobs; to protect the program was to protect the politician's career.

Some members of Congress tried to be both military reformers and porkers, but when the two conflicted, pork usually won. When a reformer, like Congressman Smith, threatened another's pork, it put the reformers outside Senate club norms. It is ok, expected even, to oppose other members on political questions, but delaying the flow of federal dollars into another's state was pushing the boundaries. The club didn't like that behavior.

With the defenders of business as usual trying to push the reformers beyond the pale of club membership, and with the reformers themselves sometimes willingly placing themselves outside membership in good standing, the reformers tended to become isolated. That is not a good place to be in a political environment where the votes are counted accurately and only the majority wins.

Blue Ribbon Coup de Grace

At the urging of John Tower in 1985, President Reagan called for yet another "blue ribbon panel" to fix the Pentagon. The deluge of public criticisms of DoD had taken its toll, and the standard response of Secretary of Defense Weinberger and his senior staff that the problems didn't exist, were grossly overstated, or had already been solved simply had not washed with the press and the public.

Senator Tower and President Reagan were responding with a well worn Washington tactic: when you don't know what you want to do, or don't want to do what you know you need to do, establish a commission to study the thing and report back in a year or two. Such commissions have the useful effect of freezing things in place: anyone who opposes a reform can simply argue that the proposed action is premature as all the ills are being studied by the prestigious "blue ribbon panel," and everybody needs to wait for it to recommend what is best.

The Tower-Reagan "blue ribbon panel" was a stacked deck: its chairman was the same David Packard who in 1972 as deputy secretary of defense oversaw the nonimplementation of the reforms recommended by the 1971 Fitzhugh Blue Ribbon Commission. Prominent among the new "Packard Commission's" members was Dr. William J. Perry, who had long opposed reformers' ideas, especially as regards technology, and who in 1978, as mentioned earlier, killed off the Fitzhugh Commission recommendation to establish an independent office to run operational testing, the same idea Senator Pryor legislated in 1983. (Perry would, of course, rise to even greater prominence as President Clinton's second secretary of defense.) To top it all off, the staff director for the new Packard Commission was Senator Tower's former staff director for the Armed Services Committee.

The new commission started issuing reports in February 1986, just in time to catch Congress' annual cycle for writing the annual DoD Authorization bill, the most likely legislative vehicle for DoD reform. The Commission's findings and recommendations were mostly vapid platitudes; some were pernicious. Most of them were replays of the recommendations made by the lesser DoD reform commissions in the 1950s, 1960s, and 1970s: DoD needed "more and better long range planning," budgets should be based on national strategy and should run for two years, not one; major figures like the secretary, his undersecretary for procurement, and the chairman of the Joint Chiefs should all be given more authority; procurement rules should be re-codified into a single document; more items should be bought "off the shelf" as commercially available items, and DoD should stop harassing defense manufacturers with investigations and let the manufacturers audit themselves. And, Senator Pryor's 1983 operational test reform should be undone by permitting the Pentagon's new centralized "acquisition czar" to control testing (the students should be put back in charge of writing and grading their own exams).[11]

Some of these recommendations sounded very reasonable. An example was the idea of buying more commercially available items, especially spare parts, to reduce the horrors uncovered by Ernie Fitzgerald. But, what actually resulted reveals much about Pentagon culture: defense manufacturers started printing catalogues of their "commercially available" products. The items were unaltered from their past noncommercial existence, but now, being in a catalogue, they were "commercially available." The reasonable sounding reform changed nothing.

The proposal to undo the 1983 test reform legislation caught the reformers' attention, and we spent much time and energy opposing it. We won that fight, but in the meantime—with the reformers energies preoccupied—most of the other Packard recommendations were codified into law. So proud of their final handiwork were the House and Senate Armed Services Committees that they honored senior members by naming the new law after them: the "Goldwater-Nichols Department of Defense Reorganization Act of 1986."

The Goldwater-Nichols codification of most of the Packard Commission recommendations quickly acquired a reputation as the ultimate in defense reform. It also reclaimed for the Armed Services Committees the lost mantle of authority on defense issues that the reformers had been stripping from them.

Later, the good name of the Packard-Goldwater-Nichols reforms started to fray around the edges. In July 2002, Secretary of Defense Rumsfeld complained of the department taking double the time it took in the past to produce new weapon systems. He also reviled the huge bureaucracy and headquarters staffs that performed little, if any, useful function, and he yearned for real commercial business management techniques in the Pentagon.[12] These are all problems the 1986 Packard-Goldwater-Nichols drill was credited with fixing.

Indeed, in 2005 the media's coverage of Pentagon management reads like just another chapter from the same book of the pre-Goldwater-Nichols era of the early 1980s. Aircraft manufacturers were found producing substandard parts at exorbitant prices.[13] Despite its huge cost, parts and labor on the V-22 "tilt-rotor" aircraft for the Marines were found to be quite shoddy, and when a conscientious employee attempted to alert the contractor, we was fired for his pains.[14] More fundamentally, GAO found DoD to have so many problems that it takes little reading between the lines to conclude it is the most poorly run major agency in the federal government.[15] Indeed, a different rating system by the Office of Management and Budget showed DoD to be one of the worst managed departments of the federal government. In 2006, a new chairman of the House Armed Services Committee, Duncan Hunter (R, CA), acknowledged the failure of the Goldwater-Nichols legislation to do anything positive about DoD acquisition management saying, "Now, 20 years later, four major studies [by GAO] were recently released that conclude essentially the same things [as had been re-discovered by the Packard Commission in 1986]."[16] The failure had been complete and widespread, except that it relieved the pressure for more meaningful reform.

Conclusion

Imposing change from the outside on an unwilling Pentagon is a steep uphill climb that is made no easier by the nature of the Pentagon itself, Congress, and journalism in America.

Congress is ill-suited to force the Pentagon to change. Members of Congress are neither in a position nor disposed by their profession to fight the long, nasty, underground bureaucratic battles that must be won if reform legislation, even when it lacks major loopholes, is to have any real impact. More importantly, being politicians whose first priority is political survival, members of Congress are just as likely to turn against reform propositions and their advocates when they become unpopular or when they attract negative attention as they are to turn toward them when they bring favorable headlines and popular acclaim.

In short, Congress is a weak and sunshine-only reed to rely on as a lever to impose change on the Pentagon. It may be a useful component for imposing some reforms, certainly any requiring legislation, but alone, it is insufficient.

Unwritten club rules in Congress, especially the Senate, make it difficult for any member of Congress to pursue reform and remain a member in good standing. However, it remains to be seen if a member who steps outside the expected code of behavior on Capitol Hill and remains a virtual outcast can actually exercise significant influence on Capitol Hill by defining with his or her behavior a new standard for ethics, understanding the issues, and doing something about them.[17]

The press also has significant limitations. It collectively lacks staying power, and in too many cases, it can be interested only in superficial, "newsworthy" issues. For important but intellectually difficult, sometimes boring, explanations for why some things are the way they are requires an extraordinary journalist with an extraordinary venue willing to publish such material. Surely, there remain today journalists acutely interested in fundamental defense issues and editors willing to print their work, but they are the exception, and there are too few of them to seize and hold the attention of the American body politic—lacking an apocalyptic event that galvanizes the nation's and the press' attention.

In short, asking Congress and the press to act as the main levers to impose reform on the Pentagon and to sustain the effort is asking for the impossible. Highly appropriate for a short term effort or for part of a larger effort, neither has the nature to be able to change the likes of business as usual in the Pentagon.

Given the likely impermanence of congressional impetus for change the Pentagon does not want, it becomes immensely easy for the Pentagon to reassert itself after a wave of reform passes. A public part of that counterreformation can come in the form of "blue ribbon" panels, such as the 1986 Packard exercise, which under the guise of change can be nothing more than business as usual reclaiming the mantle of legitimacy. By the time such occurs, most of those who earlier shouted reform from the rooftops will have scattered to the winds or may be shouting a different tune.

Notes

1. The events related here about Senator Kassebaum and Col. James Burton were first related in the author's "The Wastrels of defense." The material that follows is an adaptation of those passages and are reproduced here, with various editing changes, with permission.

2. The quotes and summaries here and below are from copies of the author's memoranda to Senator Kassebaum and her handwritten responses.

3. For more details, see James G. Burton, *The Pentagon Wars: Reformers Challenge the Old Guard*, Naval Institute Press, 1993. Home Box Office also made a TV movie out of Burton's experiences.

4. See *Weapons Testing: Quality of DOD Operational Testing and Reporting*, General Accounting Office, GAO/PEMD-88-32BR, July 1988.

5. Fred Reed, "Lets Reform the Military Reformers," *Washington Post*, Outlook, October 11, 1987, p. H1.

6. Ibid., p. H1.

7. Charles Bennett and Tom Ridge, "Military Reformers: A Defense Asset," *Defense News*, March 28, 1988, p. 32.

8. "Notes from briefing for members and staff held February 23, 1984 from 2:15 until 4:00 in SR-188 on Aegis TESTING [sic.]," February 23, 1984, unsigned.

9. See "Department of Defense Authorization for Appropriations for Fiscal Year 1985," Hearings before the Committee on Armed Services, United States Senate, Part 8, Sea Power and Force Projection Subcommittee, March 14, 28, 29, April 5, 11, May 1, 1985.

10. See *Weapons Testing: Quality of DOD Operational Testing and Reporting*, General Accounting Office, GAO/PEMD-88-32BR, July 1988.

11. See Packard Commission reports: "An Interim Report to the President," by the President's Blue Ribbon Commission on Defense Management, February 28, 1986; and "A Formula for Action; A Report to the President on Defense Acquisition," April 1986.

12. Donald H. Rumsfeld, "Why Defense Must Change," *Washington Post*, July 18, 2002, p. A19.

13. John M. Donnelly, "Plane Makers Bought Suspect Parts by the Thousands," *Defense Week*, July 3, 2003, p. 1.

14. Bob Cox, "Bell Is Facing Federal Scrutiny," *Fort Worth Star Telegram*, December 13, 2003.

15. "DoD's High-Risk Areas: Successful Business Transformation Requires Sound Strategic Planning and Sustained Leadership," Statement of David M. Walker, Comptroller General of the United States, before the Subcommittee on Readiness and Management Support, Senate Armed Services Committee, U.S. Senate, April 13, 2005, GAO-05-520T.

16. Roxana Tiron, "Lawmaker Calls Pentagon's uying System 'Terribly Broken,'" *The Hill*, April 6, 2006.

17. For further discussion of this line of reasoning, see the final chapter ("Twelve Not-So-Easy Steps to a Sober Congress") of *The Wastrels of Defense: How Congress Sabotages US Security* by the author.

CHAPTER 4

The Lost Decade

Lawrence J. Korb

Introduction

As noted in Chapter 3, by the end of the 1980s, it had become clear that the attempt to radically change or reform the Pentagon to make our armed forces more efficient and effective had ended. However, the sudden and unexpected collapse of the Soviet Union in the early 1990s gave those interested in reforming the armed forces another opportunity to reshape the Department of Defense (DoD). The collapse of the Soviet Empire was not the only development that made reform imperative. At the same time that the cold war was winding down, the information revolution was heating up and changing the way in which the private sector was operating. Some of the proponents of military reform now wanted to exploit these new technologies to bring about a Revolution in Military Affairs (RMA); that is, change dramatically the way in which the armed forces were organized, equipped, and trained to fight war.

This process of reforming the military by taking advantage of the "Revolution in Military Affairs" came to be known as defense transformation. The goal of these new reformers was to produce an innovative and high-tech U.S. military force that would become dramatically more effective by using a space-sea-air-and ground network of sensors to pinpoint enemy forces and a similar network of precision guided munitions to destroy them from long range.

In effect they hoped to replicate the success of the German military, which in the spring of 1940, married two revolutionary new technologies—the radio and the internal combustion engine—to facilitate the tactic of rapid coordinated maneuver known as *blitzkrieg*, which they used to overwhelm the larger French military in six weeks in the spring of 1940.

Another reason mandating reform of the military was that during the 1990's the international environment was changing rapidly. The collapse of the Soviet Union, the rise of globalization, and the spread of technology enhanced the power of nonstate actors like al-Qaeda; led to a rapid increase in the number of failed states, in places like Yugoslavia, Afghanistan and Somalia and the emergence of extreme regimes in Iran and North Korea.

The concern of the reformers was summed up by Bill Lind and three midlevel officers in the *Marine Corps Gazette* in 1989. They argued that military history can broadly be grouped into three "generations": pre-Napoleonic, 1805–1939, and 1939–? Each generation has specific characteristics, for example, the third generation focused on firepower and mobility, while the second generation is characterized by mass and positional warfare. As a result of their analysis, they come to two conclusions. First, forces that subscribe to a previous generation of warfare (the Prussians at Jena, the French in 1940) are almost always crushed by enemies using the stratagems of the next generation (Napoleon's attack in columns and levée en masse, the Wehrmacht's "blitzkrieg"). Second, the writers argue that the world is on the cusp of warfare's fourth generation that they described as follows:

> In broad terms, fourth generation warfare seems likely to be widely dispersed and largely undefined; the distinction between war and peace will be blurred to the vanishing point. It will be nonlinear, possibly to the point of having no definable battlefields or fronts. The distinction between "civilian" and "military" may disappear. Actions will occur concurrently throughout all participants' depth, including their society as a cultural [including public opinion], not just a physical, entity.[1]

In trying to cope with these changes, the Pentagon conducted three major reviews of its defense posture in the 1990s, that is, during the last half of the administration of the first president Bush and in the Clinton administration. Two of these; the Base Force and Bottom-Up Review (BUR) were initiated by the DoD, while the third, the first Quadrennial Defense Review (QDR) was mandated by the Congress. In addition, Congress set up an independent body, the National Defense Panel, to make recommendations on reforming the armed forces.

Base Force Review

The first and most important review was called the Base Force. It was begun in late 1989 and unveiled to the Congress in January 1991. It was largely the work of Joint Chiefs of Staff (JCS) chairman, Colin Powell and his Joint Staff.[2] As President Reagan's assistant for National Security Affairs before moving to the JCS in 1989, Powell knew that the Soviet Union was on its last legs well before he became the nation's senior military officer. He believed that when the Soviet threat collapsed, the rationale for a large standing U.S. military would be undercut. Powell feared there would be a stampede by members of Congress arguing that since there was no threat, there would be no need for a large military, and since we did not need so many guns, we could start shifting large sums of money to such things as schools or housing or crime prevention.

Powell also knew that without a Soviet threat, the U.S. military would have to be smaller. There would be very little support within the political system for a cold war-size military in a post-cold war world, particularly in a Congress then controlled by the Democrats, many of whom had opposed much of the Reagan defense buildup. Powell feared that the Pentagon's political enemies would come after it with a chain saw if there was not an overarching strategy to guide the reductions. He was also aware that abstract concepts like "maintaining stability, preventing chaos in the international arena, or establishing a new world order" would not resonate politically as a justification for maintaining a significant military force in the post-cold war period. Finally, Powell did not wish to see the U.S. military diverted into such nonmilitary tasks as peacekeeping and nation-building. In his view, and that of most of his colleagues, the U.S. military exists to deter potential adversaries and to fight and win the nation's wars not engage in operations other than war. Powell wished to lead the U.S. Army not the Salvation Army.

Therefore, upon taking office and before the collapse of the Soviet Union in the fall of 1989, Powell began planning for what he called post-cold war "Base Force." Powell's action was a reversal of the normal procedure in the executive branch. Usually the secretary of defense and his staff or the national security advisor and his staff would develop the policy and strategy and leave it to the military to execute it. However, Powell's civilian bosses, Secretary of Defense Dick Cheney, Undersecretary of Defense Paul Wolfowitz, and National Security Advisor Brent Scowcroft, did not believe the collapse of the Soviet Union was imminent in 1989 or even in 1990. In fact, even after the fall of the Berlin Wall in late 1989, Cheney argued that the U.S. military budget should be cut by no more than 10 percent over the 1990–1995 period.

Powell's Base Force envisioned a military about 75 percent of the size and cost of the military that existed when he took office. According to the timetable Powell presented to his superiors, the Pentagon would reduce its force structure and budget by 5 percent each year in real terms between 1990 and 1995. By 1995, Powell's plan would have reduced the total force of uniformed military personnel from 3.3 million (2.1 million active and 1.2 million guard and reserve) to 2.5 million (1.6 million active and 0.9 million guard and reserve). The Base Force reductions in personnel would result in parallel cuts in the number of ground divisions, ships, and tactical air wings. For example, the Army would reduce the number of active divisions from 18 to 14; and the Marine Corps from 3 to 2; the Navy the number of ships from 528 to 450; and the Air Force the number of tactical fighter wings from 34 to 26. The essentials of the U.S. military would remain the same only somewhat smaller; that is, the forces would be organized and operated in the same way as they were in the cold war.

The Base Force also changed the way the United States rationalized its force structure. In the post-cold war world, with no Soviet military threat, the United States would shift from a threat-based force to a threat-and capability-based force. According to Powell, while the U.S. military might no longer have a specific airlift requirement to move millions of tons of supplies and equipment to Europe to deal with a massive Soviet and Warsaw Pact invasion, it still needed the capability to move large amounts of material to several places around the world. Similarly, while the United States might no longer face the Red Army in the Fulda Gap in Germany, the nation still needed to be able to project power to other places around the globe.

According to Powell his Base Force needed to be capable of performing four basic missions: first, it needed to be able to fight across the Atlantic; second, it needed to be capable of fighting across the Pacific; third, it needed to have a contingency force in the United States that could be deployed rapidly to hot spots, as the United States did to Panama in 1989; and finally, it needed to possess a nuclear force of sufficient size to deter nuclear adversaries.

Powell dealt with the issue of a specific enemy by arguing that his Base Force military needed to be capable of waging war by itself, that is, without allies, against what later became known as the rogue or outlaw states.[3] According to Powell, the threat from the Soviet Union had been replaced by something quite different—demons and dangers of a regional nature against whom the U.S. Armed Forces might have to go and fight.

"Rogue States" refers to hostile third world states with comparatively large military forces and robust weapons of mass destruction (WMD) capabilities. According to those who characterize them as rogues or outlaws, these states harbor aggressive intentions against their less powerful neighbors, oppose the spread of democracy, and are guilty of circumventing international norms against nuclear, biological, and chemical proliferation. The chairman of the JCS identified six rogue states, which, in his view, posed a military threat to U.S. interests: Iran, Iraq, Syria, Libya, Cuba, and North Korea. Powell argued that U.S. forces could not be sized to defeat just one of those rogues, because that might tempt another potential aggressor, or outlaw state, to take advantage of a situation when all U.S. forces were committed against one. For example, if all U.S. forces were committed to a war in the Persian Gulf against Iran or Iraq, North Korea might believe the United States could not respond with sufficient force in a timely manner if it attempted to cross the 38th parallel. Therefore, Powell complemented his "rogue" doctrine with the two-war concept, that is, the U.S. military should be structured to handle two major regional conflicts (MRCs) simultaneously. Finally, the United States had to assume that its allies would not automatically come to its aid in the event of a conflict in the Persian Gulf or the Korean peninsula. Accordingly, Powell believed that the United States would need a force of 11 ground divisions, 10 tactical air wings, and some 6 aircraft carriers—about 400,000 troops in order to prevail in each theatre. In Powell's view, the rogue doctrine and the MRC concept without allied support justified a force that was about 75 percent of the size and structure of the military maintained during the cold war.

The Base Force analysis also resulted in some reductions in the area of conventional weapons modernization. The Pentagon terminated or reduced the production of some current-generation systems (AH-64 Apache attack helicopters,

F-16 multipurpose fighter planes, SSN-21 Seawolf attack submarines, and the V-22 Osprey tilt-rotor transport planes). However, the Base Force gave high priority to the development and production of several cold war systems: the Comanche scout and attack helicopter for the Army, the F-22 stealth air-to-air fighter for the Air Force, the F/A-18 E/F multipurpose tactical aircraft for the Navy, the Navy's new CVN-72 aircraft carrier, and the DDG-51 destroyer.

This approach to modernization put the Pentagon into an arms race with itself and was bound to cause problems by the second half of the 1990s. With the collapse of the Soviet Union, there was no real need for next-generation systems like the F-22 or new attack submarines. Moreover, since these new systems would be so expensive, the Pentagon could not replace existing systems on a one-to-one or even one-to-two basis with a procurement budget 25 percent below the cold war average.

The Base Force also gave high priority to maintaining the readiness of the remaining force structure at cold war levels. Since it was clear that the conventional forces would not have to face a sophisticated peer competitor like the Soviet Union on very short notice, this was a needlessly expensive extravagance. It required spending an increasing amount of money on operation and maintenance (O&M) per capita all throughout the 1990s. By the end of the decade, O&M spending per active duty troop had risen by 40 percent in real terms.

Powell also had strong ideas about the circumstances under which U.S. military forces should be committed. He argued that the U.S. military should be sent into battle only when three conditions were met: first, U.S. political objectives were clear and measurable; second, the country was prepared to use overwhelming force quickly and decisively to advance that objective; and third, military forces would be withdrawn when that objective was accomplished, that is, the political leaders had to have an exit strategy. Powell and most of his military colleagues did not wish to see the U.S. military become involved in more Vietnams (1962–1972) or Lebanons (1982–1983) where in their view the objectives were not clear and where the military had to fight, in Powell's words, with "one had tied behind its back." This approach to the use of military force became known as the Powell Doctrine.

For three reasons, the Bush administration accepted, uncritically, the rationale of the Base Force as well as the force structure, modernization plans, and readiness criteria proposed by Powell. First, many members of Bush's national security team did not want even as much as a 25 percent reduction in defense spending as noted earlier Secretary of Defense Cheney wanted to reduce the defense budget by only 10 percent over the 1990–1995 period, and reprimanded Powell for publicly revealing the Base Force concept. Second, the Bush administration did not want to become involved in peacekeeping and stabilization operations around the globe. It never sent forces to Bosnia and agreed only to what it thought was a limited involvement in Somalia.

Unfortunately, for those advocating real reform in the military, the 1991 Persian Gulf conflict occurred just as the Base Force was being finalized for inclusion in President Bush's National Security Strategy Report. In the view of Powell and his supporters, that conflict demonstrated perfectly the Base Force's concept of an MRC: the conflict was a limited war, fought against a state that used somewhat familiar tactics; the U.S. military was able to use its overwhelming conventional superiority to force a very quick decision, and the military was out of the theater quickly (100 hours of ground combat after 37 days of bombing). Third, Bush assumed he would have a second term in which he and his team could develop their own defense strategy. Bush's single term was dominated by the adjustment to the collapse of the Soviet Union and by the first Persian Gulf War and its aftermath.

The Bottom-Up Review

One of the severest critics of the Base Force approach was Les Aspin, chairman of the House Armed Services Committee during the Bush administration. As a graduate of the Pentagon's Systems Analysis Office, Aspin criticized the Powell-Cheney-Bush review as being "top-down," resulting in forces by subtraction that responded to the Pentagon's organizational needs rather than to real threats to U.S. interests. Aspin argued that a real "bottom-up review" was needed if the United States were to get the peace dividend it earned by spending $10 trillion to bring about the collapse of the Soviet empire and the Soviet Union. In early 1992 he presented options to the Congress that would have given this nation a completely different military at much less cost. Aspin's plan could have saved as much as $231 billion over the FY 1993–1997 period.[4]

The Democratic candidate for president in 1992, Arkansas Governor Bill Clinton, endorsed the Aspin approach, and President Clinton, "the candidate for change," appointed Aspin to be secretary of defense in order to change the Pentagon by conducting a real Bottom-Up Review (BUR).

Aspin and his deputy and eventual successor, William Perry, did indeed carry out the BUR, but despite their best efforts, it was a bottom-up review in name only. The Aspin-Perry review resulted in a military hardly changed from the Base Force. This was not surprising given the fact that Powell remained as JCS chairman and resisted any major changes, that Aspin did not have a full team of appointees in place during the review, and that President Clinton did not want any significant battles with the military hierarchy after his failed attempt to get them to drop the ban on gays.

In the BUR, the two-war concept was sanctified and the services essentially protected their vital interests. The Navy was allowed to keep the twelve carrier battle groups it had needed during the cold war. The Air Force did give up some 200 tactical fighters, but gained an equal number of strategic bombers for tactical use. The active Army gave up two ground divisions, but the Army National Guard and Army reserve were maintained at the cold war levels, and the Marines actually added a division's worth of ground forces.

Like the Base Force, maintaining cold war levels of readiness was given a top priority by the Bottom-Up Review and operations and maintenance funding per active duty troop still grew significantly. Relics of the cold war like the SSN-21 Seawolf submarine, Trident II missiles, the F-22 fighter, and Milstar satellite communications system survived the review, even though the Soviet threat that brought about their development had gone away. In addition, the Clinton administration resurrected the Marine Corps' $80 billion V-22 Osprey transport plane, and the $9 billion Seawolf submarine that Dick Cheney, the Bush administration's secretary of defense, had tried to cancel. There were some changes, but they were minor: overall military manpower was cut by another 8 percent to 2.3 million, and projected levels of defense spending over the FY 1994–1998 period were reduced by 9 percent on the dubious assumption that reform of the acquisition system would save substantial funds.[5]

The BUR pleased neither conservatives nor liberals nor military reformers. Conservatives argued that the reductions Clinton proposed to make in the Bush plan, which amounted to $127 billion, or 9 percent over the FY 1994–1998 period, made it impossible to prepare effectively for two nearly simultaneous major theater wars. In addition, these defense hawks were unhappy with the fact that in the Clinton administration the military began to be diverted into "operations other than war," or small-scale contingencies, in places such as Haiti and Bosnia. Liberals, on the other hand, were unhappy that Clinton had made such a comparatively small reduction in Bush's program. Their unhappiness was compounded when Clinton himself continually added back some of the funds he had cut and then agreed to additions the Republican Congress made to his proposals. By the end of his first term, about $100 billion of the $127 billion in cuts were restored by Clinton, or the Congress with Clinton's assent. Over the FY 1994–1998 period Clinton actually spent more on defense than the first President Bush had projected upon leaving office.[6]

The reformers felt that the BUR, just like the Base Force, had not given the Pentagon the ability to wage fourth generation warfare. Their fears were confirmed by events in Somalia. The U.S. involvement in Somalia in 1992 started as a mission to provide humanitarian aid to famine victims in Somalia, but when the Clinton administration took over in 1993 it became a military mission against the Habr Gedir clan and its leader, Mohammed Adid. Adid and the Habr Gedir were considered to be the main obstacle to peace in Somalia, and "Task Force Ranger," a collection of Special Forces units was assembled to operate against the clan. This was to be textbook example of fourth generation warfare.

The Base Force proved itself to be unsuited for this war. The U.S. military lost the "hearts and minds" of Somali citizens in the fall of 1993 when its AH-1 helicopters attacked a meeting of Habr Gedir clan elders who were discussing a peace proposal, killing several and its attempts to abduct Mohammad Adid resulted in the loss of eighteen American Soldiers, and two UH-60 helicopters because the Special Forces found themselves in a battle against thousands of Somalis. Some were members of Adid's militia, but others were unaffiliated Somalis, alienated by the seeming callousness of the U.S. troops in the area.

Quadrennial Defense Review

In order to deal with the criticisms of the Pentagon's first two efforts, Congress mandated that the Pentagon do another review, a Quadrennial Defense Review (QDR), and Congress also set up an independent panel the National Defense Panel (NDP) to review the QDR. As might be expected, the QDR and the NDP came up with different conclusions. But neither dealt with the central issues of reforming the military to deal with the new post cold war environment

First, the Pentagon's QDR, like the Base Force and the BUR, reaffirmed the two-war scenario, thus leaving in place the force structure, modernization strategy, and readiness emphasis of the two previous reviews. Perry's successor, former Maine Senator William Cohen, a Republican in a Democratic administration, was no more willing than Perry, Aspin, or Clinton to take on the vested interests in the Pentagon or the Congress. The QDR postulated that the U.S. military needed to be able to "respond" to two Desert Storm-like regional conflicts at the same time. Second, the United States needed to continue to "shape" the international environment by continuing to maintain over 200,000 troops forward-deployed to Europe and Asia and by providing forces for small-scale contingencies like Bosnia and Haiti. Third, the United States should continue to maintain 7,000 strategic nuclear weapons until START II was ratified by the Russian Duma and then drop that number to 3,500. Finally, the United States should "prepare" for an uncertain future by continuing to modernize U.S. weapons.

The QDR did propose some marginal across-the-board reductions in personnel and weaponry. It set a goal of reducing active-duty manpower by 60,000 or 4 percent, civilian employees by 80,000 or 11 percent, and reserve personnel by 6 percent. The QDR also proposed reductions of about 25 percent in the planned buys of the F-22, the F/A-18 E/F, and the V-22 osprey but did not cancel any of these cold war relics.[7]

The National Defense Panel (NDP)

The NDP, which was unveiled in December 1997, did make some useful criticisms of the QDR. First, the panel pointed out that the two-war concept was not only obsolete but is primarily a device for justifying a "cold war-lite" force structure. Second, the NDP argued that the Pentagon was still spending too much money on yesterday's weapons such as the M1A1 Abrams battle tanks and Nimitz-class carriers. Third, the NDP criticized the Pentagon for not making ground units more mobile, and for failing to exploit the potential unmanned aerial vehicles and other reconnaissance and communications systems. Fourth, it recommended that DoD add $5–10 billion in annual funding to support new initiatives in intelligence, space, urban warfare, joint experimentation,

Table 4.1 U.S. Defense Policy Reviews

	Actual Force 1991	Base Force Recommendations, 1991	Bottom-Up, 1993	Review, QDR, 1997*
Army				
Active Divisions	18	14	11	10
Reserve Brigades	57	42	42	30
Air Force Tactical Wings				
Active	22	15	13	12
Reserve	12	11	7	8
Navy				
Ships	528	450	346	306
Carriers	15	13	12	12
Marine Corps				
Active Divisions	3	2	3	3
Reserve Divisions	1	1	1	1
Total Uniformed Personnel				
Active	2,130,000	1,640,000	1,450,000	1,360,000
Reserve	1,170,000	920,000	900,000	835,000

Note: *This is the force structure that existed on July 1, 2000.

and information operations in order to transform itself into a twenty-first-century force.

However, when the JCS opposed the recommendations of the NDP, Secretary of Defense Cohen also refused to support them. Instead, in the fall of 1998, Cohen supported the JCS request to the president for more funding for the current force posture. Although the Chiefs did not receive the full $150 billion they sought over the FY 2000–2005 period, Clinton gave them $112 billion over that period, and Congress added an additional $8 billion in FY 2000 and FY 2001 alone. As a result, a decade after the cold war the defense budget had declined by only 10 percent in real terms.

Summary

Table 4.1 summarizes the results of the three policy reviews conducted by the Pentagon during the 1990s: the Base Force, the BUR, and the QDR. It shows that from 1991 to 2000, active duty manpower was reduced by 770,000 or 36 percent and reserve manpower by 335,000 or 29 percent. What is more interesting and significant than the size of the overall reduction is that the reductions in the Army, Navy, and Air Force active manpower are almost exactly the same: 36, 37, and 37 percent respectively. Moreover, the service shares of the budget remained the same throughout the decade (Army 25 percent, Navy 31 percent, and Air Force 35 percent).

The fact that the defense force of 2000 was essentially a shrunken version of the Reagan-era cold war force, or that the budget shares of the three military departments remained unchanged, should not be surprising. As the previous chapters demonstrate, the Pentagon is a very difficult organization to change radically and the JCS are very skillful bureaucratic infighters. Moreover, Powell was the most influential military officer since World War II giants like Eisenhower and MacArthur, while Clinton, because of his lack of foreign policy experience and his draft history, was the least likely president to bring about real change in the Pentagon. As a result, by the turn of the century the Pentagon and the nation were in the worst of all possible worlds. By any reasonable comparison or historical standard, the level of defense spending was quite high, and yet the Pentagon still continued to train, plan, and equip itself to fight threats from a bygone era and had not taken full advantage of the revolution in military affairs to leverage new technology to project lethal power over great distances or reorganized itself to deal with fourth generation threats.

Conclusion

After a decade of studies and panels, the U.S. military was slightly smaller than it was when the cold war ended. But its force Structure was essentially a shrunken version of the cold war force and it continued to purchase cold war era weapons that dealt with threats from a bygone era. Just as in the 1970s and 1980s the reformers had lost to the military bureaucracy.

One of the strongest critics of the Pentagon's failed attempts to make any significant reforms in the decade of the 1990s was the Republican candidate for president in 2000, George W. Bush. In his successful campaign, Bush vowed to give his secretary of defense a broad mandate to challenge the status quo and envision a new architecture of American defense for decades to come. Chapter 5 will discuss how well this was done.

Notes

1. William Lind, Col. Keith Nightengale (USA), et al., "The Changing Face of War: Into the Fourth Generation," *Marine Corps Gazette*, October 1989.

2. For a description of the process of developing and the rationale for the Base Force see Colin Powell, *My American Journey*, Random House, New York, 1995, pp. 444–458.

3. See for example Michael Klare, *Rouge States and Nuclear Outlaws*, Hill and Wang, New York, 1996.

4. Les Aspin, An Approach to Sizing American Conventional Forces for the Post-Soviet Era: Four Illustrative Options, February 25, 1992. See also Bill Clinton and Al Gore, Putting People First, New York Times Books, 1992; Powell, My American Journey, pp. 579–580; and Lawrence Korb, "Our Overstuffed Armed Forces," Foreign Affairs, 74(6) (November/December 1995), 22–34.

5. Les Aspin, The Bottom Up Review: Forces for a New Era, September 1, 1997.

6. Daniel Gouré and Jeffrey Ranney, *Averting the Defense Train Wreck in the New Millennium*, CSIS Press, Washington, DC, 1999, p. 55.

7. The analysis of the QDR and NDP is based upon Michael O'Hanlon, *How to Be A Cheap Hawk: The 1999 and 2000 Defense Budgets*, Brookings Institution Press, Washington, DC, 1998, pp. 4–20.

CHAPTER 5

Defense Transformation

Lawrence J. Korb

Introduction

In the 2000 presidential campaign, then Governor Bush's criticism of Clinton's handling of the military fell into three broad categories. First, Bush and his advisors argued that Clinton had seriously underfunded the military. By comparing the percentage of the gross domestic product that Clinton had allocated to defense to that which the United States allocated in the late 1930s, the Bush team even implied that Clinton had allowed the state of our defense forces budget to fall to pre-Pearl Harbor levels. Second, Bush argued that Clinton had overstretched the military by using them repeatedly for stability and humanitarian operations in situations not critical to the nation's security. Bush pointed out that sending the military on nontraditional missions, or operations other than war, to places like Haiti and the Balkans to stabilize those areas and prevent the killing of the innocents was not their job and undermined its readiness to conduct major regional contingencies in places like the Persian Gulf and the Korean Peninsula.

Third, Bush argued that the Clinton administration had failed to take full advantage of the Revolution in Military Affairs (RMA) to transform the armed forces to increase their effectiveness, efficiency, and flexibility.

Bush summarized the three criticisms in a speech at the Citadel in December of 1999 and promised if elected he would increase military spending significantly, use the military only for warfighting and not for operations other than war, and transform the military even if it meant skipping a generation of technology. For example, not building the F/A-22 Raptor, a stealth fighter originally designed to achieve air superiority over Soviet fighter jets that were never built. His campaign message to the nation and our armed forces was "help was on the way."

Bush's criticisms on spending and overuse of the military were more than mere campaign hyperbole, they were downright disingenuous. Clinton had actually spent more on defense than the administration of the first President Bush had projected upon leaving office. As noted in the previous chapter, while Clinton in the Bottom-Up Review had reduced the size of the active Army, he increased the number of people in the Army National Guard and the active duty Marine Corps. Moreover, Clinton kept alive two major transformational weapon systems that the first Bush administration had tried to cancel, the V-22 Tilt Rotor Osprey and the Seawolf Submarine. In real dollars, in the 1990s, the Pentagon spent $3.3 trillion, only 14 percent less than it did in the 1980s during the Reagan buildup. More significantly during the Clinton administration this nation spent almost as much on the military as the rest of the world combined. Moreover, in his 2000 presidential campaign, Bush did not follow up on his proposal to increase defense spending significantly. His platform called for increasing defense spending by only $45 billion over ten years. (This was actually less than the increase proposed by Vice President Gore who promised an increase of $80 billion.)

Nor did Clinton overuse the military. Even with the deployment to the Balkans and Haiti, the percentage of American forces deployed abroad during the Clinton years was lower than in the 1980s. On average less than 4 percent of America's active conventional forces were deployed regularly in small scale contingencies in the Clinton era.

Nor were the armed forces, as Bush indicated, not ready to carry out their traditional missions. The forces that drove the Taliban and al-Qaeda from power in Afghanistan in a few weeks and overthrew the regime of Saddam Hussein in less than a month, were recruited, trained, and equipped by the Clinton administration. Bush's first defense budget did not go into effect until October 1, 2002, a year after the invasion of Afghanistan and six months before the start of hostilities in Iraq.

Transformation and the Revolution in Military Affairs

Transformation however was another story. As we noted in the previous chapter, the president and his advisors on national security were correct in pointing out that the Pentagon had not taken full advantage of the Revolution in Military Affairs. And the president was correct in appointing a person with the stature of Donald Rumsfeld to undertake a radical transformation of the way in which the Pentagon planned, organized, and prepared to fight the battles of the twenty-first century.

Rumsfeld brought an ideal background to be a change agent for the Department of Defense. Not only had he held the post in the waning days of the Ford administration, he had also served in Congress, as White House Chief of Staff, and Ambassador to NATO. In addition, after leaving government he had served as Chief Executive of two major corporations and had transformed them from near bankruptcy into very profitable enterprises and had chaired two defense commissions dealing with major defense issues, one on National Missile Defense and one on the militarization of space.

However, despite these advantages, Rumsfeld was not any more successful in radically transforming the Pentagon than those who tried before and immediately after the cold war. There were several reasons why Rumsfeld was not able to bring about a radical transformation in the way in which the Pentagon operated.

First, his management style was inappropriate for bringing about real reform in the world's largest bureaucracy. Upon taking the helm in January 2001, Rumsfeld quickly alienated the uniformed military, the career civil servants, defense industry, and the members of the Armed Services Committees in both Houses, which oversee the Pentagon. In effect, he treated the Pentagon like a hostile takeover and ignored the input of all the components of the military industrial complex and by early September 2001, he was actually on his way out of office.

In his first eight months in office, Rumsfeld established more than a dozen outside working groups called Strategic Review Panels that proposed cutting nearly every major defense program and slashing the force structure of the Army. By excluding the Joint Chiefs of Staff (JCS) from the process and treating these career officers as change resistant bureaucrats, he alienated them and when their complaints leaked to the press, it alienated the defense industry, the Congress, and the White House and emboldened them to undermine Rumsfeld. Rumsfeld had lost and was bitter about it.

Indeed on September 10, 2001, Rumsfeld gave his farewell address to the military and civilian personnel in the Pentagon. He told them that in resisting his proposed change they were the real enemy. "Perhaps this adversary sounds like the former Soviet Union," Rumsfeld commented, "but that enemy is gone: our foes are more subtle and implacable today. You may think I'm describing one of the last decrepit dictators of the world. But their day, too, is almost past, and they cannot match the strength and size of this adversary. The adversary's closer to home. It's the Pentagon bureaucracy."[1]

However, given the events of 9/11, nobody paid much attention to the speech. Moreover, his heroic behavior on the day of the attack on the Pentagon helped him keep his job. Reflecting on Rumsfeld's actions that day, former secretary of the Army, Thomas White noted that "He's a hands-on guy and he is very good in a crisis—I think. He's physically a tough guy and he wants to be at the scene of the action. And that was—I think—his finest hour."[2]

Second, it was difficult to make drastic and painful changes when most analysts agreed that the United States was the world's only military superpower and enjoyed overwhelming global military superiority.

Third, Rumsfeld also tried to do too much too soon. Most of the components of the military industrial complex agreed that the DoD should take advantage of the RMA, the real issue was the pace and extent of the transformation. Even though the Pentagon had tried to maintain as much of its cold war structure as possible in the 1990s, it did embrace some aspects of the RMA. For example, in the first Persian Gulf War in 1991, less than 10 percent of the bombs dropped on the Iraqi infrastructure and forces were precision guided or smart bombs. Eight years later, when the United States bombed Kosovo, the percentage of smart bombs used in the attacks had grown to 70 percent. Similarly even though the Air Force and Navy were still spending most of its budget on manned aircraft, the Pentagon was already buying some unmanned drones.

And, while the RMA might make the forces more effective, the advocates argued, by providing them with what they described as information superiority, and such other claims as safety through stealth, superior striking speed, agility and mobility, and the capacity to operate in a joint fashion (none of which was demonstrated in any combat in Kosovo, Iraq, or Afghanistan), this did not mean that we could make wholesale reductions in the number of ground forces. They would be needed for Fourth Generation Warfare.

The wholesale changes that Rumsfeld was proposing would have had dramatic and mostly negative impact on defense industry and those representatives and senators who represented states and districts that were building the cold war era weapons like the F-22 Fighter Fighter and the Crusader Mobile Howitzer System. By ignoring the input of the defense industry and the members Congress, Rumsfeld ensured that they would resist many his proposed changes even more than normally.

Moreover, when industry leaders and congressmen and senators learned about Rumsfeld's proposed wholesale changes, they made their unhappiness known to the White House. Since, the White House needed the continuing financial support of the defense industry and votes from Congress for their tax programs, neither the president nor his advisors came to Rumsfeld's defense. In fact they began floating names as possible successors to Rumsfeld as secretary of defense. One name floated was Sean O'Keefe, then at the Office of Management and Budget.

Finally, the president was not able give Rumsfeld the funds necessary to make the wholesale changes he wished. Despite the president's criticisms of Clinton's underfunding of the Pentagon, President Bush was only willing to add about $4 billion a year to the $300 billion budget he inherited from Clinton. His main priority in his first five months in office was initiating large-scale tax cuts. To do this while keeping the budget in balance meant holding down the growth in defense spending, the largest controllable item in the federal budget. This came as a rude shock to the uniformed military expecting that help was on the way meant that large budget increases were in the offering.

Whatever chance Rumsfeld had to transform the Pentagon's spending priorities ended with the attacks of 9/11. From 9/11 through 2005, the regular defense budget, not including the cost of the wars in Iraq and Afghanistan, increased by 40 percent and the military was able to continue buying the cold war weapons as well as purchase some of the new transformational systems.

However, having lost some battles in the Pentagon, Rumsfeld decided to show that dominance through technology alone would work on the battlefields in Afghanistan and Iraq. Unfortunately this experiment did not work and the results were disastrous for the country and the uniformed military.

But Rumsfeld alone was not responsible for the disastrous results in Afghanistan and Iraq. Much of the blame falls on the military, particularly the Army. To understand why, we must go back to Vietnam.

In response to the failure of the U.S. military's defeat by an underequipped, yet highly motivated, insurgency in Vietnam, the DoD began focusing heavily on changing the military into a more effective conventional fighting force. Instead of recognizing and institutionalizing the lessons learned from the U.S. military's experience in Southeast Asia, the Army studiously avoided any systematic appraisal of counterinsurgency lessons learned (in Vietnam) because such an appraisal would "have suggested a responsibility to prepare for future insurgencies. One insurgency out of sight was all insurgencies out of mind."[3] Rather, in the post Vietnam period of the 1980s and throughout the 1990s, many in the defense community sought funding for and promoted the advancement and primacy of conventional means to resolutely counter the Soviet threat. Military planners began to contend that "future advances in precision munitions, real-time data dissemination, and other modern technologies, combined with appropriate war-fighting doctrine and organization" could transform war.[4]

This change was exemplified by the experience of one of the Army's most experienced officers. In a recent interview, Lieutenant General Robert Gard (U.S. Army, Retired), the first president of the National Defense University and a veteran of both the Korean and Vietnam Wars, recalled attending a training course in Fort Leavenworth, Kansas, in the early 1960s. Looking back on a lengthy and grueling course, shaking his head disappointingly, Gard recalled how there were two mornings during the ten months he spent at Fort Leavenworth that were devoted to the training of counterinsurgency tactics to new officers. "The job of the Army" Gard's sergeant barked "is to kill the guerrillas." With the ink still fresh on his Harvard doctoral diploma, Gard questioned the sergeant. "Wouldn't a counterinsurgency campaign be more effective if we were to employ other elements of statecraft concurrently? If we were to say, use political and economic means, psychological operations, as well as peacekeeping and reconstruction efforts alongside the conventional campaign to kill guerrillas?" Looking around somewhat shocked and surprised at the audacity of the student, the sergeant came back rather quickly, "We kill the guerrillas first. Somebody else deals with all that shit afterward."

While the lesson learned by Gard that day may have taken place decades ago, the implications of that Army sergeant's mindset still resonate within the armed forces today. Faced with other messy counterinsurgency campaigns in Iraq and Afghanistan, too many military leaders have continued to rely upon conventional firepower and the overwhelming force available to the armed forces to try to deal with and decisively defeat the insurgencies. Supporting this dependency is a reticence on behalf of military planners for operations other than war; a reluctance that has become strongly reinforced by a devotion to defense transformation.

As noted in the previous chapter, a renewed interest and emphasis was placed on transformation or RMA after the stunning and lopsided victory by United

States and allied forces in Operation Desert Storm. The premium placed on advanced targeting and communications systems, information technology and long-range war-fighting capacity showcased in the 1991 Gulf War was the product of a decades-long shift in DoD planning and orientation toward a technologically advanced and therefore vastly superior conventional military force, according to the advocates of RMA and similar technological agendas.

At first glance, the effective rout of Saddam Hussein's Republican Guard during Operation Desert Storm appeared to demonstrate the swiftness and efficacy possible under an RMA model. Yet what the 1991 Persian Gulf War actually proved was the ease with which any competent force could defeat a poorly-equipped, led and motivated group of reluctant conscripts. The 1991 war had the side effect of reinforcing the changes the Army had made throughout the 1980s and 1990s—"which made it an unchallenged force for short, blitzkrieg-style warfare against other states, but badly positioned for protracted ground combat, especially of an irregular or unconventional nature."[5] Ultimately, the war demonstrated the marked ability to succeed in decisive combat operations and a shocking inability to lay the groundwork for decisive political success in order to provide the conditions for a permanent peace. The technologically advanced Army knew how to win the battles but not the war.

While both the present war in Iraq and the current war in Afghanistan have seen initial success, both efforts have descended into political chaos and severe instability. In light of these recent developments one must question the wisdom of the RMA: has the DoD placed too much of an emphasis on transformation, or as transformation enthusiasts argue, has the DoD not given transformation enough time to mature?

While preliminary success in the invasion of Iraq and Afghanistan has proven the effectiveness of transformation principles in achieving some primary objectives (during decisive combat operations), a dependence on weapons systems and doctrine that comprise defense transformation has shifted the emphasis away from achieving the long-term political objectives of stability, security, prosperity, and democracy. As a result it is clear that the DoD has taken the RMA concept too far in respect to resources, emphasis, logistics, and planning. It has considered transformation as an end in itself rather than a means to achieving an end.

"Help Is on the Way"

As noted in the previous chapter the emphasis placed on defense transformation, which would become a key aspect of the Defense Department under Donald Rumsfeld, was signaled in the campaign of then Governor Bush. In a campaign speech at the Citadel in 1999 George W. Bush called for advancing the procurement of future weapons and technologies. As a presidential nominee, Bush echoed the desire of some in the defense department to "skip a generation" of weaponry and accelerate the development of advanced weapons technologies.[6] By employing advanced technology, long-range precision weaponry, and real-time communications equipment, it was thought that the American military would be able to decimate its opponents in short order at very little cost both in treasure and American casualties.

Transformation was thus justified as a means to attack swiftly and destroy the enemy with overwhelming force in order to eliminate its will to fight. Accordingly, defense transformation programs in the 1990s and through to today have focused on this shortcut to victory by designing systems whose sole aim is to persuade the enemy that, by rapid and complete destruction of his military capability, further resistance is hopeless.[7]

In order to achieve these goals, the DoD has developed and deployed systems that emphasize the overwhelming use of force. One need look no further than the Pentagon's own budget and spending patterns in recent years to get a sense of where its priorities lie. One of the more striking aspects about recent Pentagon budgets is the technologically dependant and firepower focused nature of the bulk of the some eighty weapons systems on the drawing board and nearly $1.5 trillion worth of weapons systems in various stages of development. Moreover, with over $256 billion reserved for the F-35 Joint Strike Fighter, $65 billion for the F/A-22 Raptor, $12 billion allocated for the B-2 Heavy Bomber, $20 billion for the DD(X) destroyer, (not to mention the long-term funds allocated to offensive space-based weapons), the paramount placed on firepower is undeniable.

It is difficult to dispute the effectiveness of such cold war weapons systems in the early stages of both Operation Enduring Freedom in Afghanistan as well as Operation Iraqi Freedom (OIF). The use of advanced weapons systems led to the rapid dissolution of the Taliban as well Iraqi security forces in Afghanistan and Iraq, respectively. Indeed, the U.S. and coalition forces were able to defeat Taliban forces within two months of entering Afghanistan as well as enter Baghdad within two weeks of starting OIF.

The Inherent Problems of Force Dependency

Like the announcement of the defeat of the Taliban several months earlier, on May 1, 2003, President Bush declared the end of major combat operations in Iraq. While most Americans rejoiced at this announcement, those with a background in post-conflict resolution knew that this simply meant the easy part was over.

Initial victories did however lead many defense transformation enthusiasts to claim that success in Afghanistan and Iraq proved the case for defense transformation and that these two operations had ushered in a "New American Way of War." [8] "True believers" such as Max Boot extolled the virtues of defense transformation and lauded its ability to achieve a quick and decisive victory. What the transformation faithful did not recognize was that the pursuit of a battlefield victory for its own sake discouraged thinking about and indeed planning for the second and by far the most difficult half of a war of regime change: phase IV operations aimed at establishing a viable replacement for the destroyed regime.[9] This emphasis ultimately undermined long-term political success and thus ensured instability and chaos in both theaters.

The Use of Force and Transformation: The Self-Fulfilling Prophecy

Displaying a lavish and excessive use of firepower, the initial "Shock and Awe" phase of the war in Iraq relied upon the decades of resources and planning devoted to transformation weapons and doctrine. Such a campaign was able to present, and indeed depended on, such an awesome use of conventional firepower force that Iraqi security forces could not foreseeably mount a standing defense; opting rather to melt into the streets of Baghdad and other cities. During the ground invasion, the plan designed for the invasion of Iraq by General Tommy Franks', the U.S. Commander of Central Command (CENTCOM), was "built around U.S. technological and mechanical advantages. 'Speed kills,' the general insisted to his subordinates as they wrote and rewrote the massive plan."[10]

Shortly after the initial "Shock and Awe" phase two massive "thunder runs"—monstrous charges of tanks and other armored vehicles—were executed in order to force the regime to collapse. These raids were "focused operationally on the destruction of the Iraqi army—the state's warfighting capability—and destruction of the Hussein states'apparatus" concluded Maj. Isaiah Wilson.[11]

In Afghanistan, a small number of elite U.S. forces in conjunction with proxy Afghani fighters were able to inflict a crushing initial blow to the Taliban regime by waging war at standoff ranges, with precision weapons annihilating enemies at a distance, before they could close with U.S. commandos or indigenous allies. While Taliban forces did offer some initial resistance, their fighters melted away into the safe haven of Pakistan's tribal areas in the face of overwhelming force delivered by the coalition and American troops.

The manner in which both campaigns were executed serves to highlight the effects of the decades-long emphasis placed on transformation: with overwhelming conventional force comes the tendency to rely on it exclusively. Simply put, the reliance placed upon a swift victory employing overwhelming conventional military power (embodied in years of transformational weapons systems—like the smart bombs—buildup) by defense planners within the Pentagon has led to its exclusive use in times of war.

In this sense the decades-long emphasis placed upon transformation, rooted in overwhelming military power, has become a self-fulfilling prophecy: the prominence given to transformation systems on behalf of Pentagon strategists has led to their primacy in tactical implementation. Preeminence given to hard power thus led to the marginalization of and planning for other means to pacify populations, namely stability and support operations (SASO). Such priorities have in turn compromised U.S. ability to achieve the larger political battle to win the peace in operations following the collapse of both regimes.

As British strategist Colin S. Gray contends, American devotion to firepower, "while highly desirable in itself, cannot help but encourage the U.S. armed forces to rely on it even when other modes of military behavior would be more suitable." In irregular conflicts in particular Gray concludes, "resorting to firepower solutions readily becomes self-defeating."[12] As it is becoming increasingly clear by the day, counterinsurgency fighting in which the United States is engaged in Iraq and Afghanistan clearly requires a different type of military behavior than the United States is accustomed to and even comfortable with. Here, the legacy of Vietnam looms large within a military culture that is averse to operations other than war (OOTW). While a military doctrine focused on and dedicated to winning set-piece combat operations is necessary for any military operation, the immediate post-combat phase of war requires a shift in rules of engagement, doctrines, skills, techniques, and perspectives appropriate to the mission.[13]

General Frank's maxim that "speed kills" also reflected a misconception of the situation in Iraq. "Speed didn't kill the enemy—it bypassed him. It won the campaign but it didn't win the war, because the war plan was built on the mistaken strategic goal of capturing Baghdad, and it confused removing Iraq's regime with the far more difficult task of changing the entire country."[14]

Rather than state-of-the-art, high-tech weaponry implemented with a premium on rapidity lauded by transformation enthusiasts, the military is in increasing need of soldiers that are capable of long-term goals of rebuilding infrastructure as well as providing peacekeeping and constabulary forces in order to protect civilian populations vulnerable to sectarian strife. However, calls for these capabilities have been soundly rejected by the DoD. In the Bush administration, military culture within the Pentagon is such that the administration's strategy of "Clear, Hold and Build" does not apply to the Defense Department. As noted by Bob Woodward in Bush at War, Part III, Secretary Rumsfeld has claimed that it is not the military's job to hold and build but rather just to clear in decisive combat operations. But if it is not the military's job to pick up the slack after the clearing has been done, whose is it? What other department or branch of the government has the capacity, capability, and more importantly the funding to do so?

A further obstacle to achieving success in both Iraq and Afghanistan is the paradox of force in a counterinsurgency mission. As Jeffrey Record of the Army War College points out, "extant Army force and tactical doctrines are hardly optimized for the counterinsurgent mission, which demands the utmost restraint and discrimination in the application of force. Firepower restraint, not its application is the key to winning a counterinsurgency war." In this sense, target destruction is insufficient and perhaps counterproductive in circumstances where the United States is seeking regime change in a manner that gains support of the defeated populace for the new government.[15]

Yet the search and destroy strategy continues to exert a strong pull on the U.S. military. As Andrew Krepinevich, executive director of the Center for Strategic and Budgetary Assessments and the author of *The Army and Vietnam* argues:

U.S. operations against insurgents in Iraq put too great an emphasis on destroying insurgent forces and minimizing U.S. casualties and too little on providing enduring security to the Iraqi people; too much effort into sweeping maneuvers and no enduring presence and too little into effective coordination of security and reconstruction efforts.[16]

While transformation doctrine and weaponry were designed as a shortcut to decimate the opponent in order to destroy his will to fight, this logic becomes increasingly dangerous when implemented in a counterinsurgency mission. In an environment where high collateral damage can woo a potentially neutral citizen to the opponents side, force implementation can hinder a mission's ultimate goal. The emphasis on the use of force as a means to pacify a population therefore runs the risk of divorcing military means from the political ends to which they are attempting to meet. Military planners seem to have forgotten the cardinal rule: that war is an extension of politics by other means.

Transformation at the Expense of Phase IV Operations

In spite of the incredible amount of resources and emphasis placed upon transformation principles in order to defeat the regimes in Iraq and Afghanistan, a surprisingly insignificant amount of effort was expended toward stability and support operations (SASO, Phase IV Operations) in the wake of the fall of Saddam Hussein and the Taliban. In fact as Brookings Institute Foreign Policy Studies Senior Fellow Michael O'Hanlon notes, the Army's official history of the war reveals that, despite planning very carefully and rigorously for the invasion operations, the Army barely considered the post-invasion environment itself.[17]

Despite the swift collapse of conventional forces in both Iraq and Afghanistan—characterized by the use of key transformation principles of advanced technology, long-range precision weaponry, and real-time communications equipment—a decisive victory in both operations remains elusive. The credence placed upon the effectiveness of transformation to bring a swift victory in both campaigns was such that meticulous and careful planning for the postwar environment on behalf of Pentagon planners was neglected almost entirely. So much confidence was placed upon the efficacy of transformation in its ability to bring a decisive victory in Iraq that military planners within the Pentagon became preoccupied with planning the logistics for cutting 50,000 troops from Iraq within three months after the collapse of the regime in April 2003 and by another 50,000 shortly thereafter (with most troops coming home from operations within one year).[18] Indeed, "it is difficult to escape the conclusion that certain preparations for operations like those still going on in Iraq were not made because defense planners placed primary emphasis on high-technology transformational concepts."[19]

Decisive victory over the organized armed forces of an enemy government is a beginning, not an end. In effect, in the post 9/11 world initial and decisive combat operations are conducted for the purpose of being able to conduct stability and support operations afterwards. Traditional military victory is therefore only the prelude to the SASO operations that will actually determine the outcome of the operation. The second task is generally more difficult than the first for the United States today because of the military's fixation with great superiority in conventional war-fighting techniques and capability buttressed by years of defense spending and training centered on transformation.

Shifting Priorities

After four years of war in Iraq and over five years in Afghanistan, decisive victory remains more elusive today than ever. The scramble for "fresh perspectives" and new tactics on behalf of the Bush administration serves to highlight the failure and inappropriate qualities of the means used thus far in both operations. Regime change wars seeking decisive combat victory but necessitating the support and cooperation of local populations to ensure a stable political outcome require a fundamentally different response from the conventional war-fighting tactics that the U.S. military knows so well.

This shift will require a substantial move away from a capabilities-dominated approach espoused by the Bush administration to a defense strategy that integrates both threat-based and capabilities-based initiatives. As military strategist Frederick Kagan contends "we should shorten our gaze and focus on immediate operational challenges and problems first, on visible near-and mid-term threats second, and only then on long term threats and opportunities."[20] Such a strategy must focus less resources, effort, and planning on RMA/transformation programs that offer solutions to problems of a bygone era in order to attend to the contemporary threats and challenges currently facing our nation. Taking current threats as well as budgetary constraints into consideration, this strategy would not necessarily abandon transformation programs completely nor affect long-term U.S. military capabilities. As the Center for American Progress' Quadrennial Defense Review points out, this approach would "reflect the need for transformation while maintaining current military readiness and capabilities, as opposed to the administrations practice of making transformation an end itself."[21]

The policy question is therefore not whether the United States should continue to maintain its hard-won and indispensable conventional primacy but whether, given the evolving strategic environment, it should create ground (and supporting air) forces dedicated to performing OOTW, including counterinsurgency.[22] Upon consideration of the challenges still facing our nation's military in both Iraq and Afghanistan and the Global War on Terror, it becomes clear that the U.S. military must commit significant manpower and resources to stability/peacekeeping forces in order to win the political war; provide nonmilitary solutions such as promoting economic development and making sure basic services are restored; guarantee large numbers of properly trained ground troops for purposes of securing population centers and infrastructure; maintain order and concurrently provide humanitarian relief; and facilitate a revived delivery of such fundamental services as electrical power, potable water, and garbage collection.[23]

Fortunately, there is an indication that this is where some leaders in the military are shifting their focus. The new ARMY/Marine Field Manuel released in June of 2006 deals comprehensively if not exclusively with counterinsurgency (COIN) operations. This manual, can be viewed as a "new doctrine (that) is part of a broader effort to change the culture of a military that has long promoted the virtues of using firepower and battlefield maneuvers in swift, decisive operations against a conventional enemy. Instead of massing firepower to destroy Republican Guard troops and other enemy forces, as was required in the opening weeks of the invasion of Iraq, the draft manual emphasizes the importance of minimizing civilian casualties. 'The more force used, the less effective it is,' it notes."[24] In place of military solutions, the focus must be shifted to include the need to build up local institutions and encourage economic development as a dominant strategy.

Conclusion

Despite the disappearance of the Soviet threat, throughout the 1990s and continuing today, the Army and the other services have continued to prepare for and build weapons systems as if the Soviet military was about to storm the plains of Europe any day now. Years of programs dedicated to defense transformation at the expense of a preparedness and capacity for counterinsurgency and stability and support operations have inhibited the military's ability to deal with this threat. Our nation is paying for this today. When dealing with counterinsurgency operations, the United States needs to see phase IV as the predominant stage. "After all if these operations don't succeed the war will end in defeat however stunning the initial military success might have been."[25] Incorporating the hard lessons learned in Iraq and Afghanistan into future military budgeting, planning, and training would constitute a far more practical form of transformation and real military reform.

Notes

1. Remarks as delivered by Secretary of Defense Donald H. Rumsfeld, The Pentagon, Monday, September 10, 2001, *Defense Link*, http://www.defenselink.mil/speeches/2001/s20010910-secdef.html.

2. "Rumsfeld's War," *PBS Frontline*, October 6, 2004, http://www.pbs.org/wgbh/pages/frontline/shows/pentagon/view/.

3. Jeffrey Record, "The American Way of War: Cultural Barriers to a Successful Counterinsurgency," *CATO*, 2006, p. 15, http://www.cato.org/pub_display.php?pub_id=6640.

4. Michael O'Hanlon, *Defense Strategy for the Post Saddam Era*, Brookings, Washington, DC, 2005, pp.76–77.

5. Thomas E. Ricks, *Fiasco: The American Military Adventure in Iraq*, The Penguin Press, New York, 2006, p. 132.

6. Bush speech to the Citadel, http://archives.cnn.com/2001/ALLPOLITICS/02/09/bush.military/index.html.

7. Frederick Kagan, *Finding the Target* (under the way forward section), Encounter Books, New York, 2006, p. 344.

8. Max Boot, "The New American Way of War," *Foreign Policy*, 2003, 41–58.

9. Record, "The New American Way of War," p. 5.

10. Ricks, *Fiasco*, pp. 127.

11. Ibid. 117.

12. 9. Colin S. Gray, "The American Way of War: Critique and Implications," in *Rethinking the Principles of War*, ed. Anthony D. McIvor, Naval Institute Press, Annapolis, MD, 2005, pp. 27–33.

13. "In the Wake of War: Improving U.S. Post-Conflict Capabilities," Council on Foreign Relations, 2005, p. 13.

14. Ricks, *Fiasco*, pp. 127–128.

15. Record, "The American Way of War," p. 7.

16. Andrew Krepinevich, "How to win in Iraq," *Foreign Affairs*, September–October 2005, p. 92.

17. O'Hanlon, Defense Strategy for a Post Saddam Iraq, p. 38.

18. Quote from former. Secretary of the Army Thomas E. White in Michael Gordon's "The Strategy to Secure Iraq Did Not Foresee a 2nd War," *New York Times*, October 19, 2004.

19. O'Hanlon, *Defense Strategy for a Post Saddam Iraq*, p. 77

20. Kagan, *Finding the Target*, p. 364.

21. Korb, Wadhams, Grotto, "Restoring American Military Power: A Progressive Quadrennial Defense Review," Center for American Progress, January 2006, pp. 22–23.

22. Record, "The American Way of War," p. 9.

23. Ibid. 7.

24. Michael Gordon, "Military Hones a New Strategy on Insurgency," *New York Times*, October 5, 2006.

25. Kagan, *Finding the Target*, p. 370.

CHAPTER 6

From Tethered Goats and Military Jackasses to Reform

Winslow T. Wheeler

The U.S. armed forces won dramatic victories over Iraq's conventional armed forces in 1991 and 2003. Surely, these successes are evidence that the Defense Department has solved whatever management and war-fighting problems may have existed. U.S. military training, equipment, and leadership were clearly far beyond the Iraqis, and American soldiers, Marines, sailors, and airmen and women fought with evident courage and skill. There remain some cost scandals in the Pentagon, but American military forces are certainly the best in the world, and high equipment costs are little price to pay for such dramatic effectiveness. Change, if needed, should only be at the margins. Or, so the argument runs.

The American military victories in 1991 and 2003 were dramatic, but they were also incomplete, and they also say almost nothing about the quality of our armed forces and their weapons. The victories were against tactical opponents who, with only a few exceptions, behaved in combat like a "tethered goat" with a leader who, without any qualification, was a military "jackass." American forces remain untested in the twenty-first century against a well-trained, equipped, and led conventional foe. Moreover, against irregular enemies in Iraq and Afghanistan who evidence a level of tactical skill and strategic acumen well beyond Iraq's conventional forces, U.S. forces are clearly much more severely challenged—to the point where the wars in Iraq and Afghanistan have probably been lost.

To the extent American military forces in the conventional wars against Iraq show improvement—if, indeed, that is the case—a significant part of the credit should go not to the Pentagon's managers and senior military commanders but to people those managers and commanders tried to ignore and suppress.

The Reformers' First War

In the first Gulf war in 1991, Operation Desert Storm, the Air Force's F-15 shot down thirty-four of the thirty-six Iraqi aircraft destroyed in the air.[1] The

F-16 was available in larger numbers and flew far more air to ground sorties than any other allied aircraft type.[2] The F-18 flew more air to ground sorties than any other Navy aircraft and won the navy's two air-to-air kills.[3] After the war, Iraqi prisoners of war declared the A-10 to be one of the two aircraft they feared the most (the B-52 was the other).[4] And, the commander of all U.S. air forces in the theater, General Charles Horner, said of the A-10, which he initially resisted being deployed in numbers to the theater, "It saved our ass."[5] Each of these aircraft was the result of the work of John Boyd, Pierre Sprey, and other reformers. Three of the four aircraft would never have existed without the reformers and were initially stoutly resisted by the Air Force and Navy, and the fourth, the F-15, would have been a very different, heavier, more complex, and certainly less effective combat aircraft.

These hardware contributions were the lesser ones. The reformers also made major but unheralded contributions to the initial success of the second war against Iraq. The Army's main combat force during the war, the Third Infantry Division, was reorganized per the recommendations of a lowly but brilliant major, Donald Vandergriff. He had captured the attention of Secretary of the Army Thomas White and Vice Chief of Staff of the Army Gen. Jack Keane with his probing analysis of the Army's industrial-age personnel management system in the book *Path to Victory: America's Army and the Revolution in Human Affairs*. That system treated people like interchangeable parts and constantly tore apart units and reconstituted them as soldiers were individually plugged in and out. Instead, Vandergriff helped devise a "unit manning system" that kept people together in units to train, deploy, and fight all under the same commanders (at all levels). This permitted the essential ingredient of combat effectiveness, unit cohesion, to grow.

It is interesting to note that despite many of Vandergriff's ideas later being taken on by Army Chief of Staff General Peter Schoomaker, and Vandergriff himself being called by military sociologist Dr. Charles Moskos as "the best known major in the Army" and having a "bigger impact than many that have achieved higher rank," the Army forced Vandergriff into retirement.[6] Vandergriff's case points to a larger problem with the Army, that while it may espouse innovation and adaptability from its leaders, its actions belie its words.

Even more important, the Marines had tailored their fighting tactics to the innovative, initiative-based, fast paced, adaptive-to-unfolding events methodology that Boyd preached. One assessment credited six leaders with enabling the Marines' evolution to the effectiveness in land combat it demonstrated in Operation Iraqi Freedom; one of the six was John Boyd; a second was a disciple of his (Col. Mike Wyly, USMC ret., who the Marines—like the Army with Vandergriff—forced into retirement, despite his very fundamental contributions); a third was the Marines' commandant who first urged the Corps' adoption of Boyd's thinking, and a fourth was a four star commander who thoroughly understood and strongly advocated Boyd's thinking.[7]

Another significant contribution has also gone unheralded, this one involving the first Gulf War. A few days after Saddam Hussein invaded Kuwait in

August 1990, John Boyd started flying back and fourth from his home in Del Ray, Florida to Washington, DC. He was talking with Secretary of Defense Richard Cheney, whom Boyd had met when Cheney was a congressman and had visited in his home to brief the young congressman on Boyd's thinking about conflict and strategy. With Boyd's counseling in late 1990, Cheney resisted the plan of the regional commander in the Gulf, Gen. Norman Schwartzkopf, to attack Saddam's forces head-on in a battle of attrition, a technique Boyd characterized as "hey diddle, diddle, straight up the middle" (a phrasing Cheney and others subsequently used).[8]

A new plan emerged; the Marines would provide distractions: a feinted amphibious assault and a frontal, land attack northward from Saudi Arabia into Kuwait. Meanwhile, the Army would perform a wide left hook from a concealed deployment beyond Saddam's western flank.[9] The plan was to envelop Saddam's regular army in Kuwait, but more importantly, to trap from the rear, cut off, and destroy three divisions of his elite Republican Guard. These were not just Saddam's best-equipped and trained forces, they were an essential political prop, a praetorian guard, for his regime. General Schwartzkopf came to understand that and designated the Republican Guard as the operation's number one *strategic* target. The Guard's destruction could mean the collapse of Saddam's regime without a single U.S. soldier marching into Baghdad.

Many think the plan went perfectly, even if it did not remove Saddam. It did not go nearly so well. The Army's Seventh Corps did launch its attack from well beyond Saddam's flank, as planned, but instead of enveloping the Republican Guard from its rear, Seventh Corps proceeded north too slowly and turned directly into, not behind, the Republican Guard's flank. Instead of an envelopment, the Seventh Corps' assault was a shove into the shoulder: not a sickle cut behind the Republican Guard but a piston into it from the side. It destroyed major portions of one of the Republican Guard divisions, while the others retreated, relatively intact, into the southern Iraqi city of Basra.

Mistaken, General Schwartzkopf declared the Republican Guard trapped and destroyed, and President Bush ordered an end to offensive operations. America reveled in its one-sided victory and welcomed the troops home with a heartwarming parade in Washington. Meanwhile, the elements of the Republican Guard that had escaped into Basra suppressed a revolt of Iraqi Shi'ite Moslems who, with some encouragement from President Bush, rose up to rid themselves of the hated Saddam regime. Without those Republican Guard units, it is possible—just possible—that the Shi'ite revolt could have gained enough momentum for the rest of the country, the majority of which was also Shi'ite, to rise up and dump Saddam. We will, however, never know. The Army's Seventh Corps failed to achieve the design of Cheney's plan, as inspired by Boyd.[10]

The truncated victory was also against a force significantly less impressive than what many might think.

Tethered Goat

A "very senior air officer involved in the Desert Storm air campaign," almost certainly General Horner, speaking to an author of a study of the first Gulf war under the promise of no attribution, asserted that attacking Iraq and its armed forces from the air was about as difficult as "shooting at a tethered goat."[11] There was little to no opposition from Saddam's sizeable air force, and Iraq's ground-based air defenses were either mostly suppressed by day five of the air campaign or simply avoided by allied aircraft by flying above the defenses' reach. (Those defenses, especially their most high-tech radar-directed ones, were also substantially less impressive than had been advertised.)[12] Thirty-eight U.S. and allied aircraft were shot down, but given the number of attacks flown (just under 65,000) the casualty rate was extremely low, 0.0006 percent. Over North Vietnam, North Korea, Germany, or Japan in earlier wars, U.S. air casualty rates were orders of magnitude higher.[13]

The fighting on the ground at the end of the war was even more telling. Desertions from the regular Iraqi army units in Kuwait, what Iraqi prisoners of war later described as "the footrace north [back into Iraq]," started with the opening of the U.S. coalition's bombing campaign.[14] The regular Iraqi army units in Kuwait were demoralized before the fighting even started. Contrary to an army "war hardened" from its eight-year struggle with Iran the previous decade, the Iraqi regular army was "war weary."

Iraq's regular army mostly consisted of disfavored Shi'ite units in a Sunni Moslem political/military infrastructure. The Shi'ia both reviled Saddam and were reviled by him and his regime. They received the dregs of training and equipment compared to the elite Republican Guard behind them to the north (in part for the purpose of blocking their retreat). These Shi'ite units knew they were expendable cannon fodder. Thirty-eight days of air attacks touched off massive desertions, but demoralization before the first bomb's detonation was an essential precursor.

Morale, rather than the allied bombing, as the definitive factor for the massive desertions comes as no surprise to military historians. Historically, bombardment alone, especially bombing from high altitude, does not automatically mean desertions, surrender, or collapse of competent military units. Other better-trained and motivated armies, such as both sides in the trenches in World War I and the Germans in Normandy, France, in 1944 in Operation Goodwood, experienced even more intense bombardment without breaking and with virtually no desertions. In the case of the Iraqis, the combination of demoralized troops treated contemptuously by their leadership with thirty-eight days of bombing broke the units.

Once ground operations began at the end of the bombing, "The few Iraqi units that tried to fight proved themselves so ill-trained as to be almost helpless."[15] Even the Marines frontal push into Kuwait produced almost as many Iraqi solders rushing forward to surrender as rushed north to retreat. The Army's Seventh Corps' push into the flank of the Republican Guard's Talakahna division did produce some sharp, short engagements, but the reason for Seventh Corps' failure to get behind the enemy was its commander's decisions, rather than the ferocity or skill of the opposition.

Skeptics that Iraqi incompetence in Operation Desert Storm in 1991 was a major factor in the American victory can take a lesson from Operation Iraqi Freedom in 2003 when the Iraqis had the added incentive of defending their homeland.

Bad Learners by Design

Whether they win or lose, professional militaries routinely attempt to learn from their mistakes in war. The Iraqi armed forces did almost nothing to engage in this basic process after 1991.

This was partly apparent from how Saddam deployed his forces in 2003 in the run up to the second war when it was abundantly clear an American attack was coming. In 1991, both the regular Iraqi army units and the Republican Guard were deployed out in the open on the desert floor and took their pounding—tethered goat-like—for thirty-eight days from the air. In 2003, they did very much the same thing; the major difference was that the precursor U.S. air campaign was shorter and the terrain was more irregular and built up than the billiard table-like Kuwaiti desert. In 2003, U.S. military sources told a UPI reporter, "But by deploying his divisions in open battle against the hard-driving US forces, he [Saddam] made the same mistake he had made back in 1991, he left them out in the open where annihilating US Army firepower and air power could obliterate them."[16] There were some examples of the Iraqis attempting to hide some equipment from strikes from the air, but even that was frequently done incompetently as forces were incompletely hidden or attempted to move in circumstances where they could be easily detected, found, and attacked.[17]

An apparent explanation for the inept deployment was Saddam's concern that if those forces—even the Republican Guard—appeared inside Baghdad where they might conceal themselves better and subsequently engage the Americans more effectively, they might be tempted to turn against Saddam.[18] Military considerations were passed over in favor of political ones.

In addition, Saddam was concerned that if his conventional forces became too competent, they might be able to defeat his praetorian guard and eliminate him. Accordingly, regular army units were denied ammunition, fuel, and other supplies for training, so that even if they had been deployed more appropriately, they remained unschooled in camouflage, self-defense, and even aiming their weapons.[19]

Lousy Materiel

Even after the drubbing they took in 1991, the Iraqi armed forces remained sizeable and, at least on paper, somewhat impressive. After 1991, Saddam retained about 300 combat aircraft in his air force, but in 2003, he literally disassembled it. By the start of the second war, the Iraqi air force's mechanics had unbolted the wings from many of their fighter and attack aircraft in order to hide them.[20] There is little, if any, record of Iraqi combat aircraft attempting to leave any runway to contest the U.S. domination of the skies or to bomb U.S. or allied forces.

The Iraqi navy was in even worse shape; it did not exist for any practical purpose.[21] The Iraqi ground forces were more substantial. In 2003, the army had 350,000 full-time actives and 100,000 reservists called up at the start of the fighting. It also had from 2,200 to 2,600 main battle tanks, 3,700 armored personnel carriers and other armored vehicles, and 2,400 artillery pieces, all left available after the 1991 war.[22] Only 700 of the tanks were relatively modern Soviet era T-72 models. The rest were earlier Soviet models dating back to the 1960s.[23]

While numerous, most Iraqi tanks were poorly maintained; they were even more poorly manned. The "bean count" of up to 2,600 tanks says nothing of the combat capability of the Iraqi tank force. As discussed below, the Iraqi officer corps was largely unwilling and unable to lead, and the tanks crews were ill trained and unwilling to fight. It was an utterly hollow force.

Hodge-Podge

Shortly after the first Gulf War, Saddam established a more elite *Special* Republican Guard of 15,000 to 20,000 troops and put his son Qusay in charge. The primary purpose of these units was not to be an even more elite unit for war fighting but to be a more secure praetorian guard to keep an eye on the other praetorian guard, the regular Republican Guard.

In addition, Saddam created various irregular forces. In 1995, he established a "Saddam Fedayeen" paramilitary force of 15,000 to 25,000. Their purpose was political security in the streets, such as suppressing unauthorized demonstrations. These answered to Saddam's other son, Uday.[24] There was also a Special Security Service, a Hitler Youth-like Lions of Saddam, various domestic intelligence organizations, armed Ba'ath party loyalists, and others, all amounting to several thousands.[25]

Each was intended for regime security, not Iraqi national security. "Many Iraqi combat units were better at watching each other, and at suppressing the Iraqi people, than at fighting a foreign opponent."[26] Rather than cooperating, they competed with each other for Saddam's favor. In fact, they hated each other.[27] Cooperation between them in combat, a necessity for even a rudimentary showing of competence against the American and British invaders, was simply not in the cards.

Lousy Doctrine

Along with outmoded Soviet equipment, the Iraqis employed ineffective Soviet war-fighting doctrine. It stressed monolithic, unimaginative, rigid tactics, especially frontal attacks.[28] Saddam preferred the Soviet-style centralized command principles and the smothering of individual initiative for internal political purposes, but for the few Iraqis units that chose to fight with any fervor, the head-on tactics were foolish against American firepower. One Army study of the war termed these tactics "self-defeating" against properly trained military units, such as the U.S. and British forces in Iraq in 2003.[29]

Lousy Leaders

The Iraqi armed forces were rife with material, mental, and moral divisions; these weaknesses were at their worst in the officer corps.

Each of the officer ranks in Saddam's different special, elite, regular, and paramilitary organizations were paid dissimilar salaries, given different equipment, and afforded varying privileges, all according to their political status, not their military professionalism.[30] In fact, military competence was often a criterion for selection out, not up. Many of the most competent officers in the regular and elite formations had been retired or shunted into minor jobs; some even had the occasional fatal accident. Competent officers might acquire their own following and, therefore, were a threat to Saddam.[31]

Officers still in service focused on currying favor. The preferential treatment for some and disdain for others created real discord.[32] The mutual distrust and jealousies Saddam fostered among his military and paramilitary leadership was good for his remaining on top but bad for anything approaching coordinated command and control or effective military leadership.

Moreover, to preserve any favored status they might have acquired, officers routinely lied not only to each other but also especially to their superiors about the material and moral condition of the forces they led. When Saddam convened 150 senior and trusted officers four days before the outbreak of the Operation Iraqi Freedom, he asked them to report on the material readiness and moral willingness of their units to resist an American invasion. One general present later asserted he and every other officer in the room who spoke lied about their units' readiness and their troops' willingness to fight.[33] It was an officer corps where lying, apple-polishing, noncooperation, and lack of competence in the field were the way to the top.

It was even worse at the pinnacle. To ensure Saddam's political control, no unit commander could make a move without his direct permission. Any unordered initiative his units wanted to show to fight, had there been any willingness to do so, was suspect activity in Saddam's inward-focused command center.[34] Further, Saddam himself had worse than no talent for military command. When the fighting started in 2003, he literally froze, just as he had in 1991, and the pummeling of the tethered goat started once again.

Saddam and his generals aptly demonstrated their military incapacity when they failed to take advantage of a few days' "pause" U.S. forces took in late March 2003. Bad weather and a supply shortage—and other factors discussed below—had resulted in a temporary halt on the march to Baghdad. The weather impeded air operations against Iraqi ground forces; U.S. combat units needed maintenance and supplies; resupply units were strung out along the roads from Kuwait up to the outskirts of Baghdad, and some Army commanders had panicked. The commander of the first Marine Division, Maj. Gen. James Mattis, described the Iraqi military command as "dumber than you-know-what" for failing to capitalize on this temporary vulnerability: "They were real dumb."[35]

It was command imposed from the top, and the top, in the words of one student of the war, was a "military jackass."[36]

Unwilling to Fight

Iraq's rotten leadership exacerbated Iraq's soldiers being unable and unwilling to fight. *Time* magazine told one Iraqi soldier's story: "In Mahmudiyad, Ali Mohammed ... observed an officer ordering 20 of his men to head into town to confront the advancing Americans. As they march forward, he stripped off his uniform, revealing civilian cloths underneath, and fled in the opposite direction. When the soldiers realized what had happened, they too turned and fled. . . . Soldiers who didn't have street clothes tried to buy or beg them from residents."[37]

Several Army and Marine after action reports and news articles written by embedded reporters recounted that many Iraqis units never even intended to fight. A Marine unit reported: "On the commencement of the war [we] discovered none of the [Iraqi] T62s and T72s [tanks] was occupied. . . . [The tanks were all] lined up neatly in tactical formation with Iraqis standing next to them surrendering holding out wads of cash to the Marines."[38] Another Marine simply told the press, "The Iraqis weren't putting up much of a fight."[39]

Damaged Iraqi tanks were empty of Iraqi corpses inside; they had been abandoned by their crew before the fighting started.[40] Even some Republican Guard tankers simply fled the threat of battle for safer regions.[41] Units called in to fill the gaps deserted as well: One regular army unit was sent to the town of Dawrah to replace a Republican Guard unit that had already fled. According to an Iraqi observer, when this new unit heard there were two U.S. tanks seven miles away, the soldiers "dropped their weapons, changed their clothes and ran."[42] Whether from embedded journalists or military after action reports, account after account spoke of Iraqi desertions after little or no fighting.[43]

Lousy Tactics

Some individual Iraqis also demonstrated real bravery and neither deserted nor surrendered: individuals and small units attacked U.S. tanks and other armored vehicles with assault rifles, stood in the open to fire antitank rocket propelled grenades, or hurdled themselves in pickup trucks at prepared U.S. defenses. These self-defeating but personally brave tactics were fundamentally foolish; like Saddam's inept frontal assaults at higher levels, they simply presented American firepower with easy targets.

When the fighting reached urban areas all along the U.S. march north to Baghdad and in Baghdad itself, the conventional Iraqi forces seemed unaware of the opportunity to entangle U.S. forces in close house-to-house fighting where America's technological and firepower advantages lessened. There was also no coordinated effort to impede the invaders' access to Baghdad by systematically destroying the bridges leading to the city. According to one report, the Iraqis failed to destroy a single bridge leading to Baghdad.[44]

There were some uncoordinated efforts by some paramilitary units to ambush Marines and Third Infantry Division units on and near bridges. From the descriptions by the embedded press, these efforts were harrowing for the U.S. units on the receiving end, and U.S. casualties did occur, but the tactics the Iraqis used were the same foolish headlong plunges in the open into American firepower. American command of the roadways and bridges from Kuwait to Baghdad was never seriously challenged. The timing of the U.S. entry into Baghdad was under U.S. control, not Iraqi.

Even the attacks on U.S. supply vehicles behind the lead combat units, while harrowing for the targets, especially the 507th Maintenance Company and the individuals of that unit who were killed and captured, were poorly executed and uncoordinated. Some lead U.S. combat units were experiencing real shortages of ammunition, food, medical supplies, and spare parts.[45] A sustained, coordinated effort by the Iraqis to interdict lines of supply and communication, which were incompletely protected by U.S. personnel not prepared by virtue of training and equipment to defend against sustained attacks, could have pushed beyond its limits a supply situation descried as stretched to the breaking point.[46]

Most Incompetent Army in the World

Indeed, some authorities assert the Iraqi armed forces were the worst in the world. Maj. Charles Heyman, editor of *Jane's World Armies*, an independent, country-by-country analysis of the world's armies, found "They [the Iraqis] were the most incompetent army in the world."[47] Even elements of the U.S. Army tend to agree: a study performed by the Strategic Studies Institute of the Army War College in Carlisle, PA, found Iraqi incompetence to be the critical element in the victory in Operation Iraqi Freedom.[48]

The trouncing administered to Saddam's armed forces was meaningless as an indicator of American military prowess. Congressmen and women and senators often assert U.S. armed forces are "the best in the world;" some even assert "the best in history." But, what proof of "best" is there in defeating a foe of such overwhelming incompetence? It is empty, politically driven rhetoric.

Triumph of Technology?

Second only to the wars against Iraq "proving" America's armed forces the best in the world is the technological hubris these "victories" gave rise to. Much was said of Operation Desert Storm in 1991 bringing a revolution in warfare thanks to the triumph of aerial technology in attacking ground targets. At the Government Accountability Office, this author spent four years assessing the various claims, not just from manufacturers but also from senior commanders (most of them in the Air Force) and top civilian managers. Put simply, the claims of brilliant success for high-tech systems were grossly exaggerated. Some claims went beyond exaggeration to what could only be fabrication.[49]

In Operation Iraqi Freedom in 2003, similar technological miracles were promised before the campaign—and declared after it was over—even before the data were available. Unhappily for the technological fantasies, however, a source as mainstream as the Army War College, in its study mentioned above, found that the Iraqi's incompetence, not American technology, was the determining factor in the 2003 war.[50]

More specifically, much ballyhooing was proclaimed about a new generation of technology to "remove the fog of war from the battlefield" through a system of sensors, computers, and communications equipment. In the form of the Army's $160 billion "Future Combat System," this "system of systems" is supposed to be able to inform both commanders and troops in the field not just where the friendly forces were but also where is the enemy. With this information, commanders in remote headquarters could inform forces in the field not just where was the enemy, but because they could view the entire battlefield, they could tell the tactical units exactly what they had to do to prevail. So sure are the advocates of this system that Army vehicles would be able to sacrifice armor in favor of radios and computers: with such precise information on the enemy's location and movements, fires could be centrally directed from headquarters such that the enemy's more lethal antiarmor weapons would never get close enough to friendly vehicles to do them any harm. It would be a true revolution in warfare.

It all failed miserably in Operation Iraqi Freedom where prototype systems were deployed. An example occurred at "Objective Peach" where Lt. Col. "Rock" Marcone, a battalion commander in the Third Infantry Division, was fighting. Despite having the appropriate equipment, he was "almost devoid" of any information about the strength or location of Iraqi forces. At night, the situation grew worse; he was not left uninformed; he was misinformed. He was advised one Iraqi brigade was in his area, but three appeared to confront him with a threat he was not fully prepared to fight.[51]

Marcone's experience was no isolated event. Equipped similarly to burn off the fog of war from the battlefield, a Marine commented, "We had terrible situation awareness."[52] Even when the communications links worked, the system didn't: some units complained they received too much information for them to process, much of it useless. In other cases, tactical units became so disgusted with the equipment that they simply turned it off.[53] That was a comment the author heard anecdotally from several sources. Worse still, when the equipment seemed to be working and was left on, commanders who were scores, or even hundreds, of miles away attempted to micromanage units in the field.

This was a behavior encountered in previous wars: the commander in the field observing the enemy and having a feel for the actual situation being counter-directed by a more senior commander many miles away with no grasp of the situation at hand. Predictably, the effects can be not just a fumbled military engagement but also a commander and unit in the field demoralized for future operations because they know they are not trusted by remote senior commanders who may again misdirect the troops "at the sharp end" and cause their demise.

Unfortunately, such experiences were not the only reasons for American units in the field to question their own leadership.

"The Harder We Work, the Behinder We Get"

On May 1, 2003, on the aircraft carrier *Abraham Lincoln*, President Bush declared the "end of major hostilities." Given subsequent events, he would have been more correct to declare the "start of the more deadly phase." In the months after Bush's declaration, hardly a day passed without American casualties. By mid 2007, the insurgency remained full-blooded and had claimed almost 3,500 American dead and 25,000 wounded.

The change in the nature of the conflict has become all too familiar to Americans: drive by shootings, suicide car bombs, command detonated explosive devices; in other words guerrilla tactics. By October 2003, up to 35 such attacks occurred per day,[54] and before the January 2005 elections, they increased to 150 per day, before they "reduced" to over 50 per day. By mid-2007, they remained well above that level while much of the violence had spread into intercommunal warfare, primarily—but not exclusively—between the Shi'a and Sunni communities. Without the "military jackass" in control, operations in Iraq were proving to be nothing like the "cake walk" some American jingoists glibly predicted before the war.

The insurgents have evidenced themselves to be far more than the Saddam "dead-enders" Secretary of Defense Rumsfeld tried to dismiss in 2004. The insurgency evolved into a witch's brew of previously separate and even nonexistent elements, including Sunnis, foreigners with Syrian, Saudi, al Qaeda or other connections, and others, previously unpolitical and nonhostile, who became incensed with the Western presence and behavior in Iraq. Using both traditional guerrilla tactics and new ones, these disparate elements all contributed to the chaos in Iraq. They lacked coordination and even a cohesive outlook, but they shared common goals: making the Americans pay for their adventure in Iraq and punishing the new regime the American occupation fostered, even if it meant butchering innocent Iraqi civilians for the purpose of demonstrating the fecklessness of the foreign and collaborationist security apparatus. Indeed, some elements sought out civilian Iraqi targets in order to foment civil war. By 2006, it was unclear whether the insurrection against the American occupation was the course of future violence or whether it was the growing sectarian conflict or, more probably, some combination of the two with one or the other predominating at any given time in response to immediate circumstances. The year 2007 brought no change, other than an increase in the number of U.S. troops deployed into the chaos.

This concoction of different attackers with different motivations and different targets comprised a new form of warfare first predicted in 1989 by a small number of insightful thinkers, including Bill Lind (formerly of Senator Hart's staff in the days of the Congressional Military Reform Caucus). They dubbed it "Fourth Generation Warfare."[55] It was a new evolution of the guerrilla strategy and tactics articulated by Mao Ze Dong in the 1930s and refined by the Vietnamese communists in the 1950s, 1960s, and 1970s. It added elements of religion, culture, and globalism to the communist's nationalistic, anticolonial doctrine. Moreover, much more so than earlier guerrilla strategies, it gave primary emphasis to mass media operations, such as on Al Jezerra and CNN, as a means to spread fear in the West and resentment among the faithful. Beyond "guerrilla warfare with a new twist," as many serving generals see it, however, this Fourth Generation Warfare is a way that small, decentralized insurgent teams, with a common ideology, can take on their seemingly more powerful conventional-minded opponents. They use simple but very modern technology to attack the linear-thinking, complex technology militaries of the West, many of which seem stuck in what these analysts dubbed Second Generation Warfare—exemplified by the set piece battlefields and shallowly thinking commanders of the First World War.

By 2006, the U.S. military services had still found no way to contain the insurgency. They had barely evolved a doctrine. Unbelievably, when they first encountered the insurgency, they not only denied its existence but also had no military doctrine for guidance on how to cope with it. They had literally defined it out of existence. As a result, some U.S. tactics, such as the flattening of Fallujah in 2004 to attack insurgents there, appears to have increased their fervor and even their number more than it eliminated and deflated them. Overall American behavior comprised a virtual recruitment poster for al Qaeda recruits to not just hurry to Iraq to kill Americans but to thicken, unite, and motivate the ranks of America's enemies in the broader war with terrorism.

In October 2003, *USA Today* disclosed a memo Secretary of Defense Rumsfeld sent to his senior colleagues in the Defense Department. In it, he reflected an outlook that was both grim and confused. He asked, "Is our current situation such that the harder we work, the behinder we get?" and further "We lack the metrics to know if we are winning or losing the global war on terror. Are we capturing, killing or deterring and dissuading more terrorists every day than the madrassas and the radical clerics are recruiting, training and deploying against us?"[56] Rumsfeld's puzzlement that whatever he and his colleagues might do the only result was continued chaos seems as appropriate for the duration of the conflict as it was for 2003.

Rumsfeld's memorandum also revealed an obliviousness to serious problems that were encountered in the "easy" part of the conflict before May 2003, as well as to what was emerging thereafter. In fact, in the conventional phase of the war, before May 2003, there were obvious signs of incompetence in the Army's senior command, and after May 2003, it became apparent to those willing to observe that a major cause of the insurgency was the occupation itself.

Assessing the U.S. Army in Iraq

An uncompromising advocate of reform in the U.S. Army has been retired Colonel Douglas Macgregor. Decorated for his performance in Operation Desert Storm as an armor commander in the only significant tank engagement with the Iraqis in 1991, MacGregor wrote the groundbreaking book *Breaking the Phalanx: A New Design for Land Power in the 21st Century* advocating radical reform of the Army's industrial age force structure. Like others, MacGregor also suffered the fate of the outspoken reformer and retired as a full colonel. Just as he had been before he retired, Macgregor continued as one of the Army's most severe critics, especially of its senior commanders. In an essay released by the Straus Military Reform Project of the Center for Defense Information in Washington in 2006 and titled "Fire the Generals!," Macgregor wrote a litany of revealing criticisms. His cauterizing essay, reproduced as Appendix I makes several key points:

- The Army was utterly unprepared to fight the conflict in which it found itself immersed in 2004. It lacked not only appropriate doctrine but also a willingness to understand the nature of the conflict it was in. As Macgregor relates in one of many telling examples, when Gen. George Casey assumed command of coalition forces in Iraq in 2004, he asked to meet the headquarters' counterinsurgency expert. His staff was puzzled; they had no such expert.
- Senior Army commanders repeatedly made tactical errors in directing their forces because of their mindset that they were facing a Soviet Union/cold war style opponent. Worse, when the March to Baghdad encountered Saddam's Fedayeen irregulars using tactics the U.S. commanders did not expect, some of those commanders panicked and sought a "pause" in operations to slow down the pace of events to permit them to figure out how to respond. This plodding, reactive—almost passive—approach was also demonstrated in other situations, such as when Army commanders wanted days to prepare to march from Baghdad to Tikrit in the face of virtually no opposition.
- Although the Army had adopted "jointness" as a mantra for its operations involving other services and disparate types of units, in practice, there was no such thing. Instead of "joint," operations and logistics were ad hoc and not designed for war, certainly not the one that developed.
- Most importantly, despite twelve years of experience in the Persian Gulf after the first Gulf War, the Army's generals did nothing to prepare to cope with the complexity of operating in a Muslim Arab country or thinking about how the next conflict ought to be fought differently from the last war. As a result, the American occupation of Iraq became

a virulent source of the insurgency against it, a characteristic not just ignored by the Army's high command but facilitated, even encouraged, by it.

Macgregor concludes that at the core American military leadership is poorly prepared for real war—the kind that occurs on battlefields against real enemies and where actions taken have life and death consequences, rather than the political playing fields in Washington where bureaucratic behavior, even extreme careerism, are utterly unexceptional. Dilatants in Washington, DC, who babble on about American armed forces being the best in the world, even history, would be well advised to read Macgregor's powerful essay.

Addressing the Problems from Within

If senior military and political leaders cannot, or will not, lead military reform, who can? A different reformer, still another retired Army officer, Major Donald Vandergriff (mentioned above), has spent his career, both in uniform and as a civilian, thinking about how to prepare military officers for the battlefield. His work, published in several books, studies, articles, and monographs (noted in the bibliography section), provides the all-important link between the professional and ethical failures Macgregor described on the battlefield in Iraq and what can be done to eliminate those failures in Washington. Vandergriff's work is a prime example of profound reforms that can make a significant difference.

In an article "From Swift to Swiss,"[57] Vandergriff describes how to build from the ground up an officer corps that knows how to think under stress and understands the necessity of responding to facts and events as they exist, rather than staying within the existing lanes of preestablished dogma. This article appears as Appendix II. In it, Vandergriff describes the "industrial era" personnel system the Army adopted shortly after the turn of the century as an attempted reform to permit the United States to contend on the linear, attrition battlefield of the First World War (a form known to some as "second generation warfare"). That industrial outlook on military personnel, especially officers, saw soldiers as interchangeable parts, trained to perform in a set way against a preconceived array of circumstances. As warfare revealed itself to require more fluid, adaptive, thinking responses to both known and unforeseen circumstances, this personnel system was shown to be completely inappropriate, not just in twenty-first century Fourth Generation Warfare, but even on the Third Generation battlefields of World War II, where German units often outperformed Americans on a unit for unit basis.[58]

Vandergriff sought to learn from this essentially Prussian, not Nazi, model and found a whole new approach to military officer training. This model sought ways to develop officers who could make rapid and effective decisions in the chaos of the battlefield. It was an approach to officer development developed by a Swiss educator, Johann Heinrich Pestalozzi, who developed his theories on education in the late 1700s. His theory was that students would learn faster on their own if they were allowed to "experience the thing before they tried to give it a name." It sought to teach students to identify the core of a problem and to react appropriately to it, rather than use a recipe approach. It is an attempt to teach military leaders—at all levels of the military hierarchy—how to think, rather than to react without thinking on the battlefield.

Imagine the difference between the thoughtful, fast reacting (and also rigorously ethical) officer corps that Major Vandergriff's education techniques seek to develop as opposed to the senior Army commanders Col. Macgregor describes in the Iraq War, where adherence to preconceived notions, panic, and other behavior inappropriate to the evolving circumstances seem more predominant. It is a stark choice between politically correct military failure and adapting appropriately to evolving and demanding circumstances to succeed on the battlefield.

It is perhaps encouraging that as a civilian adviser to the Army, Vandergriff's ideas on how to produce an "adaptive" officer corps have won advocates in some senior corners of the Army. If these ideas are embraced, it is possible for America's Army to avoid in the future the professional and ethical failures Macgregor described in Iraq. Unfortunately, however, for Vandergriff's ideas to take hold and for the officers imbued with them to rise to senior command will take many years. And, more importantly, it will require those in command now, many of whom are the problem, to foster an environment in the military services where thinking, adaptive, ethical officers both remain in the armed forces and are promoted. Frankly, the outlook for that is not propitious.

Necessary but Insufficient

The kind of redress sought by Col. Macgregor and Maj. Vandergriff would go far to improve American military performance on twenty-first-century battlefields, but their ideas only partially address America's defense problems. That portion of the Defense Department that preoccupies itself with the development and acquisition of technology, and with the management of its more than two million military personnel and almost three-quarters of a million civilian workers, also needs reform—at least as much as the parts of the military services that fight wars. According to both the GAO and OMB, the DoD is one of the worst managed agencies in the federal government.

The Pentagon's ills were described in detail by another of the core military reformers, Chuck Spinney, in long and detailed testimony he delivered to the Committee on Government Reform and Oversight of the House of Representatives in 2004. Spinney's testimony is especially relevant because it directly ties his understanding of the Department's pathologies—based on his thirty-plus-year Pentagon career—to some solutions.

Spinney's testimony is presented as Appendix III. It describes the Pentagon's core management failing as ignoring the consequences, especially in the form of budget costs, of both past and future decisions. This double breakdown makes it impossible for decision makers to assemble the information needed to form a coherent defense plan.

Essential to the pathology is a repetitive bias to understate future costs in a two-step bureaucratic strategy, identified by Spinney as "front loading" and "political engineering." Front loading means a "low-balled" estimate of costs of a program or policy to facilitate approval in the Pentagon and Congress. In the second, "political engineering" phase, the goal is to point out the jobs and other benefits that accompany a program and thereby raise the political stakes before the true costs of the front-loaded program become apparent. By the time the real costs emerge, the political cost of a termination is perceived by decision-makers in Washington as prohibitive.

In response, those decision-makers cut back production rates to wedge the reduced program into the available money. This overall process permits too many "low-balled" weapons to get stuffed into the budget, and it allows ever-rising pressure to grow the entire defense budget. The inevitable lower rates of production naturally decrease the rate of inventory replacement, which increases the age of weapons and makes them more expensive to operate, thereby driving up the costs of the operating budget. Thus, you get a shrinking, aging, less ready defense inventory at increasing cost.

The first priority is to fix the Pentagon's accounting problems to make it difficult, if not impossible, to ignore the cost consequences of past and current actions. In a set of follow-on recommendations explained in detail in Appendix III, Spinney aims to continuously improve Pentagon managers' ability to shape and adapt to unfolding change: to strive to improve the "fit" of plans to reality while coping with unpredictable events.

As an attempt to combine the operational realities of making a coherent set of strategic and budgetary decisions based on reliable data rather than wishful thinking or willful misrepresentations, Spinney's outline of a method to address the Pentagon management problem is unique and demands close and careful attention. His prescriptions will strike most Pentagon managers and think tank pundits as strange, if not impractical, because it lacks easy prescriptions for a thoroughly theoretical solution that requires no one to make any unpleasant sacrifices: the decision-making methodology that got us to our current situation.

Whither Reform?

There is scant reason for smugness in an easy victory against a tethered goat commanded by a military jackass, to say nothing of a continuing failure to deal competently with an insurgency. Indeed, given the absence of meaningful U.S. tactical success and our overall strategic insolvency, thus far, in Iraq and clearly also Afghanistan, there is reason to remain gravely concerned about America's inability to cope with a foe we can hardly identify, cannot pacify, and cannot ignore. It is even reasonable to ask, if the United States refought the war in Vietnam with the armed forces and especially the civilian and military leadership we have today, would there be any difference in the outcome? After decades of "reform," we seem to have ended up all to close to where we began.

In a 2006 article he wrote to explain why firing Secretary of Defense Rumsfeld for his many failures would very probably *not* result in any significant improvement in our armed forces face, Bill Lind, one of the original military reformers, pointed out why just removing Rumsfeld will accomplish virtually nothing as long as the culture remains unchanged.

As Lind points out, Rumsfeld is focused on technology as a solution: "His focus is 'Transformation,' a broad effort to replace manpower with high technology that will guarantee American military dominance far into the future, over all potential state opponents."[59] It was this same technology that failed so completely to remove the fog from the battlefield not only against the more indistinct insurgents in Iraq and Afghanistan, but which repeatedly failed to deliver the same promise against the grossly inept—and readily locatable—conventional foe in the "easy" phase of Operation Iraqi Freedom.

Rumsfeld pursues a "false promise of winning through technology,"[60] a focus which, as the reformers to a man point out, means a military that remains "focused inward on rules, processes, and methods; maintains rigid hierarchies that feed centralized decision making; prizes obedience over initiative; and depends on imposed discipline." It is something entirely different from an "Army focused outward on the enemy, the situation, and the result the situation demand[s] [where] leaders at all levels [are] expected to get the necessary result regardless of rules or even orders."[61]

Under the rubric of "Transformation," "Revolution in Military Affairs, "Net Centric Warfare," and endless other vapid descriptors, Rumsfeld, indeed the Pentagon's leadership and all too many in the world of pundits (i.e., aspiring successors to Rumsfeld) sees war as "a matter of putting firepower on targets." This is a result believed to guarantee success through "precision weapons" and centralization in command reinforced by other technologies, especially computer systems that will, it is believed, enable generals in remote headquarters to observe, if not control, the movements of every soldier—both enemy and friendly—to inevitable success. It was, Lind points out, just such a mentality and technology that were a major reason for the failure of Operation Anaconda in Afghanistan in 2002, thereby permitting bin Laden to escape, as one minor example. And, it was why Germany so easily defeated France in 1940 and why crudely equipped guerrillas defeated the American superpower in Vietnam.

The technological schemes, when laid over a cold war force structure with people managed by an out of date—industrial age—personnel system, carry heavy baggage with them: "obedience is demanded and initiative is shunned." "Rigid hierarchies and stovepiped information flows all feed the centralized control of high-tech fires that are the basis of 'Transformation' and the other buzz words. Far from being progress, they embrace concepts that reinforce the culture of technological dogma that is the ball and chain that [modern, 'high tech'] militaries drag behind them. Worse still, as these same concepts pull the American military backward, war is moving on into a fourth generation where events are fluid, the enemy indistinct, and the conflict itself only secondarily military."[62] Our fourth generation enemy and our predictable, top heavy, inflexible, inward focused American armed forces "are ships passing in the night, to the great advantage of the Fourth Generation," according to Lind.[63]

The most serious problems are not at the bottom of our military forces; they are at the top. Americans soldiers, Marines, sailors, and pilots have fought with undeniable courage and determination in both Iraq wars, no matter what the quality of the opposition. The core problem is the overall direction of both the fighting forces and the Pentagon structure that is supposed to support them.

Thus, Lind concludes in his short essay that even if Rumsfeld were to be replaced, a hierarchy that sees things precisely the same way will remain: "We will continue to lie becalmed between a dinosaur-inhabited Scylla and a techno-fantasy Charybdis called Transformation, as we lose two Fourth Generation wars in Iraq and Afghanistan. Perhaps those defeats will do for us what Jena did for Prussia and propel us toward genuine military reform."[64]

It is not just sad but unnecessary that the real impetus for reform of America's armed forces may have to come from yet another military defeat. Perhaps the realization will occur that after the debacle of Vietnam we remain just as vulnerable to defeat from foes with no budget or technology to speak of. As the reformers have prescribed, methodologies exist for real reform, but the will and the leadership are lacking. It may require yet another military embarrassment combined with a sufficiently large number of taxpayers no longer willing to pay an extraordinarily high cost for a shrinking, aging, less ready military that refuses to adapt to new evolutions in the nature of warfare. If we are lucky, it will not come to either, but from the appearances of the course America is on, it may require both.

Notes

1. *Gulf War Air Power Survey, Volume V, A Statistical Compendium and Chronology*, contract study for the Secretary of the Air Force, Washington, DC, 1993, pp. 653–654.

2. Ibid., p. 418.

3. Ibid., pp. 653–654, 418.

4. "Operation Desert Storm: Evaluation of the Air Campaign," U.S. General Accounting Office, GAO/NSIAD-97-134, p. 148.

5. William L. Smallwood, *Warthog: Flying the A-10 in the Gulf War*, Brassey's, New York, 1993, p. 96.

6. Dr. Moskos made this comment in the office of the Army Personnel Chief in February 2004.

7. George Wilson, "Marine Corps Evolves into Sophisticated, Fluid Fighting Force," *Government Executive* Daily Briefing, April 4, 2003.

8. Robert Coram, *Boyd: The Fighter Pilot Who Changed the Art of War*, Little Brown & Co., Boston, 2002, pp. 422–424.

9. Ibid., pp. 422–424.

10. For a more detailed discussion of the failure of the 7th Corps left hook, see "Pushing Them Out the Back Door" in the Epilogue of James G. Burton, *The Pentagon Wars*, Naval Institute Press, Annapolis, MD, 1993, pp. 243–256.

11. Footnote 22 in Chapter 5 of *Battlefield of the Future*, "War and Hyperwar," by Col Richard Szafranski, USAF, in *Aerospace Power Chronicles*, Air University Press, Maxwell Air Force Base, Montgomery, AL, 1983.

12. For further analysis of Iraq's "Integrated Air Defense System," see "Operation Desert Storm: Evaluation of the Air Campaign," pp. 82–107 and 205–207.

13. Analysis of data in *Gulf War Air Power Survey*, p. 651.

14. Data collected for "Operation Desert Storm: Evaluation of the Air Campaign."

15. William S. Lind, "What Great Victory? What Revolution?" essay written in the aftermath of the 1991 Gulf War, in the author's files.

16. Martin Sieff, "Why Baghdad Fell Fast: Saddam No Stalin," *United Press International*, April 16, 2003.

17. Dr. Stephen Biddle, Col. James Embray, Col. Edward Filiberti, Col. Stephan Kidder, Dr. Steven Metz, Dr, Ivan Oelrich, and LTC Richard Shelton, "Toppling Saddam: Iraq and American Military Transformation," Strategic Studies Institute, Army War College, Carlisle, PA, April 2004, pp. 24–26.

18. Lance Gay, "Iraq Ignored History, Was Doomed to Fail Again," *Scripps Howard News Service*, April 9, 2002.

19. Biddle, "Toppling Saddam," pp. 27–31.

20. Gay, "Iraq Ignored History, Was Doomed to Fail Again."

21. Anthony H. Cordesman, *The Lessons of the Iraq War; Main Report*, Center for Strategic and International Studies, downloaded from CSIS Web site at www.csis.org, p. 23.

22. Ibid., p. 42.

23. Ibid., p. 47.

24. Molly Moore, "A Foe that Collapsed from Within," *Washington Post*, July 20, 2003, p. 2.

25. Cordesman, *The Lessons of the Iraq War*, p. 47.

26. Ibid., p. 23.

27. Moore, "A Foe that Collapsed from Within," p. 3.

28. Thomas Withington, "What If We Battled a Real Army?," *Long Island Newsday*, August 27, 2003.

29. Biddle, "Toppling Saddam," p. 24.

30. Moore, "A Foe that Collapsed from Within," p. 3.

31. Cordesman, *The Lessons of the Iraq War*, p. 50.

32. Moore, "A Foe that Collapsed from Within," p. 3.

33. Ibid., p. 3.

34. Martin Sieff, "Why Baghdad Fell Fast: Saddam No Stalin," *United Press International*, April 16, 2003.

35. Elaine Grossman, "Marine General: Iraq War Pause 'Could Not Have Come at a Worse Time,' " *Inside the Pentagon*, October 2, 2003.

36. Cordesman, *The Lessons of the Iraq War*, p. 26.

37. Terry McCarthy, "What Ever Happened to the Republican Guard," *Time Magazine*, May 5, 2003.

38. "Brief on 1 MarDiv, Observations," as appearing in "Operation Iraqi Freedom, After Action Reviews and Lessons Learned," U.S. Marine Corps reports e-mailed to author.

39. 1st L. Jennefer Jordan, "Lessons Learned on the 'Highway to Hell," *Marine Corps News*, May 20, 2003.

40. McCarthy, "What Ever Happened to the Republican Guard."

41. Wilson, "Marine Corps Evolves into Sophisticated, Fluid Fighting Force."

42. McCarthy, "What Ever Happened to the Republican Guard."

43. For example, see U.S. Army Officer, 3rd Infantry Division, "With the 'Marne 500' in Iraq," *The Urban Operations Journal*, March 2003, p. 3; "Operation Iraqi Freedom, Task Force 2-7 Infantry (Mechanized)," Ralph Hammond, Chief Collective Trng and ABCA/International Programs, Doctrine and Collective Training Division, Combined Arms and tactics Directorate/Infantry School, Ft. Benning, GA., report e-mailed to author; McCarthy, "What Ever Happened to the Republican Guard"; Moore, "A Foe that Collapsed from Within," p. 1; Grossman, "Marine General."

44. Cordesman, *The Lessons of the Iraq War*, p. 25.

45. See "Army Takes Its War Effort to Task," *Los Angeles Times*, July 3, 2004.

46. Biddle, "Toppling Saddam," p. 199.

47. Withington, "What If We Battled a Real Army?"

48. Tom Bowman, "US Technology, Inept Enemy Led to Iraq Victory, Army Says," *Baltimore Sun*, October 13, 2003; See Biddle, "Toppling Saddam."

49. For a lengthy exposition of the details, see "Operation Desert Storm."

50. See Biddle, "Toppling Saddam."

51. David Talbot, "How Technology Failed in Iraq," *Technology Review*, November 2004.

52. Ibid.

53. Ibid.

54. Rajiv Chandrasekaran, "Attacks on Troops on Rise, Commander Says," *Washington Post*, October 23, 2003, p. A 27.

55. See William Lind, Col. Keith Nightengale, Capt. John F. Schmitt, Col Joseph W. Sutton, and Lt. Col. Gary I. Wilson, "The Changing Face of War: Into the Fourth Generation," *The Marine Corps Gazette*, October 1989. This article also appears at www.d-n-i.net.

56. Dave Monitz, "Defense Memo: A Grim Outlook," *USA Today*, October 22, 2003.

57. See Donald E. Vandergriff, "From Swift to Swiss," *Performance Improvement*, February 2006, p. 30.

58. For an excellent analysis of how and why German units outperformed American in World War II, see Martin van Creveld, "Fighting Power: German and U.S. Army Performance, 1939–1945," Greenwood Press, Westport, Conn., 1974.

59. William S. Lind, "Fighting the Last War: Rumsfeld's Resignation Is Less Important than a Reordering of U.S. Strategy," *The American Conservative*, June 19, 2006, p. 27.

60. Ibid., p. 29.

61. Ibid., p. 29

62. Ibid., p. 29.

63. Ibid., p. 29.

64. Ibid., p. 29.

CHAPTER 7

Conclusions: What Is Military Reform?

Winslow T. Wheeler

We can deduce from the foregoing some conclusions about what military reform is and, equally importantly, what it is not. Meaningful reform involves a certain way of thinking about and acting on questions of national defense. We shall address here some ways meaningful reform can be identified while also pointing out some ideas that sound like reform but are not.

To dispense with some of the easier questions first, we can describe what military reform is not.

Military Reform Is Not a Question of Political Party or Ideology

The active membership of the Congressional Military Caucus consisted of Republicans and Democrats and liberals, moderates, and conservatives; for example, Congressmen Newt Gingrich on the right and Congresswoman Barbara Boxer on the left were equally active and legitimate reformers in the 1980s in the House of Representatives. Opponents to military reform, and those indifferent to it, have also come from all stripes. For example, Senator John Tower opposed just about every reform initiative proposed, and a liberal Democrat who was often involved in defense issues, Senator Dale Bumpers of Arkansas, was consistently indifferent to fundamental reform ideas, as described in this book.

Timing also makes a difference. In the twenty-first century, both Gingrich and Boxer have dropped military reform ideas like last week's fish. Today, former Congressman Gingrich advocates most, if not all, of the ideas described below that demonstrate what reform is not. As a U.S. Senator, Barbra Boxer has rarely, if ever, shown any significant initiative on defense issues, and when she does talk on them, reform content is consistently absent.

Military Reform Is Not a Function of Budget Size

It is heresy in Washington, DC, to fail to use money as an expression of political support—either for a government activity, such as education, or for politicians themselves. However, the size of a defense budget is almost without meaning for the quality of the military forces it supports, or fails to support. Smaller budgets can—and have—meant a stronger force, and larger budgets can, and do, mean a weaker force. If both were not true, and if a disparity in the cost of forces would accelerate victory for the richer side, then France and Britain would have defeated Germany in 1940, America would have won the war in Vietnam, and President Bush would have won the wars in Iraq and Afghanistan long ago.

The proposition is just as true for hardware. Cheaper weapons can—and have—been far more effective than expensive ones. World War II is crammed with examples: the cheap, simple Soviet T-34 tank was far more effective than Germany's more costly, better machined Panzers Mark III and IV. Even more important, the brilliant Soviet design generated a total tank force that was far more effective than the force that included Germany's super tanks, the Panther and the Tiger, which appeared on the battlefield only in puny numbers because of their complexity and resultant cost and unreliability. In fact, high expense can be a sign of an ineffective weapon: expense usually means complexity and suboptimal numbers; complexity means unreliability; low numbers exacerbate the unavailability of unreliable systems, even if the high-cost weapon were to be individually effective, which is often not the case.

Military Reform Is Not a Technological Agenda

Some attempt to couch their technological fantasies as reform; however, such agendas are almost always business as usual consisting of inflated cost and hype. "Revolution in Military Affairs" (RMA) and "transformation" are just two of many slogans used today to mask a tired, decades old technological agenda with reform-like terminology. Indeed, such buzz words usually mean at their core the advocacy of very specific technological agendas and the antithesis of real reform. For example, a "revolution in warfare" was declared to have occurred in Operation Desert Storm with the advent of "one bomb, one target" precision attacks, and it was supplemented with descriptions of the F-117 "stealth" bomber, which this time—it was promised—made the revolution a real one. It was pure balderdash. "One bomb, one target" was a rare event in Operation Desert Storm.

While many video tapes are shown on TV from Desert Storm and other conflicts to "document" precision air to ground strikes, those aircraft hangars, bridges, and tanks being hit with a single guided bomb are often not what they appear. The narration usually fails to point out the documented results. In the 1991 Persian Gulf War, bridges, for example, were destroyed only after an average of ten tons of guided munitions were employed against them. The tape released to the public may have simply been the last attempt. In the case of the destroyed tanks (a favorite of the "one bomb, one target" hypesters), research showed that only a small percentage of the destroyed tanks inspected after the war were hit by anything at all from the air. Most were either destroyed by the Iraqis themselves or hit by ground-based antiarmor systems.

More recently, the Army has postured a "revolutionary" development with its "Future Combat System" (FCS). A "system of systems" that will employ a host of sensors, computers, and communications gear, it promises to remove fog and chaos from the battlefield by telling our headquarters and combat units where every enemy unit on or near the battlefield is. In fact, it promises to do so with such precision and regularity that Army combat vehicles will no longer require heavy armor. So precise will be our intelligence and so promptly will it be effectively communicated to unit commanders on the battlefield that we will know where every single antiarmor weapon in enemy hands is hidden, and we will be able to "zap" them all from beyond their own range with our own long-range precision targeting systems. Ergo, heavy armor to resist the tens of thousands of rocket propelled grenades and all, repeat all, other antiarmor systems will no longer be needed. It is the penultimate promise—under the RMA banner—of the military dilatants in Washington, who have been on the hunt to remove "fog" and "friction" from the battlefield with highly complex communications equipment tying together networks of military forces, quite literally, since the 1930s.

We saw this concept in operation in Iraq in 2003 when commanders received prototypical FCS-like systems. The information was too regularly too late, too unclear (thereby creating its own "fog"), or misleading (creating not just fog but friction as well). Perhaps, even worse, the centrally funneled intelligence inherent in systems like FCS facilitated interference from remotely located headquarters with the decisions of unit commanders in the field, who understood in Nisaryiah, for example, much better what was the situation than a colonel or a general sitting behind a desk in Qatar, or the Persian Gulf or even Tampa, Florida. It is a system that epitomizes micromanagement from above at its worst and that can foster mistrust and entropy among combat units and with commanders back in headquarters. That is what we want to do to the enemy, not to ourselves. Some of the more prescient field commanders in Iraq in 2003 responded by simply turning the FCS-type systems off.

The agenda behind the FCS is nothing new. It was the same kind of concept the French used in 1930 to attempt to manage the battlefield from central headquarters under the moniker "methodical battlefield." In 1981, the military reformers warned us of its many American predecessors (variously called the World-wide Military Command and Control System and the Joint Tactical Information Distribution System) in the form of a " . . . futile attempt to 'manage' the battle through a complex set of communications links to central command posts in favor of allowing military commanders the flexibility (command initiative) to respond quickly to the changing circumstances always present on a real (as opposed to a theoretical) battlefield."[1]

Gimmicks like the so-called RMA persistently fail on the battlefield, but they will live on in theoreticians reveries and highly priced corporate proposals. The same agenda will appear under a new moniker when the failure of RMA sinks into the Washington, DC, think tank community; it is as predictable as the sunrise.

Reorganization Is Not Automatically Reform

We have learned from endless reorganizations over the history of congressional investigations, blue ribbon commissions, and the like that reshuffling the organizational deck in the Pentagon can as often be a step backwards, as forwards. A good example was the creation of an "acquisition czar" in the reforms of the Senate Armed Services Committee and the Packard Blue Ribbon Commission in the mid-1980s. The declared intent was to repair the disastrous procurement experience of the Pentagon in the late cold war. High-cost weapons had sent the budget into the stratosphere, but all the spending only produced lesser numbers of mediocre, if not unworking, weapons. And, of course, there were scandals galore. There was a clear need for change, and the "acquisition czar" was the approved response.

Subsequent history has shown that reorganization to be a complete failure. Under the new structure, costs went up even more steeply; inventories went down, and scrutiny (not performed by the "czars" but by others) into the performance of many of the most prominent weapons shows that effectiveness was well below what was promised. At one point, John Boyd ruefully remarked, "What do you expect when all you change is the room assignments in the bordello?"

Some explanation of the failure of typical reorganization proposals can help to explain why many ideas that "sound good" often result in either no change at all or a worsening situation. The penchant for many organizational reforms has been to centralize: to put more authority in the hands of one man or office. A seemingly logical reaction to problems, to "streamline" cumbersome bureaucracies and to designate someone as clearly in charge of cleaning up a mess, such proposals often fail. They do so for the simple reason that they tend to put decision makers out of touch with reality by removing them even further from "ground truth" in terms of what soldiers need and what they think of what they get. Such streamlining also ignores, even eliminates, mechanisms that can bring real improvement: such as a system of checks and balances from multiple offices working on solutions and coming up with several candidate ideas, rather than a centralized system producing one "school" solution, unchallenged by any competition.

Put another way, multiple competing bureaucracies can be a good thing—if they can be forced by creative leaders to actually compete not for funding and status but on how best to get the job done. However, any such proposal is too counterintuitive for most people, especially politicians—both in Congress and the halls of the Pentagon. How many congressional hearings and blue ribbon commissions have endorsed "expanding the bureaucracy"? Too often, reform efforts are hobbled by what is politically acceptable.

What are the indicators that a proposed reform could be for real—more than political cosmetics, indiscriminately throwing money at the problem or reorganizing to strangle the marketplace of ideas? What are the characteristics of real reform?

They can be articulated in three realms: the physical, the mental, and the moral. Again, the easiest first, and also the least important: the physical issues, such as hardware, or weapons.

Weapons: Is Less More?

Time and time again, successful generals have commented that had their soldiers or airmen changed equipment with the enemy, the result of the conflict would have been the same. General Norman Schwartzkopf made such a statement after he defeated Saddam's forces in 1991, but of course, the advocates of high tech ignored the statement in their analysis of the reason for the victory. Similarly, when I was in Israel in 1983, the Chief of Staff of the Israeli Air Force stated to me and a group of congressional staffers that had his pilots flown Syria's Migs and if the Syrians had been flying F-15s and F-16s, his pilots still would have had the same exchange ratio of 83-0, in Israel's favor, in the Israeli invasion of Lebanon in 1982. Moreover, history is full of examples of the side with the superior equipment being the loser: in 1940, many French and some British tanks were superior to most German tanks in terms of both armor and firepower. In the air war over Europe in 1944 and 1945, Germany flew the highly superior Me-262 and other more obscure high-performance fighters but, of course, lost quite decisively. In that case, much of the aerial victory was due to the brilliant— but relatively conventional—design of the low cost American P-51 fighter (once it was equipped with the British Merlin engine—a modification that was adamantly opposed by the high command of the U.S. Army Air Corps).

Of course, it is preferable to have superior equipment, but only if it is available in sufficient numbers to have a real impact on the battlefield and especially if it is crewed by well motivated and thoroughly trained personnel. The point was obvious in the two wars against Iraq: the Iraqi armed forces were equipped with competent Soviet equipment in many cases but the troops and pilots were simply not willing to fight, and when they did so it was done incompetently. They simply made easy targets out of themselves.

The same results have occurred in training facilities for American pilots. A former editor of the Navy's *Topgun Journal*, James Stevenson, has reported the success that American instructor pilots have over their students. In the past, instructors flew cheap, simple F-5 aircraft; the students flew "more capable" (and more complex and expensive) F-14s, F-15s, and other "superior" aircraft. And yet, even though the students were proficient, they virtually always lost in encounters with the better trained, more experienced instructors.

Even though the quality of equipment is less important than other considerations, inferior equipment can needlessly cost peoples' lives, and it can cost battles. What then distinguishes a military reformer's view of superior equipment?

Pierre Sprey wrote the consummate briefing on what distinguishes superior weapons. His briefing, "What Quality vs Quantity Issue?,"[2] addressed the conventional wisdom prevailing in the 1980s that the reformers advocated large numbers of cheap but less effective weapons, rather than what others preferred: smaller numbers of more effective, but admittedly costly, weapons. In refuting the paradigm, Sprey pointed out a few of history's many examples of the better weapon also being more simple and, therefore, cheaper and more reliable. He cited as examples rifles, tanks, artillery, naval combatants, air to air missiles, and—of course—fighter aircraft, where it was the more complex, more expensive version that was the loser in terms of performance in combat. It was not a question of high tech versus low tech; it was instead a question of the smart use of technology to assist the human operator versus the advocacy of technology in its own right, with little thought for either the human operator or what lessons history shows to be the real criteria for a successful weapon.

He argued that "You can't design for superior effectiveness if you can't define it." Further he stated:

- "to understand effectiveness, study combat, not technological promises";
- "combat effectiveness is always irreducibly multidimensional";
- "two essential measures are always '*rate*' *of kill* [not kill rates in canned individual jousts] and *numbers in combat.*"

He applied these criteria in a study of air-to-air combat. His criteria for assessing the effectiveness of fighters—in order of importance—were

1) surprise (which aircraft sees the other first; most air to air kills occur when the loser is not even aware he is under attack),
2) numbers in the air (that is, the total number of actual combat sorties that can be flown, both per day and over the long term),
3) ability to maneuver to a firing position (not just speed and turning, but more essentially agility both in acceleration and deceleration and in switching from one maneuver "transient" to another), and
4) demonstrated weapons lethality, especially for exploiting split second opportunities (not theoretical kills generated by computer models, which are literally never a true representation of real-world combat).

The result of Sprey's—and Boyd's—application of these criteria, against an Air Force (and Navy) bureaucracy that fought them every inch of the way, was the F-15, F-16, F-18, and A-10—the most successful combat aircraft America deployed in decades. Sprey and Boyd did lose some fights with the Pentagon's aviation bureaucracy and each of the designs gained additional—performance killing—weight and, thus, cost, as a result. But, the essential quality of the basic concepts survived—to varying degrees in the different aircraft. Today, there is virtually no one in either the Air Force or the Navy who argues that any of those aircraft should have been traded in for what the Pentagon's aviation bureaucracy originally wanted and drew on their own design boards. (It was a classic example of the benefit from "competing bureaucracies.")

Put simply, the Sprey criteria, which rely so much on a study of real-world events (combat's actual lessons), have proven themselves on actual battlefields. Sadly, they are lessons that the Air Force ignored in designing its new genera-tion fighters, the F-22 "Raptor" and the F-35 "Joint Strike Fighter," which are both overweight, overcost, and—according to Sprey's proven criteria—losers, not winners.

The reformers emphasized the use of new technology in weapons, but the "high tech" they sought was both simple and proven on the battlefield. Moreover, they did not seek to trade in quality for quantity; they insisted on both.

They also asserted that weapons are the lowest rung of what counts in military combat.

Mind Over Matter

A higher rung on the ladder of what counts in conflict is the realm of the mental. The mental dimension includes several subsets, including organization, some, but not all, "people issues," and matters of tactics and doctrine. In each case, an independent point of view, focus on ground truths (empiricism), and results where it counts—on the battlefield, not in corporate laboratories or Power Point briefings—are all central. Academics, top down thinking, and behaviors not rooted in the realities of war are not just irrelevant but counterproductive.

Two examples are useful on the subject of organization. In the 1980s, Col. Macgregor (see Appendix I) wrote in his book *Breaking the Phalanx: A New De-sign for Landpower in the 21st Century* about how to reorganize the Army to bet-ter adapt to post-cold war conflict. The Army's traditional division structure was more relevant to combat with the Soviet Union, and it was an impediment to the form of conflict more likely in the post-cold war age, which required rapid transport to regional battlefields and, more importantly, the ability to adapt better to previously unforeseen circumstances. Macgregor recommended a new, flatter, more compact but also more powerful brigade structure, which could more eas-ily move to distant conflicts and which shucked the unnecessary, higher, thicker command structures that came with larger divisions. Put simply, it was a structure that sought to adapt to new realities.

The Army adopted Macgregor's thinking but only in the most superficial man-ner. It started a reorganization into "brigade combat teams" called "modulariza-tion," but it simultaneously shrank existing brigades by weakening their combat arms. This expanded the number of brigades, but it made each one weaker. It also—not accidentally—expanded the number of brigade headquarters. The reor-ganization became an opportunity to accommodate the bureaucratic requirement to establish command billets for the Army's excessive number of senior colonels and junior generals. A constructive and fundamental reform was perverted by selfish bureaucratic impulses to turn away from combat needs toward careerist ones.

Another organizational reform that showed promise but that was also attacked by the Pentagon was the independent testing office, discussed in Chapters 2 and 3. There, the simple yet important idea of an office independent of corrupting influences in service and procurement bureaucracies was fought to a standstill by those same bureaucracies; they fully understood the threat to their domination of the DoD acquisition system.

There are some positive examples of reorganizations: prominently, the Truman Commission. Truman's initiative was a new congressional adjunct (it literally expanded—not streamlined—the bureaucracy) led by an individual who evidenced independence in the most positive and important sense. His habit for hard work, listening to the evidence, and taking action consistent with the evidence— without much regard for prevailing conventional wisdom or established entities— gave his new bureaucratic creation a value far in excess of any negative attributes resulting from the increases in staff and the administrative activities needed to carry off hundreds of hearings and dozens of reports. It was another clear example of the counterintuitive benefits of "expanding the bureaucracy." More than just another nameplate on a door on Capitol Hill, it was a beehive of activity of people who were led by a man uninterested in currying favor with business as usual.

Ironically, but not surprisingly, the initially unwanted commission made Truman a star. Truman became a political idol, then vice-president, then president. Not bad for an operation few took seriously at the beginning and some— including the White House—tried to brush aside.

The same kind of direct connection between empirical realities and bureaucratic output can be seen in the typically reformist procurement recommendation to "fly before you buy," that is, to fully test a new piece of hardware in combat-realistic conditions before billions of dollars are spent to put it into full production. A seemingly simple prescription, it requires persistent wars inside the bureaucracy to ensure the tests are (1) conducted, (2) not compromised by performance enhancing unrealism, and (3) honestly reported. It is a good example of the simple thing being extremely difficult to do. It is also a classic example of a reform that many rhetorically embrace but that few actually carry out in a meaningful sense, especially when the advocates of business as usual fight back and the going gets tough.[3]

In the reforms and reorganizations he recommended in Appendix III, Chuck Spinney sought to ground the Pentagon's book-keeping, cost estimates, and budgets in reality, not political, careerist, or conventional bureaucratic agendas. His recommendations have the consistent theme of trying to force government processes to interact with reality.

In a similar vein, Ernie Fitzgerald (see Chapter 2) kept on trying to narrow the gap in the Pentagon between its own rhetoric about "cost effectiveness" and reality. In his case, he sought to introduce the Department's business operations to private sector notions of efficiency and free market competition. He recoiled in disgust against the empty rhetoric of "adopting business practices" that disguised an agenda that was far more socialist than free market in its methods and results.

Similarly, Thomas Christie, who spent four decades working in the Pentagon and who served as one of the more successful directors of the reform-inspired operational testing office, argued in an important article in the U.S. Naval Institute's magazine, *Proceedings*, that great progress could be made to improve the Pentagon's very broken hardware acquisition system if managers there simply implemented the directives, regulations, and laws—as written.[4] His point is that most of those regulations, etc., would have some positive effect if they were implemented as intended. Instead, loopholes and imprecise wording are exploited by managers seeking to get along with business as usual: for example, tests that the laws seek to be realistic are not, and contracts are awarded after competitions that occur in name only.

The difference between rhetoric and realities can also be seen in various people-related issues. Members of Congress, for example, virtually always tout how much they "support the troops." This support frequently comes in the form of higher pay, pensions, health care programs, benefits for veterans and their survivors, housing, and day care centers—all of which the politicians happily advertise as evidence of profound support. Not only does such conventional "support for the troops" often ignore their real needs; it can act against their real needs.

For starters, it attracts to the armed forces people whose interests may revolve around material benefits, rather than any sense of service or sacrifice. Put simply, it puts emphasis in the wrong place: on the material, not on deeper characteristics. More importantly, emphasis on issues such as training for military personnel is often ignored by Congress as it shoves dollars at material benefits and at hardware procurement and research. In the case of the latter, the shoving often comes in the form of pushing "earmarks" ("pork") that Congress adds to defense budgets in ever-increasing amounts. Support for hardware procurement, even outside any member's political district, is also popular because major hardware items are often accepted as the measure of whether America is strong or weak or whether a politician is pro-defense, or not.

The focus on hardware often comes at the expense of other spending that is more important. Both Pentagon's budget requests and Congress' modifications to it frequently value "modernization" (hardware) above readiness issues, such as training, education, and selecting the best possible people for recruitment and promotion. Frequently, decisions are made inside the military services to reduce military personnel for the express purpose of making a few hundred million dollars more available for a hardware program that is out of control on the measures of cost, schedule, and performance. Not only is the force structure shrunk to support problematic weapons, an emphasis is put on hardware above people. As General Schwartzkopf and the Chief of Staff of the Israeli Air Force said, better trained, well-motivated people are more important than whether they operate the latest, high-cost weapon. The focus and money lavished on hardware by the politicians in Congress and the Pentagon would clearly be better spent on "people" issues.

Perhaps the ultimate example of perverse thinking on people versus hardware is the penchant in Congress to raid spending accounts for training and other forms of personal readiness to pay for the pork and nonpork hardware Congress adds to defense bills.

A genuine reform agenda for people issues would also emphasize what Major Donald Vandergriff urged in Appendix II: support for a more fundamental education for military leaders, not the kind provided in graduate schools where most "fast track" officers go. There is a much bigger pay-off for military effectiveness in thinking, adaptive leaders and soldiers than there is acquiring a business management degree. There is also more value in the kind of education Vandergriff advocates than there is in training in the form of learning "cook book" procedures for addressing preselected problems with a menu of preselected responses. It is an area devoid of congressional interest today, and the signs of real interest in the Pentagon are just barely beginning to emerge thanks to Major Vandergriff's efforts.

Another expression of "mental" approaches to military reform comes in the form of military tactics and doctrine. Some of the reformers most important contributions were not the aircraft they forced the reluctant Air Force and Navy to buy, but their thinking about "maneuver warfare" and what some started to call "decision cycles," the "Boyd cycle," or the "OODA-loop."

John Boyd, Bill Lind, and a few others had some impact on the Army and—much more so—on the Marines Corps with their thinking. After the abject failure of "attrition warfare thinking" in Vietnam (where combat was seen as an effort to simply locate and "service" targets through technology), the reformers talked about an entirely different concept. As discussed in the reformers Capitol Hill briefing (discussed in Chapter 2), "maneuver warfare" thinking grew out of some of the lessons that emerged at the end of World War I and the beginning of World War II. Far more than the simple repositioning of military forces to get at the less protected flank of the enemy, it was a different way of thinking about combat and the enemy. It sought not just to surprise the enemy or to attack where he was weak, but to get inside his mind, understand him, exploit the lessons, and pull him apart.

That was the basis of John Boyd's "OODA-loop." An insight he learned in air combat, the OODA-loop consisted of *observing* the enemy, *orienting* to the relevant issues at hand, *deciding* on an appropriate course of action, and *acting* in a manner to effectively execute the decision. The side that cycled through successive OODA-loops faster and better than the other would invariably emerge the winner. Much more than simply making decisions rapidly, it is a concept rich in implications for acting on the battlefield (and elsewhere). It is perhaps best described in print on pages 334 to 339 of Robert Coram's biography of John Boyd, *Boyd: The Fighter Pilot Who Changed the Art of War*. Understanding how to operate the OODA-loop is a gateway to military reform thinking.

Seeking far more than high-speed tanks and aircraft, the reformers sought high-speed minds; but not just quick acting minds and rapid decision making, but quick appreciation for what the realities were on the ground and in the enemy's head and then rapidly adapting to what would exploit the mental and physical situation at hand. The military unit—not just commander—that can do that quicker and better than the enemy will have a gigantic, even insurmountable, advantage on the battlefield.

This approach to the problem of winning on the battlefield—by collapsing the enemy mentally (and morally) as well as physically—is the essence of military reform. It is explained at length in many published works that can provide more detail and thoroughness than can be presented here. There are perhaps three best sources to direct the reader to achieve a summary understanding: perhaps the best is the above-mentioned biography of John Boyd by Robert Coram. Another is Bill Lind's *Maneuver Warfare Handbook*.[5] Finally, the reader can get a rapid introduction to these ideas here in Appendix IV, which is Chuck Spinney's summary biography of John Boyd. It is titled *Genghis John* and was published in the *Proceedings* of the U.S. Naval Institute Press, shortly after Boyd's death in 1997. Few who have written about Boyd understand him better than Spinney; his description of Boyd's thinking and work in *Genghis John* is short but perceptive.

The ultimate articulation of the mental dimension of defeating the enemy is what some describe as military doctrine. More than a recipe for how to move on the battlefield, it can, and should, be a mental orientation to how to think about problems and how to operate consistent with that thinking. In the beginning of the twenty-first century, the new problem is how to think about the kind of warfare being fought in Iraq and Afghanistan. Some perceptively point out the principles appropriate and effective for fighting conventional enemies can actually prove to be ineffective, even self-defeating, in the context of the new form of warfare, "4th Generation Warfare."

Orienting to the fighting in Iraq and Afghanistan, a seminar led by Bill Lind wrote what the Army and Marine Corps failed to produce in time: military doctrine for this new form of warfare. Lind's seminar's doctrine, *"FMFM 1-A: Fourth Generation War,"* appears in Appendix V. It is a prime example of the kind of adaptation the reformers typically advocate to a new development of realities on the ground, and it represents profound thinking on a problem that America's armed forces have very clearly not solved: how to win in Iraq and Afghanistan.

As important as they clearly are, these "mental" dimensions are not the most important.

The Moral Imperative

The demarcation between mental and moral issues is not always clear. For example, in the discussion above, the mental effort to write competent, relevant laws and regulations can quickly become moral issues when the time arrives to show the willpower to implement those regulations as the authors intended, rather than as others might prefer. A properly written law is meaningless if it is ignored or if its loopholes are the only part bureaucrats make use of. The matter rapidly becomes one of ethics and spine.

Moral issues should be viewed as much more powerful than mental, and they are certainly infinitely more decisive than the physical issues. It is not a new insight. In the early nineteenth century, Napoleon noted, "In war, the moral is to the physical as three is to one."[6] We see the maxim played out time after time on the battlefield as competently equipped, even trained, soldiers collapse before opponents because of a lesser will to fight, confusion, fear, and ultimately panic.

What then are the key moral issues? (Note that we are not referring just to morale.) What moral characteristics improve our chances for success on the battlefield, and in other human endeavors, and how can those elements be exploited to our advantage and to destroy the enemy?

Moral issues occur at several levels. They start within military units, such as squads, platoons, and companies of soldiers. There, research has identified the group's moral cohesion as key. "Unit cohesion" can be identified as those bonds of trust and respect between soldiers that help them endure the extraordinary stress of military combat: that form a bulwark against the impulses soldiers can feel in the midst of great chaos and danger to flee. They do not want to be seen by the other members of their unit as cowards or to let them down, and they believe they can count on their buddies to stand and fight. Time and again, literature from combat veterans and research on the matter points to the human bonds between the members of the military unit as absolutely critical: most soldiers do not fight for pay or simply because they are trained to do so. Also, they do not fight because of "god, mother, or country." Much modern research shows they fight because of the buddy next to him in the foxhole and his other buddies nearby.[7]

Specific reforms can make those intra-unit bonds grow and strengthen. Key among them is to retain individuals in a group. It may be simplistic logic, but it has escaped American military organizers for the last century. As pointed out by Vandergriff and others, throughout the twentieth century the American Army existed on industrial era principles that saw people as interchangeable cogs. It pulled apart units after their initial training, assigned people as individual "replaceable parts" into other units going to combat, and then plugged them into and out of other units throughout a soldier's career. Only recently has the Army began to revive a halting effort started in the late 1970s to retain soldiers in units and to attempt to nurture the bonds of unit cohesion that are key to optimum effectiveness on the battlefield.

More importantly, however, those human bonds of trust and empathy should exist not just on the horizontal plane among combatants in a military unit. They must extend vertically through a military organization and, more importantly, to their civilian overseers and, ultimately, to the society in general.

At the lower levels of the ascending scale, a unit that does not trust its immediate commander can fail at several levels: it can fail or refuse to understand his instructions, it can deem his instructions impossible to fulfill, or it can sabotage the implementation of the orders of a superior who is not trusted or is held in contempt. Conversely, a commander who does not know and trust his own units can fail both them and his superiors. If he fails to understand intimately the units below him, he will not know their strengths and weaknesses, what they can and cannot do, what they think they can and cannot do, and how to motivate them to do what they think is impossible.

Further, if a commander does not trust his subordinates, he may attempt to micromanage them in such a way that they cannot adapt to unfolding circumstances on the battlefield (of which the commander may or may not be aware). Telling soldiers not just what the commander wants them to do but how they are to do it will almost certainly reduce the unit's ability to adapt—to find their own creative ways to achieve the assigned goal given the immediate circumstances on the battlefield. Long and detailed, even written, orders can—but do not have to—be a sign of absent bonds of trust and understanding between a commander and the units under his command. A commander's moral attitude toward the units in his command can enhance their military effectiveness or depreciate, if not destroy, it.

An indicator of a commander's trust of the people in his command can be "mission orders" where the commander communicates goals (sometimes expressed as his "intent") without detailed or "cook book-style" orders about exactly how he wants the unit to achieve those goals. Put simply, "Take that hill," or better, "Destroy that enemy unit," rather than, "Approach that hill from such and such a location, at precisely such and such a time, using these weapons there, and those weapons here; and consuming no more than thus and such time and ammunition, and report back to me at every fifteen minute interval." The reader can easily imagine which commander a competent subordinate would rather work under. Under "mission orders," the commander will trust the unit to achieve the goal, if at all possible, in the manner they see fit but also in a manner consistent with the commander's overall guidance (for example, by avoiding civilian casualties to the fullest extent possible).

Military reform puts the highest priority on the bonds of trust and understanding running both vertically and horizontally in a military organization. Sometimes, others appreciate the importance, but in practice put other things first.

At the higher levels where the effects of the characteristics are more pervasive and thus more powerful, the same kind of bonds should run from military organizations to their civilian leaders in the Pentagon and to the White House. Suffice it to say that those bonds were well broken in 2006 when various Army generals called for the resignation or firing of the secretary of defense, Donald Rumsfeld.

(Those same generals were clearly at fault as much as Rumsfeld for their own failings in the war in Iraq. See Appendix I.) The bonds were not broken by just one
party but by both, but perhaps for different reasons: by careerism on the part of
the generals, arrogance on the part of Rumsfeld, and by an absence of trust by
both.

The same issues extend to the final civilian authority in the White House, especially on matters of strategy. When the president takes the nation into a conflict—
with or without Congress' and the nation's informed and willing consent—there is
an implicit understanding between the president and the military that he has not
asked the uniformed services to do anything that runs counter to the moral fiber
of the nation. Breaking that implicit trust (either consciously or unconsciously)
can lead to the collapse of support for the conflict both in the civilian population
and in the military ranks.

A majority of American civilians and a substantial part of the military felt that
to be the case in Vietnam, as evidenced by all the unrest about the war and the low
morale in the military, the high indiscipline, and numerous attempted murders
of officers (known as "fraggings"). The moral failures explain America's defeat in
Vietnam as much as anything else.

The American war in Iraq is no less controversial on the moral level and
demonstrates just as vividly the consequences of a breakdown of trust between
national political leadership, civilians controlling the Pentagon, the military, and
the nation. No event epitomizes that failure better than the Abu Ghraib prison
scandal: the torture and abuse of Iraqi civilian detainees in the American-run
prison in Iraq.

The president declared accused terrorists and alleged enemy combatants, such
as those held at the U.S. facility in Guantanamo, Cuba, to be beyond the purview
of the Geneva Convention for the treatment of prisoners of war. The secretary of
defense seconded the president's sentiments. Implicitly, the message ran down
the military hierarchy. When the ultimate consequences arrived in the form of
photographs of "unauthorized" abuse of detained Iraqis at Abu Ghraib, the finger
pointing started, most of it downhill. While the Army conducted several studies,
all of which placed the blame with subordinates, the secretary of defense and the
president expressed their shock and protested their own innocence.

One of the results of that scandal was the entrance of a moral wedge between
the prosecution of the war and the American public. That wedge ultimately consisted of much more than just the Abu Ghraib prison scandal; the failure of the
Bush administration at the moral and grand strategic level was massive and pervasive.

• The war was initiated through the conscious selection of a cause that was initially horrifying to the general American population but ultimately fraudulent (Iraq's weapons
  of mass destruction). The false pretext for the war (it is almost irrelevant whether the
  falsehoods were conscious lies or not) laid the seeds for discord and dissention among
  Americans and between us and our allies.

- The Bush administration went to extraordinary manipulations to extract the functional equivalent of a declaration of war from Congress in October 2002, immediately before congressional elections when the politicians on Capitol Hill were especially vulnerable to questions of patriotism. And yet, the president never sought to amend the original legislation—and thus the legal circumstances for continuing the war—when the real facts became known.
- The predictions for the cost of the war, both in terms of dollars and lives (both American and those of Iraqi civilians) were ludicrously optimistic. We drove a wedge not only between ourselves, but also between us and the Iraqis and the rest of the world. We did so when we should have been trying to make skeptics and outsiders empathetic to our success, not apathetic or even hostile.
- We failed to properly equip our own soldiers with needed equipment while Secretary of Defense Rumsfeld callously attempted to dismiss his own oversights with statements like "You go to war with the Army that you have." These and other self-launderings were not the kind of leadership that would seem appropriate for a civilian who sends military personnel into combat.
- The Bush administration and its supporters from both parties in Congress continuously tried to pillory any who warned of possible pitfalls and setbacks—that turned out to exist—and to label any criticism as defeatism, if not traitorous behavior. These actions again increased our internal divisions and provided an unseemly stage for outsiders to observe as they decided what was their own attitude toward America and its war.

The list can go on. In time, the wedge grew—without relent—to make the war a driving force in the defeat of the president's agenda and the Republican majority in the congressional elections of 2006. It was precisely the kind of breech between the national civilian leadership, the military, and the general American population that makes our side weaker, owing to entropy, dissention, and broken trust.

But that is, literally, just the half of it. Abu Ghraib and the other moral failings made the enemy stronger: not only were the Americans showing the world that their actions belied their rhetoric about democratic values for Iraqis, the prison and the other self-contradictions became a rallying cry for the enemy. In an age of modern communications, it was a more effective a rallying point than "Remember the Maine" or "Remember Pearl Harbor" ever were in earlier centuries.

These and similar problems started and enlarged the cracks in the moral bonds we should have been closing and strengthening among Americans and our allies. They created the moral isolation of the Bush presidency and the Rumsfeld Pentagon from the rest of the nation. They also tended to make external parties, whom we would want to make sympathetic to our success, neutral, if not hostile, and they tended to give the enemy a unifying theme, a reason to fight and to persist. While we fractured our own unity and will to fight and alienated uncommitted parties, we unified the enemy and strengthened his resolve.

In every respect, we did things exactly wrong. Ultimately, we created a situation where it became increasingly difficult, to the point of impossible, to end the conflict on terms favorable to ourselves. We also sowed the seeds for future conflict. Still worse, through our ineptitude to cope with the enemy on the political-military battlefield of fourth generation warfare, we showed the enemy how to defeat us.

The bankruptcy of America's enterprise in Iraq has been complete at the grand strategic level.

Activity on moral issues that weakens one side and bolsters up the other is what we want to do the enemy, not what we want to do to ourselves. It is not just bad strategy-making; it is, quite literally, aid and comfort to the enemy. It is the kind of moral leadership that loses wars.[8] It was grand strategic failure at the top, and that crippling failure was compounded by many others lower down in the system. The failures were thorough and complete on the level of conflict that decides wars.

At the highest and most powerful level, careful attention to—and behavior consistent with—a high moral plane is the essence of military reform. The responsibility to exercise it falls first on the civilian and military leadership at the top. If they fail at that level, the nation is doomed to failure.

In conclusion, many people have over time proposed a galaxy of ideas to "reform" America's armed forces, but as we have witnessed, those ideas can sometimes be more corrosive than constructive. The American military reformers who emerged in the 1970s made an extremely valuable contribution by providing an empirically tested framework for distinguishing real military reform from proposals that may sound good but in practice cannot or simply do not work as promised. That framework to assess future ideas may be one of the most valuable contributions from that unique group of individuals.

The future of American military reform, with or without the involvement of the individuals who have to date comprised the effort, is most uncertain. It is very unclear—at best—if the American national security and political communities have the insights to identify what is wrong in the current system and, more importantly, it is unclear if those communities have the collective character to undertake what is needed to effectively reform the existing system. In the past in other nations, it has required a humiliating defeat to provide the impetus for real reform. If America is lucky, the nation's national security community will undertake reform before any such unhappy event.

The path is available for those who care to take it.

Notes

1. Jeffery G. Barlow, editor, "Critical Issue: Reforming the Military," The Heritage Foundation, 1981, Washington, D.C.

2. See Pierre Sprey, "What Quality vs Quantity Issue?" at www.d-n-i.net Web site. (To be installed there.)

3. For a detailed description of just how difficult it can be in the Pentagon's bureaucracy to fully and realistically test hardware and honestly report the results, see James Burton's *The Pentagon Wars*, which is listed in the annotated bibliography of this book.

4. See Thomas Christie, "What Has 35 Years of Acquisition Reform Accomplished?" US Naval Institute *Proceedings*, February 2006.

5. See William S. Lind, *The Maneuver Warfare Handbook*, Westview Special Studies in Military Affairs, Boulder, Co. 1985.

6. This popular maxim can be found at http://www.napoleon-series.org/research/napoleon/c_genius.html.

7. For example, see Wm. Darryl Henderson, *Cohesion: The Human Element in Combat*, National Defense University Press, Washington D.C. 1985, and Martin van Creveld, *Fighting Power: German and U.S. Army Performance 1939–1945*, Greenwood Press, Westport, CT, 1974.

8. For a more thorough discussion of the role of moral issues in the formulation and conduct of strategy, see John Boyd's discourse on strategy, "The Strategic Game of ? and ?," at http://www.d-n-i.net/boyd/pdf/strategy.pdf.

Fire the Generals!*

Douglas Macgregor

American failures in Iraq are often laid at the feet of the White House and the civilian leadership of the Pentagon. The top military leadership deserves just as much of the blame.

When Gen. George Casey took over as commander of U.S. and coalition forces in Iraq during July 2004, he asked his staff in Baghdad to set up a meeting with the headquarters' counter-insurgency expert. His request was met with silence. Incredible as it may seem, after fighting what American military authorities had been calling an insurgency for over a year, the Army's headquarters in Baghdad had no experts on counter-insurgency operations.[1]

A year later, Casey returned to Washington and told members of the Senate that more American troops would hurt, not help, matters in Iraq. He insisted that the large American military presence in the country "feeds the notion of occupation" and actually extends "the amount of time that it will take for Iraqi security forces to become self-reliant."[2] Even in areas of the country where American forces were showered with flowers when they arrived in April 2003, they are now under attack.[3]

In war, military strategy is supposed to reduce the probability of armed conflict, to persuade those who might fight not to fight, and when necessary, to win at the least cost in lives and treasure in the shortest possible time. In Iraq, America's top generals achieved the opposite outcome. Meanwhile, many of today's top generals are repeating the Vietnam pattern of speaking critically of the Pentagon's leadership in private, while eagerly accepting public praise and promotion from the secretary of defense for deferring to him in everything.[4]

American soldiers, sailors, airmen and marines are rightly lauded by the American public for their courage and sacrifice in the fight for Iraq, but the high quality

---

*Reprinted with the permission of the Center for Defense Information.

of American soldiers and Marines at battalion level and below cannot compensate for inadequate senior leadership at the highest levels in war. Today, the senior leadership of the U.S. armed forces in general and, the U.S. Army in particular, is overly bureaucratic, risk averse, professionally inadequate and, hence, unsuited to the complex military tasks entrusted to them. The Bush administration has a preference for compliant, sycophantic officers who are fatally dependent on the goodwill of the secretary of defense and the president who promoted and appointed them.

It is bitter to contemplate, but Americans now confront issues of the utmost gravity:

- first, the lack of character and competence apparent in the most senior ranks;
- second, the willingness of the civilians in charge, from the commander in chief to the secretary of defense, to ignore this problem; and,
- third, the probability that future American military operations will fail if generalship of this quality persists.

The Roots of the Problem

Finding generals who are competent and ethical practitioners of war—officers who will communicate to their civilian superiors the truth of what is really happening and what actions and resources are required for success—has never been easy. In American history, armies and their generals have been treated as afterthoughts, producing a pattern of emergency improvisation in wartime to replace generals who could not shake the habits and mindset of an unprofessional garrison army culture.

President Abraham Lincoln struggled with such incompetents for the first two years of the Civil War until he found someone who won battles. The man was Ulysses S. Grant, an officer no one in the Army's command hierarchy wanted. Long before America entered World War II, Gen. George C. Marshall, an officer who had waited 36 years for promotion to flag rank, ended his first year in office as Army chief of staff in 1940 by retiring 54 generals. After the Japanese attacked Pearl Harbor, Marshall continued to replace hundreds of generals and colonels, elevating men like James Gavin, a captain in 1942, to brigadier general and division commander in 1944. When Gen. Matthew Ridgway assumed command of the Eighth Army in Korea, he was no less ruthless than Marshall had been with commanders in the field who did not measure up.

So, what has changed? Why, after three years of inconclusive action in Iraq, have none of America's top generals been fired?

One reason is the absence of capable enemies to fight.[5] Since 1990, America's enemies have had no navies, weak air forces, weak to non-existent air defenses, and incompetent armies that lacked both the will and the training to fight effectively. Our superb combat soldiers and Marines easily overpowered their enemies regardless of what decisions or actions the senior military leadership took. Emergency improvisation was not needed.

The inevitable consequence of this situation is that there is no political constituency for excellence in generalship; no politician who will galvanize public opinion and demand results from generals. Consequently, while Americans can force the removal of homeland security officials from office or specify with great precision the intellectual and professional attributes of a Supreme Court justice,[6] they don't make similar judgments about generals. They don't make judgments because, for the most part, they don't know what generals are supposed to do in war or peace.

In war, this condition is dangerous because the nation's three- and four-star generals are the key figures who interface between policy and action. They decisively shape and implement the military component of national strategy that is consistent with American policy goals, ensuring that results are attained within the framework of the mission, and taking into account intangibles such as the reputation of the American people. They determine the metrics that measure success or failure, and they create the command climate that motivates subordinate commanders to take prompt action to overcome any and all difficulties.

Two important corollaries must be mentioned. In war, for generals to succeed, they must be men of character and integrity, accepting risk and uncertainty as the unchanging features of war. They must also demonstrate a willingness to stand up and be counted, to put country before career and, if necessary to resign.[7] Generals also must be students of their profession and of their enemies. They must be able to put themselves in the position of their enemies, avoid rigid adherence to ideas and methods that are ineffective, and adopt what works while concentrating their minds on the essential tasks. These attributes have been largely absent in the U.S. senior ranks, both on the road to Baghdad and in the occupation of Iraq that followed.

The Failure of Military Leadership in Iraq

From the moment the idea of invading Iraq was suggested by the administration of President George W. Bush, in the aftermath of Sept. 11, the Army's three- and four-star generals were thoroughly convinced that U.S. ground forces would have to fight a long, bloody battle with Iraq's Republican Guard divisions for control of Baghdad, and they were unwilling to undertake such a war without a ground force on the scale of Desert Storm.[8]

Even after 3rd Infantry Division's armor crossed the Euphrates River on March 23, 2003, and moved 300 miles in 96 hours to a point just 50 miles south of Baghdad at the cost of only two American lives, the fear of fighting without a disproportionately massive ground force in place persisted.[9]

When the use of attack helicopters in a pointless deep attack failed—an operation characterized by extraordinary general officer incompetence that included a failure to integrate the mission with the U.S. Air Force and the Army's rocket artillery[10] —Lt. Gen. William Wallace, commander of the U.S. Army's V Corps, and Maj. Gen. David H. Petraeus, commander of the 101st Airborne Division, were quick to conclude that "the war was in dismal shape."[11] In what was just the first in a series of misjudgments of the true situation on the ground in Iraq, preconceptions of warfare rooted in the sterile field exercises of the Cold War led Gen. "Tommy" Franks, Gen. David McKiernan, Third Army Commander, and Wallace to the wrong conclusions. These generals persuaded Secretary of Defense Donald Rumsfeld and Bush to halt all ground offensive operations until after the Air Force bombed Iraq's meager and ineffectual forces.

Had Saddam Hussein and his generals known of the Army generals' meeting near Najaf, and the deliberations in Washington, D.C., that followed, they would have doubled over in laughter. Iraq's defense was really a giant confidence game conducted by the country's political and military charlatans. Maj. Gen. Jim Mattis, commander of the Marine division who was stationed forward with his lead combat element, saw through the veil. He later said, "I didn't want the pause. Nothing was holding us up."[12]

Nevertheless, the attack on Baghdad was put on hold. Without sustaining any significant casualties, the senior Army generals remote from the fighting clung to the illusion that Iraq's armed might was too great to challenge without extensive bombing. In reality, the only obstacle to victory lay not with Iraqi resistance, which was always negligible, but in the minds of the Army's commanding generals. Grudgingly, Bush and Rumsfeld acquiesced and approved the halt. The delay lasted from March 26 until April 1, when, reportedly, only the threat of being removed compelled McKiernan to resume the attack.

Baghdad eventually fell to a single armored brigade of the 3rd Infantry Division in an action known as the "Thunder Run." However, the criticality of speed in the attack, of dramatically out-pacing the enemy's decisions and actions, had been lost. Roaring into Baghdad with tank guns blazing without the unnecessary delay could have achieved precisely what Rumsfeld and the president wanted, such as the early capture of Saddam Hussein who was in the city at that time. However, the wrong generals with the wrong thinking at the top made this outcome impossible.[13]

When Baghdad fell, Rumsfeld held a video-teleconference with Franks, asking him how soon the Army could get a tank brigade to Tikrit. Franks consulted with McKiernan, and answered "10 days." The Army generals were opposed to any task that did not involve days of planning and a preponderance of force disproportionate to mission requirements. Rumsfeld was furious, but rather than waste time arguing with the Army's senior leaders, Rumsfeld told Franks to ask the Marines. Less than 12 hours later, Marine Task Force Tripoli,[14] under the command of Brig. Gen. John Kelly, was on its way to Tikrit.

By failing to press on and accept minimal risk to their flanks and rear, the top generals in Washington and on the ground in Iraq missed the opportunity to enter the capital, and force the surrender of the Ba'athist leadership. Saddam Hussein and his entourage escaped and the first of many opportunities to psychologically dominate the enemy was thrown away. Gen. George C. Patton would have been deeply depressed by the whole affair. Yet no one at the top of the Bush administration set out to remove these officers and replace them with more aggressive, confident commanders.

There were few political incentives for action by the administration, given the realities on the ground in Iraq. The predictions by Army and Marine four-star generals' (active and retired) of a three-month campaign against a determined Iraqi enemy and the inflated numbers of troops they insisted were required to win were never right, and the Bush administration knew it.[15] If what the Army generals in command did or did not do was irrelevant to the ultimate outcome, why make an issue out of the Army generals' demands for a few days' halt just 50 miles from Baghdad? Why bother replacing three- and four-star generals who refuse to attack, when Iraq's military position was always hopeless whether the fight against Iraq's Ba'athist Fedayeen in pick-up trucks lasted five days or 10?

Glowing reports from the journalists embedded with the superb soldiers and Marines who actually did the fighting persuaded the American public that the generals in charge had just executed an immensely successful lightning offensive to Baghdad. Only Mattis offered a truly honest appraisal of the enemy. He said, "The [Iraqi] generals were dumber than you-know-what, they were real dumb."[16]

Their Weakness Conceals Our Own

The details of the campaign that removed Saddam Hussein's regime from power are beyond the scope of this essay, but the victory was due principally to the extraordinary weakness of the Iraqi enemy. That weakness concealed serious flaws in the readiness, deployment and composition of the American ground force, flaws that would come to light after the fall of Baghdad.

The offensive's greatest weakness was in the organization and composition of the attacking American ground force. In the Middle East, the offensive capacity of American armor is America's trump card in land warfare, but armor constituted a mere fraction of the force that attacked to Baghdad and, in time, its effect was dissipated by dispersing much of it to light infantry formations that sustained unnecessary casualties without it.

In addition, American command and control (C2) structures were unchanged from 1991. Like the headquarters that fought the first Gulf War, the C2 headquarters in Operation Iraqi Freedom were an improvised collection of single-service headquarters, each fighting its own war according to its own thinking–Army, Marine or Air Force. In practice, operations and logistics that should have been joint were ad hoc and not designed for war, certainly not the long war that developed.

In maneuver warfare, supply is a potential showstopper. As the Army discovered during the first Gulf War, fuel is by far the most important logistical requirement. Thanks to gas-guzzling tank engines that were never modified or changed in the 12 years that separated Desert Storm from Iraqi Freedom, it took about 120 sorties of fuel tankers every 24 hours to keep the armor in the 3rd Infantry Division moving. In addition, the deployment of other Army ground forces was confused and slow. Although the attack did not start until the United States was ready, the 101st Airmobile Division was still off-loading at Kuwait ports on March

23, 2003, when the offensive began. Spare parts were in short supply. Body armor was inadequate.

Further, despite 12 years of experience in the Persian Gulf, the generals had done nothing to prepare Army forces to cope with the complexity of operating in a Muslim Arab country.[17] The Army's chiefs of staff between 1991 and 2003 lost sight of their interwar duty: preparing for the next conflict and thinking about how it ought to be fought differently from the last war.[18]

Fortunately, the actual fighting potential of the Iraqi Army was nil.

How to Create an Insurgency in 30 Days

As American generals triumphantly occupied Saddam's palaces, so reviled by many Iraqis, chaos and criminality ruled Iraq for 30 days. No fresh American troops arrived, trained and organized to conduct post-conflict stability operations. Thousands of Iraqi Army soldiers and officers who co-operated with American forces by choosing not to fight stood by, waiting for direction from the U.S. military leadership to assist in the restoration of order.

The same generals who had attacked Baghdad so reluctantly again declined to act.[19] What happened next in Baghdad was an eerie replay of Operation Just Cause, the U.S. Army's invasion of Panama in 1989. Then, the Army generals focused on capturing Panamanian dictator, Manuel Noriega, but they neglected the importance of minimizing Panamanian Defense Force (PDF) casualties. Instead, the Army generals destroyed the PDF and created the conditions for chaos and criminality when the fighting ended, to the point where some Panamanians contend that Panama has still not fully recovered from the consequences.

By the time U.S. Ambassador Paul Bremer arrived in Baghdad in May 2003 to announce the disbanding of Iraq's governmental structures and its military and police forces, Iraq was in ruins. Directing the Army and Marine Corps to occupy and effectively govern Iraq simply completed the process of the country's total destruction.[20] Even though McKiernan had previously met privately with Iraqi generals who handed him lists of Iraqi Army officers who could be used to command a rapidly reformed Iraqi army, McKiernan did not protest the Iraqi military's disbanding. The hundreds of thousands of disgruntled former Iraqi soldiers who were thus set loose were to prove a valuable source of recruits for the rebellion then in its infancy.[21]

American soldiers and Marines soon discovered that Iraq's population did not wish to be governed by foreigners, especially Christian Americans and Europeans.[22] Violence escalated quickly in response to U.S. arrests of Muslim men on the street. They were often apprehended in front of their families, dragged away in handcuffs with bags over their heads for interrogation and incarceration.[23] Even when innocent Muslim men were released, they were further humiliated by returning under guard in broad daylight to where they had been captured—cuffed and hooded.[24] Predictably, a climate of hatred, suspicion and resentment began to emerge.

The growing violence signaled to journalists the emergence of fundamentally new conditions in central Iraq. During a video-teleconference Maj. Gen. Raymond Odierno, commander of the 4th Infantry Division (mechanized), was asked, "Aren't we just basically seeing an increasing amount of guerrilla warfare here? And to follow up . . . aren't soldiers really in greater peril now, because you basically have to go root these folks out, as opposed to during the combat phase when you used a lot of heavy armor and airpower to knock off the organized groups?"[25] Odierno's response is instructive because it reveals an unwillingness to see any evidence for the emergence of a new conflict:

> . . . This is not guerrilla warfare; it is not close to guerrilla warfare because it's not coordinated, it's not organized, and it's not led. The soldiers that are conducting these operations don't even have the willpower. We find that a majority of the time they'll fire a shot, and they'll drop the weapon and they'll give up right away. They do not have the will. And in most cases, I'm not sure they really believe in what they're doing. And so, when I talk about organized guerrilla warfare, it's a very complex organization that plans very complex guerrilla operations. That is nowhere close to what we're seeing here in my AO (area of operations).[26]

The deteriorating conditions in Iraq explain why Gen. John Abizaid's appointment in July 2003 to replace Franks was greeted with real hope. Abizaid, an American of Lebanese ancestry who is fluent in Arabic, was popular with the Army's active and retired four-star generals. To the politicians, he seemed like the politically correct choice to pursue the Bush administration's objectives in Iraq at that point in time: public security, electrical power, and jobs for millions of young men without work.

However, other than publicly confirming in July 2003 that U.S. forces did in fact face a "classic guerilla-type campaign," he did not alter the deployment of U.S. forces or change military policies or tactics. He presided at meetings and exhorted everyone to turn as much responsibility as they could over to the Iraqis (despite the fact that Iraq's military, police, and administrative bodies had been disbanded), but he did not interfere with the conduct of operations on the ground in Iraq. His visits with Army division commanders and their staffs produced no new directions in tactics or behavior.[27]

Was there anything Abizaid could have done to change the course of events in Iraq? He could have insisted that the American military administration vacate Saddam Hussein's former palaces and make themselves less visible to an Arab population already deeply humiliated by the foreign military occupation. He could have withdrawn U.S. ground forces from vast areas of Iraq where there was no insurgency and the U.S. military presence was not needed. These forces could have been redeployed to Sunni Arab-dominated areas where the violence was increasing. There the troops could have isolated and secured the population from infiltration and intimidation by the insurgents.

Simultaneously, Abizaid could have systematically exploited the obvious fault lines within the growing insurgency, the lines between rival Sunni tribal leaders, "foreign fighters," and Ba'athist "diehards." He could also have made the case to the Arabs of Iraq and the rest of the Arab world that America's presence in Iraq was not imperial, but *temporary*—pointing out that as soon as Iraq's military and administrative structures were restored, American military forces would leave the country. Knowing that America intended to leave Iraq would have disarmed many Sunni Arabs who would otherwise fight to drive out American ground forces. Instead, Abizaid supervised the construction of a series of large bases indicating an American intention to stay indefinitely.

Four decades ago in Algeria, where the French refused to depart Algeria under any conditions, the Arab revolt against French rule gained popular support.[28] Despite the commitment of 400,000 French troops to suppress the revolt inside an Arab and Berber population of 10 million people, a population larger than Iraq's Sunni Muslim community, French forces could never do more than suppress the rebellion temporarily. Fighting broke out again like an ulcer the moment French troops left an area they had fought to secure.[29] In the end, the French abandoned Algeria. Surely, Abizaid was aware of this fact.

Abizaid could have intervened with his division commanders to halt the inhumane treatment of the Sunni Arab population and put an end to the counterproductive incarceration of thousands of military-aged males. Perhaps most important, knowing that a popular rebellion in the form of an insurgency can only be successfully suppressed by indigenous armed forces, Abizaid could have insisted that the Bush administration fund a program to shift the American military role from direct combat to training and material support for indigenous Iraqi forces.[30] Early in the life of the occupation, the Bush administration was prepared to spend whatever it took to succeed in Iraq. If strongly recommended by Abizaid, there is little doubt that funding for this purpose would have been forthcoming. Getting Iraq's former soldiers back in uniform as quickly as possible would have starved the insurgency of the manpower it needed to flourish.

But little of substance changed and the Army's occupying forces settled into a routine of checkpoints, patrols, and raids designed to flush out the enemy with the means at hand. As in Vietnam, those means were primarily firepower. Simultaneously, the pursuit of Saddam and his lieutenants—particularly in the areas under the control of Odierno, and Maj. Gen. Charles H. Swannack, Jr., commander of the 82nd Airborne Division—continued, on the assumption that Saddam somehow represented the center of gravity in what was now a rapidly growing insurgency. Because of their ruthlessness, these operations backfired, fueling the fires of rebellion inside Iraq's Sunni Arab community.[31]

In Abu Sifa, one sun-baked village north of Baghdad, the practice of arbitrarily imprisoning males cleared entire farming communities of fathers, sons, brothers, and cousins.[32] Barbara K. Bodine, a State Department official who served in Iraq for 12 months during 2003 and 2004, summed up the consequences of the clumsy, brutal occupation saying: "We underestimate our daily humiliation of

Iraqis ... We don't understand when someone kills a brother, it calls for revenge killing."[33]

The excessive use of force and the policy of treating any Arab suspected of opposing the U.S. military occupation as a "terrorist" had another unintended effect. Thousands of recruits and sympathizers joined the rebellion from inside and outside the country. Reacting to the discovery of foreign jihadists inside Iraq and compounding the misapprehension of the problem, military spokesmen in Baghdad and Washington argued that unrest in Iraq was now largely a function of external interference from Syria and Iran. This was never the case. It was always the intrusive U.S. military occupation that was the fundamental problem, but it was easier for the generals inside the Green Zone to blame foreign fighters for Iraq's turmoil instead of changing course and developing a new counterinsurgency strategy.[34]

The capture of Saddam Hussein in December 2003 gave the generals in CENTCOM an opportunity to trumpet victory. They did not mention that telephone service, and the availability of electricity and of cooking and heating fuels, were no better than they were before the occupation began. Criminality was on the rise and unemployment remained around 50 percent.[35] Something was terribly wrong.

Iraq Explodes

In light of the widespread abuse meted out to Arab citizens of Iraq, including the hideous practices at the Abu Ghraib prison, for which no American officer has yet to be called to account, it was no surprise when al-Qaida's supporters, along with thousands of Iranian agents, streamed into Iraq to exploit the rapidly growing Arab hatred of American troops. Thanks to the new infusion of knowledge and expertise into the insurgent forces, Army and Marine Corps' Humvees, thin-skinned vehicles used for patrols along predictable routes, became easy targets for mines, roadside improvised explosive devices (IEDs), automatic weapons fire, and rocket propelled grenades.[36]

Despite the rising numbers of attacks on American soldiers and Marines in Humvees, Abizaid and Army Chief of Staff Gen. Peter Schoomaker let the numbers of armored fighting vehicles and tanks in Iraq decline.[37] In fact, Schoomaker ordered the 1st Cavalry Division and the 3rd Armored Cavalry Regiment, both preparing to deploy to Iraq in the first months of 2004, to bring only one in six of their Abrams tanks and Bradley fighting vehicles. In light of American losses, senior Israeli defense officers advised using heavily armored vehicles and more tanks,[38] but the top U.S. generals persisted in arguing for presence patrols in wheeled vehicles.

The Army's general officers did not routinely accompany platoon and squad leaders on patrol to understand the environment and what was needed to survive in it, creating an unhealthy divide between senior leadership and the soldiers on the ground. Had the generals done so, they would have known what a sergeant on patrol in Ramadi meant when he told a journalist, "You can have my job. It's easy. You just drive around all day and wait for someone to bomb you. Thing is, you have to hate Arabs."[39]

As it became more and more obvious that Saddam's capture in November 2003 was irrelevant to the course of the on-going rebellion against the American military occupation, Lt. Gen. Ricardo Sanchez, Wallace's successor at V Corps headquarters in Baghdad, tried to get his arms around the problem. But, like so many other officers and civilians inside Iraq's Green Zone, he was living in an unreal world. Sanchez, an officer whose thinking was rooted in sterile exercises and simulations of conventional Cold War conflict, could not grasp the complexities of Iraq's condition. In August 2004, more than 16 months after he assumed command, he remained wedded to a campaign plan for military operations that, according to officers in Sanchez's headquarters, "was totally nondescript. It had no concrete objectives."[40]

In April 2004 Iraq exploded in violent resistance. Things came to a head in Fallujah, a city of 300,000 not far from Baghdad that achieved rock star status in the Arab world for supporting relentless attacks on occupying American forces. Many American soldiers and Marines thought that Fallujah would become an object lesson for those in Iraq who directly challenged American military authority— a tailor-made opportunity to dominate the enemy psychologically. It also looked like a great opportunity for the generals in Baghdad, using heavy armor, which has proved decisively effective in urban warfare, to isolate, surround, and crush masses of enemy fighters, foreign and Iraqi, inside the city. But, it was not to be.

In a teleconference with Bush and Rumsfeld, Abizaid advised against an all-out assault on Fallujah, making the case that such an attack would jeopardize political stability throughout the country. Abizaid argued that it was not the destruction of the enemy in Fallujah and the indirect effort to educate others resisting the coalition that mattered. Rather it was to seize control of the city of Fallujah through other, less destructive means to show restraint by limiting collateral damage— and American casualties. Abizaid was unable to recognize when force can be used to psychologically dominate the enemy and when it needlessly empowers enemy resistance.

When Sanchez informed Mattis of the teleconference and the decision not to go into Fallujah, Mattis reacted by quoting Napoleon Bonaparte, "First we're ordered in, and now, we're ordered out. *If you're going to take Vienna, then, by God, sir, take it.*"[41] But Fallujah was not taken. Instead, former Republican Guard officers were sent in to organize a local force that never lived up to its obligations while fighting continued in other cities throughout the spring and early summer, and Marines and soldiers continued to die in and around Fallujah.

When Fallujah was finally seized, in November 2004, the operation was the ultimate expression of a reactive strategy. The town was never completely sealed off and, as in so many previous operations, most of the enemy were already gone when the generals' set-piece battle plan was set in motion. The taking of Fallujah after Bush's reelection in November 2004 was slow, deliberate, even incidental, almost unwanted, and only to be conducted with the minimum amount of force necessary to defeat the resistance that was standing between U.S. forces and control of the city.

Again, the widespread use of light infantry instead of heavy armor demonstrated that once the infantry on foot becomes involved in a symmetrical fight pitting AK 47 and rocket-propelled grenades against M16s, our soldiers and Marines take serious losses. These losses inevitably prompt the extensive use of destructive air and artillery strikes because light infantry lacks the protection, firepower and mobility to advance in the face of enemy fire without serious injury. As a result, Fallujah was destroyed. Ironically, the failure to use the right kind of force at the start—heavy armor—resulted in more destruction, and further alienation of Iraqis, than should have been necessary.

We've Destroyed the Insurgency . . . . Again!

After Fallujah's destruction, the generals in Baghdad claimed the back of the "insurgency" was "broken," but resistance to the American military occupation actually grew stronger, not weaker. Iraq's Arab insurgents or rebels learned from the first generation of foreign jihadists and domestic insurgents destroyed in the war and became far more sophisticated in terms of developing bombs, booby traps, IEDs and ambushes. The Sunni fighters and the Shi'ite militias both rearmed and reorganized, and due to the deepening hostility of all Muslims they had an inexhaustible supply of recruits.

The explanation most apparent to many observers in the military services for the many false claims of victory over the "insurgency" is that the top generals in Washington and CENTCOM, like their Vietnam era predecessors, were offering themselves up as media props for their misguided civilian masters in Washington. No general wants to be the first to raise his head out of the deepening trench of difficulties into which the military and the administration may be digging itself, and cry foul, especially when continuing to dig is rewarded with promotion. Under the Bush administration, it has always been easier for generals to move up than it is for them to speak up.

Lloyd George, Britain's World War I prime minister, observed that his commanding generals' official accounts of events at the front were anything, but accurate.

> The reports passed on to ministers were, as we all realized much later, grossly misleading. Victories were much overstated. Virtual defeats were represented as victories, however, limited their scope. Our casualties were understated. Enemy losses became pyramidal. That was the way the military authorities presented the situation to ministers—that was their active propaganda in the press. All disconcerting and discouraging facts were suppressed in the reports

received from the front by the War Cabinet—every bright feather of success
was waved and flourished in our faces.

In the case of Lloyd George, he did notice and he did complain, rather than lead
the deception.

Elections in Iraq eventually provided a diversion of sorts, prompting the Bush
administration to argue that as democracy took hold in Iraq, the insurgency would
weaken because al-Qaida and the opponents of the country's government had
nothing to offer Iraqis or the people of the Middle East. The Bush administration's
message lost steam as it became clear that tribalism, sectarianism and corruption
were the real determining factors in the outcomes of Iraq's elections. As the sectarian violence of February 2006 showed with a vengeance, Iraq is fragmenting
into three, distinct states; a fact that journalists visiting Kurdistan or Basrah could
easily recognize.[42]

To Casey and his commanders in the fall of 2005, it was obvious that American
interests in Iraq could not easily recover from the serious mistakes of the first
18 months or the unchanging climate of mutual hatred between Americans and
Arabs. But American casualties had to be reduced or political support at home
for the continued occupation would fail. The decision to keep the majority of
American ground forces inside the large fortified bases established during the
last three years of the occupation became critical. But, in the space between the
bases, conditions were beyond the control of U.S. forces. And the effort to train
indigenous Iraqi police and military forces, which started in earnest much too late,
proceeded far too slowly. The circle was now complete.[43] The American occupier
always had other interests and concerns, both domestic and foreign, while the
Arab insurgents had only one focus: drive the U.S. forces out and resist Shi'ite
domination.[44]

Nearly three years into the fight for Iraq, during the fall of 2005, Abizaid's
advice to Congress to "stay the course" began to fall flat. His mantra that, "Since
Desert Storm in 1991, U.S. forces have not lost any combat engagement in the
region at the platoon-level or above,"[45] was not convincing. It is a fact that American soldiers and Marines inflicted many more casualties on the Arab insurgents,
but it is the insurgents who control events by virtue of the fact that they initiated
most of the contacts, and their attacks have not diminished; they have expanded.

Like Lyndon Johnson's generals during the Vietnam era, Bush's generals are
politically skilled, energetic officers whose briefings can be impressive, but their
leadership in war arouses no faith. In modern conflict, trends outweigh episodes
or individual battles in their importance, and the trends are bad.[46] By the time
Gen. George Casey arrived in Baghdad in November 2004 the Army generals'
fight was not simply with a resilient opponent in central Iraq. Casey and his generals were also fighting to prop up not only a failed strategy but also a blinkered
civilian leadership in Washington. It remains a sad commentary on the generals
that they have shown so little spine in the face of a disastrous occupation and an
incompetently run war.

Imposing Accountability

Long periods of peace during the Cold War cultivated a bureaucratic mindset inside the Department of Defense, a mentality that is at odds with winning wars that require creative thinking and aggressive action. The resulting tendency is to promote those officers to high rank with whom the four-star generals at the top are comfortable, officers much like the four-stars themselves. These rising officers exhibit good bureaucratic skills with an over-riding instinct for personal self-promotion and they reap the rewards for "going along."[47] Such officers are only as good as the tactical doctrine they know, because they have learned not to ask what else might work. They are obviously not good enough.

Americans should reflect on the fact that U.S. military performance for over half a century has not been the mythic success that the generals encourage the public to believe. America's war on the Korean Peninsula ended in a stalemate. America lost in Vietnam. Grenada was an operational embarrassment in a fight with almost no enemy at all. Panama can be called a success despite its flaws, but it could not have been a failure given the weakness of the Panamanian Defense Force. Military incompetence enabled terrorists to drive U.S. troops out of both Lebanon and Somalia. The severely deteriorated situations in Haiti, Bosnia and Kosovo are scarcely tributes to the generals' skills in peace support operations. The 1991 Gulf War was a grossly exaggerated victory, characterized by very little direct fire ground combat, against a weak and demoralized enemy. America's intervention in Afghanistan and its 2003 invasion of Iraq were both carried out against far weaker enemies to the point where there was almost no serious opposition by conventional forces.

What is needed is a selection system for promotion to flag ranks that tests competence in training and deployments and that holds officers accountable for their performance in military educational institutions and certainly on the battlefield.

Leo Strauss, a leading American political philosopher and early advocate for neo-conservative thinking confronted similar challenges at the University of Chicago from professors who contended that "all points of view are equal . . . and that anyone who argues for the superiority of a distinctive moral insight, way of life, or human type is somehow elitist or antidemocratic and hence immoral."[48] The university professors who opposed Strauss, like the generals, were comfortable with the ambiguity of cronyism and the opportunity to advance individuals on the basis of loyalty alone, not performance. In the profession of arms, a profession that involves life and death decisions, competence, not cronyism, must be king.

In retrospect, appointing Mattis to assume command of the ground force after the fall of Baghdad would have helped immeasurably. He was not only aggressive in combat, but he had also taken the trouble to study the British and French experience with counter-insurgency and stability operations. Immediately advancing Mattis to three stars, something Marshall and Patton would surely have done, would have sent a powerful signal that professional competence and character under fire trump all other considerations in wartime. Unfortunately, the civilians in charge bowed to service parochialism and appointed an Army general, because Army troops constituted the majority of the ground force and because the civilians were unfamiliar with how ground forces should fight and how generals should command them.

Today, Winston Churchill is remembered for readiness in wartime to reverse course, to replace ineffective military commanders, to change tactics, and adopt new, more promising strategies. He believed that results, not sentiment, counted most in war.

Frustrated with the miserable performance of British generals in the opening battles of World War II, Churchill told Sir John Dill, chief of the Imperial General Staff, "We cannot afford to confine Army appointments to persons who have excited no hostile comment in their careers ... This is a time to try men of force and vision and not to be exclusively confined to those who are judged thoroughly safe by conventional standards."[49]

Today, there is no one holding elected or appointed office on the American political scene like Churchill and no political "constituency" for excellence in generalship. There needs to be—and it should not be a party matter—because the consequences of mediocre generalship are serious.

Notes

1. George Packer, *The Assassin's Gate: America in Iraq*, New York, NY: Farrar, Strauss and Giroux, 2005, page 446.

2. Greg Jaffe and Yochi J. Dreazen, "As Bush Pledges To Stay In Iraq, Military Talks Up Smaller Force: Some Top Brass Say Troops May Be Fueling Insurgency; Two Political Tests Ahead," *Wall Street Journal*, Oct. 5, 2005, page 1.

3. Ellen Knickermeyer, "Baghdad Neighborhood's Hopes Dimmed by the Trials of War," *Washingtonpost.com*, 27 September, 2005. The new ABC-Time Oxford Research International poll conducted in Iraq during December 2005 states: "There's other evidence of the United States' increasing unpopularity: Two-thirds now oppose the presence of U.S. and Coalition forces in Iraq, 14 points higher than in February 2004. Nearly six in 10 disapprove of how the United States has operated in Iraq since the war, and most of them disapprove strongly. And nearly half of Iraqis would like to see U.S. forces leave soon." See Anthony Cordesman's "The True Meaning of the Iraqi Election: A 'Trigger,' Not a 'Turning Point,'" Report for Center for Strategic and International Studies, Washington, D.C., Dec. 14, 2005, page 5.

4. Seymour M. Hersh, "Up in the Air. Where is the Iraq war headed next?" *New Yorker*, issue of Dec. 5, 2005. Hersh claims that the generals are, "... deeply frustrated, but they say nothing in public, because they don't want to jeopardize their careers. The Administration has 'so terrified the generals that they know they won't go public.'"

5. Michael Howard, *The Franco-Prussian War*, London, UK: Methuen, 1981, pages 15-19. The French Army from 1830 to 1870 was an army with a reputation for excellence against enemies far weaker than itself. But victory over Arabs, Berbers, Russians and Mexicans, enemies whose administration, training and small unit leadership was demonstrably worse than the French Army's, provided all the justification that was needed to halt reform and let the generals preserve a system that for all its faults still worked well enough. When war came with Prussia, however, the same generals exalted in the French press for their brilliant leadership in previous campaigns, shocked the French nation by surrendering their forces to the competent and effective Prussians in the space of only a few months. The French generals were quite capable of defeating weak enemies, but they were incapable of defeating a competent adversary.

6. George F. Will, *Restoration: Congress, Term Limits and the Recovery of Deliberative Democracy*, New York, NY: The Free Press, 1992, page 108.

7. T. Harry Williams, *McClellan, Sherman and Grant*, Chicago, Illinois: Ivan R. Dee, publisher, 1991, (first published in 1962), page 42.

8. Mackubin Thomas Owens, "With Eyes Wide Open: A Strategy for War with Iraq," *National Review Online*, Aug. 14, 2002. The demand for perfect information is reinforced by the mistaken notion that "knowledge is a weapon" and the fanatical assertions about the feasibility and necessity of "information dominance" through "net-centric operations." Knowledge is not a weapon. Weapons are weapons. Knowledge is what allows the soldier to aim the weapons he has at the right targets. Both are necessary, as are armor, firepower and mobility to survive and respond to the unexpected, which is what any enemy wants to achieve – especially if he has inferior forces.

9. Elaine M. Grossman, "Inside the Command Center: Decision to hasten ground attack into Iraq presented new risks," *Inside Defense*, March 18, 2004, page 1.

10. Rick Atkinson, Peter Baker and Thomas E. Ricks, "Confused Start, Decisive End; Invasion Shaped by Miscues, Bold Risks and Unexpected Successes," *Washington Post*, April 13, 2003, page A01. U.S. intelligence eavesdroppers reportedly detected 50 cell phone calls in the target area as the Apaches approached, a crude but apparently efficient Iraqi early-warning system. A thrown master switch in one town shut off all the lights, a signal for a barrage of fire that threw up a wall of lead.

11. Rick Atkinson, Peter Baker and Thomas E. Ricks, "Confused Start, Decisive End; Invasion Shaped by Miscues, Bold Risks and Unexpected Successes," *Washington Post*, April 13, 2003, page A01.

12. Elaine Grossman, "Marine general: Iraq war pause could not have come at worse time: Mattis believed Marines vulnerable to attack," *Inside the Pentagon*, Oct. 2, 2003, page 1.

13. Megan Scully, "Analysts: Army Would Play Pivotal Role In Conflict With Iraq," *Inside the Army*, Aug. 19, 2002.

14. 3 Light Armor Battalions, 1 Infantry Company, 1 Artillery Battery and supporting aircraft.

15. General Tommy Franks with Malcolm McConnell, *American Soldier,* New York: Harper Collins, 2004, page 370. In the book McConnell wrote for Franks, he cites Franks as anticipating "up to 90 days of decisive combat operations."

16. Elaine Grossman, "Marine general: Iraq war pause 'could not have come at worse time': Mattis believed Marines vulnerable to attack," *Inside the Pentagon*, Oct. 2, 2003, page 1.

17. See Jason Vest's article, "How the Pentagon sent the army to Iraq without a counterinsurgency doctrine," *Bulletin of the Atomic Scientists*, July/August 2005.

18. Strongly recommend that the reader consult *Operation Iraqi Freedom: Third Infantry Division (mechanized) After Action Report*, Final Draft, May 12, 2003. Centralized control over supply at division and higher levels left the combat units with too little of what they needed. Trucks had largely been eliminated from much of the structure – and logistics C2 was not touched at all. All of this was sold through National Training Center experience (where an army of contractors made it work) and business management techniques that in no way considered a complex, noncontiguous battlefield and corps- and army-size operational battlespace – much less a thinking and lethal enemy. In other words, logistics transformation very consciously followed a business model rather than a combat model. Sad to say you could get promoted by being "efficient" and saving money and be long retired before a war got people killed.

19. Jon Lee Anderson, *The Fall of Baghdad*, New York, NY: Penguin Press, 2004, page 250.

20. Mark Fineman, Warren Vieth and Robin Wright, "Dissolving Iraqi Army Was Costly Choice. The masses of enlisted men could have been used for reconstruction and security. Now the U.S. faces terrorism and building a new force." *New York Times*, Aug. 24, 2003, page 5.

21. Sources wish to remain anonymous.

22. Rashid Khalidi, *Resurrectin Empire: Western Footprints and America's Perilous Path in the Middle East*, Boston, Mass.: Beacon Press, 2004, page 55.

23. Stryker McGuire and Rod Nordland, "The Decent Thing. America's tough tactics have miffed the British, who have a softer post-conflict style," *Newsweek*, May 24, 2004.

24. Scott Wilson, "U.S. Troops Kill 2 Iraqis After Ambush. Baath Loyalists Hinder Efforts In Fallujah." *Washington Post*, May 23, 2003, page 13.

25. *Official Transcript*, Department of Defense Office of Public Affairs, June 18, 2003.

26. *Official Transcript*, Department of Defense Office of Public Affairs, June 18, 2003.

27. Bing West, *No True Glory: A Frontline Account of the Battle for Fallujah*, New York, NY: Bantam Books, 2005, page 24.

28. Bard E. O'Neill, *Insurgency and Terrorism: Inside Modern Revolutionary Warfare*, Washington, D.C.: Brassey's (US), Inc. 1990, pages 80–81.

29. Andrew Scott with Donald Clark, R. Bruce Ehrman, John W. Salmon, Jr., Harold Shill and Frank Trapnell, *Insurgency*, Chapel Hill, NC: The University of North Carolina Press, 1970, page 116.

30. Amatzia Baram, "Who are the Insurgents? Sunni Arab Rebels in Iraq," *Special Report by the United States Institute of Peace*, April 2005.

31. Adam Zagorin, "A Pattern of Abuse: A Decorated Army Officer Reveals New Allegations of Detainee Mistreatment. Did the Military Ignore His Charges?" *Time*, Sept. 23, 2005. Also, see Joe Klein, "Saddam's Revenge," *Time*, Sept. 26, 2005. Also, "A Year of Crucial Missteps," *Time*, Sept. 16, 2005.

32. Jeffrey Gettleman, "As U.S. Detains Iraqis, Families Plead for News," *New York Times*, March 7, 2004, page A4.

33. Bradley Graham and Walter Pincus, "U.S. Hopes to Divide Insurgency," *Washington Post*, Oct. 31, 2004, page A29.

34. James Risen and David E. Sanger, "G.I.'s and Syrians in Tense Clashes on Iraqi Border," *New York Times*, Oct. 15, 2005, page A3.

35. Adriana lins de Albuquerque, Michael O'Hanlon and Jelly Associates, "OP-CHART: Military and Economic Trends in Postwar Iraq," *Wall Street Journal*, Feb. 11, 2004, OP/ED page.

36. Hal Bernton, "Lack Of Vehicle Armor Keeps Troops On Edge," *Seattle Times*, Oct. 21, 2004, page 1.

37. Aleksandar Vasovic, "U.S. Forces Adapt to Environment in Iraq," *Associated Press* via *Washington Times*, Dec. 23, 2003, page 2.

38. Arieh Sullivan, "IDF to US: Use More Armor in Iraq," *Jerusalem Post*, Sept. 14 2003, page 1.

39. John Koopman, *McCoy's Marines: Darkside to Baghdad*, St. Paul, MN: Zenith Press, 2004, page 299.

40. Elaine Grossman, "Measuring Casey's progress: Until Last Month, Iraq Campaign Plan Lacked Specific Benchmarks," *Inside the Pentagon*, March 31, 2005, page 1.

41. Bing West, *No True Glory: A Frontline Account of the Battle for Fallujah*, New York, NY: Bantam Books, 2005, page 121.

42. Associated Press, "Sunni, Secular Parties Join In Distrust Of Vote Results," *USA Today*, Dec. 22, 2005, page 4. Edward Wong, "Turnout in the Iraqi Election is Reported at 70 Percent," *New York Times*, Dec. 22, 2005, page 1.

43. Greg Jaffe and Yochi J. Dreazen, "As Bush Pledges To Stay In Iraq, Military Talks Up Smaller Force: Some Top Brass Say Troops May Be Fueling Insurgency; Two Political Tests Ahead," *Wall Street Journal*, Oct. 5, 2005, page 1.

44. Suggested to the author in remarks by Steve Daskall.

45. General John Abizaid, Commander, U.S. Central Command in remarks to the students and faculty of the Naval War College, Dec. 2, 2005. The audience comprised primarily War College students who are mid-grade/senior military officers.

46. "Iraq Civil War Could Have Domino Effect," *Associated Press*, Oct. 26, 2005.

47. Leslie Wayne, "US: Former Pentagon Officials Find Wealth with Contractors," *The New York Times*, June 19, 2005, page 3.

48. James Mann, *Rise of the Vulcans*, New York, NY: Penguin Books, 2002, page 26.

49. Ibid, page 63.

Douglas Macgregor is a former Army Colonel and a decorated Gulf War combat veteran. He is the author of *Transformation Under Fire* (Praeger, 2003), *Breaking the Phalanx: A New Design for Landpower in the 21st Century* (Praeger, 1997), and *The Soviet-East German Military Alliance* (Cambridge University Press, 1989). His newest work, *Character Under Fire: The Battle of 73 Easting*, will be appear later this year. Macgregor wrote this article for the Straus Military Reform Project at the Center for Defense Information in Washington, D.C.

From Swift to Swiss*

Tactical Decision Games and Their Place in Military Education and Performance Improvement

Donald E. Vandergriff, Major, U.S. Army retired

In today's arena of military transformation, the newest bandwagon everyone is jumping on is "reform military education." This comes about in light of the complex problems faced by Army leaders in Afghanistan and Iraq (Wong, 2004). The Army's education and training doctrine was developed to deal with second-genera-tion or industrial war. The existing system did all right to prepare Army leaders, especially its junior officers, to adapt to the unexpected demands of the ongoing wars in Afghanistan and Iraq. Nevertheless, the Army leader development system has to do better. As a result, think tanks and military task forces are proposing all kinds of changes to military education, at the levels of joint education, midlevel officer career courses, and senior-level war colleges (Scales, 2004).

My response to all this is, "Wow! You guys just don't get it!" Why focus our efforts to change education on people whose character is already set by years of process in our antiquated personnel system? The solution to our problem is adapting our military education system alongside the evolving generations of war, which calls for a different military mindset. I say, "Why not begin the reform where it all begins?" If leaders in the Department of Defense, in Congress, and in the think tanks really want to "transform" the force, then they should start with the next generation of potential leaders. Earlier is better—transform how the Army trains its new aspiring leaders into an adaptive leader's course, as illustrated by White (1988). White explores the essence of German military professionalism, as exemplified by the 19th-century Prussian military. His volume focuses on the most important Prussian military reformer, Gerhard Johann David von Scharnhorst, who in 1801 founded the Militarische Gesellschaft (Military Society) in Berlin. The Gesellschaft became the focal point for the transformation of the Prussian army from a robotic war machine into a modern fighting force that was instrumental in defeating Napoleon in 1813 and 1815.

*This article originally appeared in *Performance Improvement*, February 2006, vol. 45, no. 2. © 2006. Reprinted with permission of John Wiley & Sons, Inc.

Of course the first responses will be, "How much will it cost?" and "What are the political costs?" My answer is that it will not cost much, if anything, to prepare the next generation for the leadership challenges the United States faces today and in the future.

The proposal outlined here is one part of a holistic solution. In turn, this can impact the way the Army recruits (markets), develops, educates, and trains its future leaders. A thorough study of history and a detailed analysis of present and future environments allows one to predict what the Army would ask officers to do in the future. Defining the end state—instilling adaptability in new leaders—made it possible to put to practice (by trial and error) concepts that build adaptability and intuition in cadets before they go on as commissioned officers to lead soldiers.

The ROTC department at Georgetown University (the Hoya Battalion) is already putting to practice many ideas on how to better educate and train cadets. They have done it without raising their budget or adding to their personnel with outside contractors. The Hoya Battalion has done it entirely with the cadre the Army gave us through its personnel assignment system. As a result, the program has finished among the top five in the nation over the last two school years, 2003–2004 and 2004–2005.

The cadre of the program, the noncommissioned officers and officers, accomplished this goal by adhering to a few principles:

- Continue to develop the program based on the lessons from war.
- Be open to well–thought-out ideas.
- Always set an example.
- Place as much ownership for the program in the hands of the cadets as is possible.
- Don't let your ego get in the way of encouraging cadets how to think.

The bottom line is that this climate drove all members of the organization to do the best they could in preparing their cadets for the future by using the most effective methods in education and training (Gill, 2004).

The goal of the Hoya Battalion was to create leaders of character who are ready, willing, and able to make the right decisions in the face of adversity, be that the enemy, subordinates, peers, or superiors, on or off the battlefield. In addition to this goal, the Hoya Battalion evolves parallel to a learning organization, where the students leave the program and continually seek education as a self-discipline.

The cadre or teachers of the Hoya Battalion used several techniques within the curriculum they devised under the Program of Instruction (POI) to assist them in achieving the end state. One tool is the Tactical Decision Game (TDG), which provides an efficient and effective way to teach intuitive decision making—or, as the Army calls it, rapid decision making—in aspiring leaders. The TDG, though an important tool in developing adaptability, is but one aspect of the entire POI of a true adaptive leader's course (see Figure 1).

The POI of the Hoya Battalion puts into context when and where education and training fall.

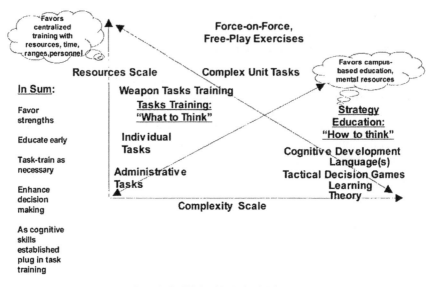

Figure 1. The POI of an Adaptive Leader's Course.

Cognitive Development (CD) occurs earlier because it is more complex and imparts a longer-lasting lesson through difficult shared experiences. Some of these experiences occur during training, but again, using the scale in Figure 1, the Hoya Battalion understands that training requires more tangible and expensive resources. Correctly done, training is resource intensive, while education is intellectually expensive. This combines into Knowledge Development (KD), which is one aspect of experience or gaining intuition. TDGs are but one tool of the cadet's evolution toward learning adaptability (Schein, 1997; Senge, 1990; Stewart, 1987).

TDG is a cheap tool, but an intellectually expensive centerpiece of the Hoya POI. By using the term "intellectually expensive," I mean that TDGs put demands on the instructor that go beyond most "ease on instructor" or "turnkey" curriculums used today. There is an art to teaching. It requires an instructor who understands war, is proficient in the technical aspects of the profession of arms, and who is a good leader. One last important asset: The instructor must have an imagination. With these ingredients, the instructor will find many ways to use the TDG to teach decision making and to build character. But first it is necessary to understand the history behind TDGs.

Background to "Why"

TDGs are used to teach leaders how to think and to train and reinforce established ways of doing something, such as task training. The technique can be traced back at least to the Chinese general and military theorist Sun Tzu, who was advocating their use more than 2,500 years ago (U.S. Marine Corps, 1989).

The way of educating and teaching Georgetown cadets called for in previous cadet command regulations evolved out the industrial age way of war (second-generation warfare) and centered on the rote memorization of process, or what is today called the Military Decision Making Process (MDMP). MDMP evolved from a scientific way of organizing thoughts in the preparation and execution of missions. It went so far as to tell commanders and their staffs that certain decisions should be made through events and time on a matrix. Additionally, MDMP evolved into the way the U.S. Army prepares civilians to become officers. TheArmy's education system has centered on memorization of the process, or the "checklist approach," to war fighting. (For more of the history behind this evolution and an understanding of why the U.S. Army went this way, see http://www.d-n-i.net/vandergriff/rha/index.htm; see also Vandergriff, 2002.)

The MDMP was created by U.S. Army Major Eben Swift in 1897. At the time of the emergence of the philosophy of scientific management, based on the theories of Frederick Taylor, Swift's methods were seen as the basis for a professional military education. The source of his process has a twist of irony to it, however. Swift's approach was based on his examination of a French interpretation of a German book on tactical decision games by a Prussian officer named Verdy du Vernois (1877; Gray, 1995). In du Vernois' system, most calculations and die rolling were eliminated in favor of an umpire who would determine results based on the situation and his own combat experience. War games had become a mainstay of German military training. Du Vernois proposed to eliminate the written rules and govern opponents by tactical rules that would become obvious during the course of the game. The French organized du Vernois' book of tactical decision games by structuring the games and their presentation.

Swift went even further, organizing the answers to the game into what we now call the five-paragraph operations order (Swift, 1906). It is important to note that, at the time, more U.S. officers spoke French than German. Swift then institu-tionalized his game at the Army's Staff College at Fort Leavenworth. Over time, the Swift method evolved into our task, condition, and standard approach to task training, and our crawl-walk-run approach to education and training systems (Dastrup, 1982). The Leavenworth methodology for teaching problem-solving skills has remained constant since the 1890s, when Swift introduced an educational technique known as the applicatory method, under which lecture, recitation, and memorization gave way to hands-on exercises in analytical problem solving, such as map exercises, war games, and staff rides—all designed to teach students how to think, not what to think. By the late 1930s, such exercises accounted for more than 70% of total curriculum hours. The applicatory method survives in the form of practical exercises; terrain walks; staff rides; and the capstone exercise, Prairie Warrior, which relies heavily on computer simulation (Swift, 1906).

At the heart of the reforms led by Gerhard Scharnhorst shortly after the destruction of the Prussian army at Jena in 1806 were ways to develop officers who could make rapid decisions in the chaos of the battlefield. Prussia's military education of its officer cadets was based on an education approach developed by a Swiss educator, Johann Heinrich Pestalozzi (B.I. Gudmundsson, personal email communication, December 16, 2004).

In the late 1700s, Pestalozzi developed his theory that students would learn faster on their own if allowed to "experience the thing before they tried to give it a name." More specifically, the Prussians used Pestalozzi's methods to educate leaders on how to identify the core of a problem and then deal with the centerpiece of the problem without "wasting time working their way to finding a solution" (see http://www.cals.ncsu.edu/agexed/aee501/pestalozzi.html).

The new education system, along with other radical Scharnhorst reforms such as strenuous selections of officers from a broad base of the population, gave the Prussians what they sought—a professional officer and noncommissioned officer corps. In the center of Europe, surrounded by several potential enemies, the Prussians had to be able to mobilize rapidly. Their officers had to prepare hard in peacetime to be ready when war began. From the very beginning of a Prussian (later German) cadet's career, TDGs were used to sharpen the students' decision-making skills and to provide a basis for evaluating them on their character (Gatto, 1991).

Prussian cadets had to solve problems with many variables under different conditions and then explain their decisions to the instructor and class. The problems the cadet was given were complex and dealt with units three levels above his own (in the case of cadets, platoon = company, battalion, and regiments). The instructors wanted to find out what the cadet would do when presented with a complex problem. They were not concerned with what the cadet had already learned, but with the cadet's willingness to present and solve the problem. These scenarios were timed. When time was up, the cadet presented his solution. Instructors and peers evaluated decision-making ability, not how tasks were accomplished (Morsy, 1994, pp. 21–45).

The TDGs introduced the cadets to the unknown, with the result that cadets wanted to know more and asked questions. They also sought to answer for themselves what they did not know. Also, the students were given orders that conflicted with the situation on the board and were forced to resolve the conflict between the two.

Another technique the Prussians used to teach decision making was to change the original situation or the orders while the cadet was preparing his solution to the initial problem. This forced the student to either challenge the original order because it was out of date or accept the old order and live with the consequences. Most of the time, the TDG was also presented under limited time, creating even more stress. But it was when the cadet briefed his solution that the major part of the learning took place, not only for the cadet but for also for his peers (Morsy, 1994, pp. 44–45). "It is not so much 'training' and 'pretraining.' That is to say, they serve to develop habits that are conducive to the use of all sorts of other methods, to include more elaborate simulations and field exercises, to study tactics" (B.I. Gudmundsson, personal email communication, December 16, 2004).

The cadet would have to present his proposed solution in front of his peers, instructors, and sometimes visiting officers. The great von Moltke, chief of the Prussian general staff from 1858 to 1888, frequently visited corps' district academies (where the Germans produced cadets) and would sit in on these games and even frequently oversee the instruction, present the situation, and then guide the discussion afterward (von Moltke, 1993).

The Prussians went beyond using TDGs to teach; they also used them in their evaluations. Weak performance on graded TDGs was grounds for failure on an exam or for expulsion from the academy. Signs of weak character were grounds for failing an exam, or worse, for a repeat offender, for expulsion from the course. The inability to make a decision or defend one's decision in the face of adversity was grounds for not being commissioned (Bald, 1986; Rothenberg, 1986).

Short of performance on an actual battlefield, there were several measures that demonstrated what type of character the cadet possessed. If the cadet changed his original decision to go along with the instructor-recommended solution, he was seen as a failure, as having weak character. Weak character was also demonstrated if the cadet stayed with a poor or out-of-date decision from higher because that is what the instructor ("higher") told him to do. The worst thing a cadet could do was to make no decision at all (Beihefte, 1877).

The contrast between the Pestalozzi approach and today's "crawl-walk-run" or "lecture-demonstration-practical application" system used in leader development curriculums is dramatic. This contrasting American approach was born out of necessity in World War I. The U.S. Army, arriving on the field of battle unprepared for large-scale war, followed the French military approach to education based on the philosophy of René Descartes. Descartes was a famous mathematician who broke down engineering problems in sequence, making it easier to teach formulas to engineering students. This approach was translated into French military training, where the French found it easy to break down military problem solving into processes (checklists) to educate their officers and their awaiting masses of citizen soldiers upon mobilization (see Figure 2) (Kirkland, 1990; see also Coffman, 1986; J.H. Hays, 1978; F. Kirkland, personal communication, April 12, 1998).

The Cartesian approach allowed the French (and later the United States) to easily teach a common, fundamental doctrinal language to many who were new to the military. It significantly reduced the time it took to master basic military skills. The downfall of this approach is that it simplifies war (complex problems) into processes where the enemy is only a template, not a free-thinking adversary with a very important voice in determining how the plan might be executed. The Cartesian approach also slows down a decision cycle by turning the planners' focus inward on process instead of outward on the enemy. The problem with this approach is that it does not fit in with the problem at hand. It is the same thing with operations research, which is a powerful tool for solving certain well-defined

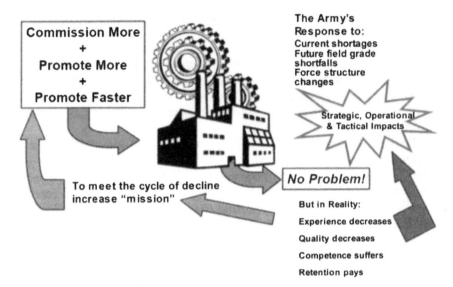

Figure 2. The Impact of the Mobilization Doctrine and the Industrial Way of War.

problems. The problem that we have with or in the Armed Forces is that we try to apply it to all sorts of inappropriate problems.

The French, relying on a massed citizen army in the late 19th and early 20th centuries, had to find a way to instruct many citizen officers quickly in military doctrine. Additionally, because of the casualties of World War I and the advance of modern weaponry and its destructiveness, the French needed a way to teach its officers how to control these resources to concentrate firepower so they could compensate for their lack of unit skills on the battlefields. They used an orderly and systematic approach to planning that was similar to the MDMP (Doughty, 1986; Vandergriff, 1998).

When the United States arrived in Europe in 1917 with its new Army, led largely by citizens who had been transformed into officers almost overnight, soldiers needed to learn the fundamentals of the profession of arms quickly. All U.S staff officers and commanders attended French schools in planning and controlling forces in combat. The United States and France were the victors in World War I and saw that victory as a justification of their training process. When the French developed methodical battle in the interwar years, the United States copied it with all its accompanying process-focused education. The U.S. Army carried this over to its education and training, as well as its doctrine (Hays, 1971; Lane, 1973; Weigley, 1971).

The Germans, on the other hand, invested far more time and rigor in developing leaders who could decide faster in fluid situations. They also promoted a military culture that encouraged initiative among subordinates, after a thorough and very tough accession process. (I must allude to the fact that we must use caution when adapting the education methods of the pre-World War II German cadet officer schools to U.S. Army ROTC. Their methods were sound but were sup-ported by an ability to make harsh cuts without much question from the chain of command, which was tolerated in their culture of the day. The best voice in this matter is found in Daniel J. Hughes' 1986 "Abuses of German Military History;" see also Higgins, 1985; Lind, 1985; Tiberi, 1985.)

The French and the United States, in contrast—and to be fair, out of desperation because their larger societies did not put a premium on funding and supporting professional preparedness peace—practiced Progressive era personnel theories and opened the net wide to accessions, to be democratic and fair. Missing was a hard "filter" up front to judge character under stress prior to awarding a commission. It was felt that new officers could learn on the job either in peacetime duty or in war. This was a very harsh way to develop and prepare leaders. Both countries felt that they were the victors in war without examining why they were the victors, and they ignored mistakes (Hays, 1971, pp. 105–114).

How to Use the TDG as a Decision-Making Teaching Tool

Today and in the future, TDGs will assume more importance in developing and sharpening cadets' tactical skills without an extensive and expensive commitment of resources. To be sure, experience is one of the most valuable aspects of teaching and training, but it is also costly. The Georgetown POI encompasses military history, essays, and varied education techniques, which carry over easily to the field. A new curriculum combined with a new operating environment and training philosophy will provide an opportunity to learn from the successes and failures of earlier warriors. Surveys of cadres taken by the author (2000–2004) garner similar responses regarding the use of TDGs: "There is no task-condition and standard;" "How can I grade this?" "The cadets need to be taught more before given this [TDG];" "This is something they should learn later [after they are commissioned and later in their careers]."

When thinking how to use the TDG, a cadre can also consider it a tactical exercise without troops. The cadre is only limited by imagination. There is a lot that can be done with the TDG. The cadre can use it in a written exam, like writing an Operations Order (OPORD) to plan for the scenario for a test. Along with the written portion, there will often be a sketch or plan that a student is required to do in developing his or her own plan. The scenario should also define who you are, why you are there, what your assets are, your mission or objective, and the threats against you. The instructor can change or adjust all of these based on what he or she wants to achieve and the level of proficiency of the class. Although the Hoya Battalion wanted the cadets to "experience the thing before you try to give it a name," the cadets attempted problems they could manage. By exposing the cadets to too complex a problem, a program may discourage them early on from taking risks and thinking boldly about their solutions (Vandergriff, 2003).

As the cadre gets comfortable with TDGs and gets a feel of how the cadets are evolving into them, the cadre can adjust all aspects of the TDG to teach critical thinking skills. For example, they can be vague in certain areas of the OPORD. This forces cadets to make assumptions or educated guesses. The Hoya POI also taught the cadets how to ask questions and not to ask dumb questions. Asking dumb questions means that they need to learn how to listen the first time and how to take concise notes quickly. Telling cadets "there are no dumb questions" is counterproductive to teaching them how to think. Allowing them to ask dumb questions gives them bad habits. There isn't much time for questions over the tactical radio. Everything done in an adaptive leader's course falls back to teaching the cadet how to deal with the stress of combat.

The POI encourages cadets to seek more knowledge when they ask pertinent questions. The instructor will now do this through the cadet brief-back of their solution. Cadets give their solutions to their peers, who will in turn evaluate the cadet's decision. The instructor is there to guide the discussion. He is also there to encourage the theme of classical education. Because of this session, cadets will seek to gain more knowledge on their own.

The instructor is also the referee, adding reality to cadet solutions with "Not possible" or "In reality, this is what this so and so can do for you in this type of terrain" type responses. Or the instructor asks probing, Socratic questions such as, "Is your course of action in keeping with the spirit of the commander's intent?" or "What caused you to change the mission you were given by higher?" These repeated sessions build character—adaptability and intuition—over time.

The major benefit of this type of education is that cadets can be put into situations that are either impractical or too expensive to enact in the field or in an electronic simulation. Cadets can go over hundreds of scenarios without ever leaving the classroom. This establishes a solid foundation in understanding decision making prior to moving to the field and more costly training. This is not a substitute for free-play force-on-force exercises but a useful adjunct. If you find a particularly relevant scenario, you can enact it live.

General Guidelines

The following are a set of general guidelines to follow when using TDGs. They are not designed to be restrictive but to ensure that cadets get the most out of the situation. Cadets know that most TDGs are written to appeal to a wide international audience. Teachers will have to take the time to translate the TDG into Army language (some TDGs are downloaded from the *Marine Corps Gazette*). Your particular ROTC battalions may develop different operating procedures, but don't get caught up in arguing about specific procedural points; there will be plenty of time for that during debrief. The *Marine Corps Gazette* TDG website is http://www.mca-marines.org/Gazette/tdg.htm; it includes archives of years of past TDGs with solutions.

The main thing to remember is to encourage the cadets to treat the situation as if they were living it. In many of the scenarios, cadets have fractions of a second to react, and allowing them to ponder the situation for hours reduces the benefits of the exercise. Spontaneity is the key. Tell the cadets that their first reaction is probably the best one. Again, it is a good tool to build character, especially when the rest of the class is attacking your course of action. No matter what the course of action, if the cadet thinks he or she is right, he or she should defend that course. Instructors must divorce themselves from their egos to support a cadet's decision, which may contradict the teacher's solution (Kilpatrick, 1951).

Also, instruct the cadets to give as much detail as possible in their answer. We have the cadets imagine that they are giving orders to their unit, or explaining their actions to their battalion commander. In several cases, teachers read scenarios to them with their eyes closed and without the benefit of taking notes. In single-person scenarios, have cadets describe the techniques they would use and why, what considerations they are taking into account, and what follow-ups they would perform. In team scenarios, have them describe what each cadet is doing and why, what their actions and reactions are. With a time constraint, this approach teaches you how to manage time and how to prioritize tasks, an effective tool to lead subordinates with limited time to plan and execute a mission.

The Hoya Battalion also employs other factors that add stress on top of most cadets' own self-induced stress in the scenario. Teachers play a war movie on TV or loud music, open the windows during the winter, have a radio speaker in the classroom continually updating the enemy and friendly situation, and whatever else we can think of to approximate the distractions felt in the heat of battle.

Finally, have fun with TDGs. There is no "right" answer, only better answers. All responses have some benefit and highlight unique perceptions of the problem. There is nothing to stop you from coming up with more than one response. Recognizing, however, that there are many ways to approach a problem, we do not limit the student to one pass or fail school solution. This is hard when using the TDG to evaluate decision-making ability during an examination, but it can be done. Cadre uses four evolving questions when grading the TDG exams and quizzes:

1. First and foremost, was a decision made?
2. If so, was it communicated to subordinates effectively?
3. Was the decision made in support of the commander's intent (long-term contract) and mission (short-term contract)?
4. If it was not, the instructor asks whether the cadet's solution was based on changing conditions that made it a viable decision even if it violated the original mission, but supported the intent.

Failure on the TDG comes from not making any decision or, in the course of briefing their course of action or while the teacher is grading the TDG, when the cadet changes his or her decision because the instructor challenged his or her choice. The cadet demonstrates the need to go along with the instructor ("higher"). Even if the teacher feels that the cadet's decision is a sound one, he or she may challenge or test the cadet's character in the face of adversity, to see how much the cadet believes in himself or herself.

From Process to Performance Improvement

TDGs transferred into decision-making games are applicable to the nonmilitary world. They are value added in many ways to an organization's leadership development or simply in the way it goes about planning for operations or in war-gaming future concepts and ideas. First, it is important to provide contrasts to the development of adaptability, as well as to talk about possible problems with this rapid approach to decision-making ability.

The Army educational approach evolved parallel with the same approach used today in the U.S. public education system called "competency-based education." Both evolved from Taylorism, or scientific management (Lane, 1973, p. 40; Weigley, 1971, p. 24; see also Hays, 1971, pp. 3, 10). The use of testing in the Leave No Child Behind initiative is the extreme example of this. "Teach the test" and "train for the test" derive from this educational (training) approach. Peter Kline in *Why America's Children Can't Think,* calls this approach to education "fill-'em-up" education. He goes on to describe this approach:

> . . . [I]f we assume that children are born with nothing on their minds, and that it is the business of education to fill those minds with the things that Everyone Should Know, as if we were programming computers, then there might be some sense in a lock-step curriculum. (2002, p. xiii)

Both systems, public education and Army training, developed to rapidly prepare as many people as possible to do critical but basic wartime tasks. Competency-based education is seen in almost every aspect of Army institutions that deal with leadership development, from curriculum development and use to how leaders are evaluated (using long competency-based leader traits lists) to how instructors are certified to teach (Center for Army Leadership, 2005, pp. 6–8).

Industrial age organizations seek to achieve routine and habit through standardized procedures. Complex tasks are broken into simple steps that are assigned to organizational positions to ensure that employees are both interchangeable and easily replaced. Bureaucratic hierarchies tend to value quantifiable assessment of specific aspects of complex managerial tasks (Reed, Bullis, Collins, & Paparone, 2004).

How does competency-based education translate into training? Following the traditional three-part distinction among the domains of learning (psychomotor or doing, cognitive or thinking, affective or feeling), training emphasizes the

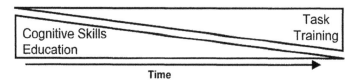

Figure 3. "How to Think" Serves as the Foundation to "What to Think."

psychomotor domain of learning. Training that is done in the cognitive domain is generally at the knowledge level and lower part of the comprehension level.

Criterion objectives are most appropriate for training and in most lesson plans or training support packages. That is, under a given set of conditions, a student will exhibit a specific behavior to a certain predetermined level or standard.

Training is essentially a closed system. The trained individual knows the "right answers," how to do things the "approved way," or how to arrive at the "school solution."

Under these conditions, the products of each student in every situation look the same. Objectives, job requirements, and skill levels are constraints with training. Yet time required for training can vary because of the aptitude, experience, and previous skill level of the student. With training, a task analysis translates into the curriculum including a complete listing of skills and knowledge required for the graduate to demonstrate competence.

Implications for Performance Improvement

The belief that task and the analysis decision-making process should serve as a baseline runs counter to how to develop cognitive skills ("how to think" rather than "what to think;" see Figure 3). What should occur is that CD should take place earlier; even college may be too late. Nevertheless, this must also involve Emotional Development (ED). The two combined become knowledge translated into experiences (KD; U.S. Dept. of the Army, 1999; Jacobs & Jacques, 1987; Magee, 1999).

Imagine seeing two bars perpendicular to one another on a horizontal plane. The bottom bar is CD. The bar on top is task training to achieve task proficiency. As the cadets or leaders begin their leadership development, the Army should "introduce them to things before giving them a name" in an environment that is painful but safe, so they seek the answer.

I have seen the adaptability approach in action, have lived it, and helped develop it; and the learning curve is remarkable, given at least average intelligence and the motivation to learn. The gradual integration of task training to gain proficiency is smoother, and students learn how to integrate tasks in a holistic view (Basseches, 1984; Graves, 1981, as cited in Wilbur, 2000; Lasky, 2001).

As described earlier, the Army approach to leader development originated through its experiences with and through the nation's mobilization doctrine for

World Wars I and II. In turn, this demanded that the Army get millions up to a basic level. It could achieve this through task proficiency.

The nation could not imagine that the military trade required thinking or even smart people. The leaders that evolved from World War II did so because the promotion system the Army had in that war became a true meritoc-racy—you were killed, succeeded and were promoted, or you failed and got relieved—through default. As soon as wars such as World War II were over, the nation forgot the lessons it should have learned, easy in the "glow of victory" ("We did nothing wrong because we won" or "Why study the Germans? They lost two wars").

Another reason the Army could emphasize task proficiency first is because the pool it drew on from the U.S. population at the time possessed a high degree of CD (Ambrose, 1983, pp. 433–457). In making this determination, the Ambrose study examined only those variables that could be gleaned from the officers' records, which fell into four general categories: age; service school attendance and ratings; length and type of service prior to World War II; and demonstrated measurable efficiency prior to World War II. In the end, however, the study found the strongest correlation between rank achieved and an officer's General Efficiency Rating (GER). The GER was the average of an officer's numerical efficiency ratings, adjusted by his branch to compensate for the peculiarities of rating officers and the difficulty of assignments (U.S. War Department General Staff, Memorandum for the Assistant Chief of Staff, G-1; all references are taken from U.S. War Department, Army Ground Forces, Report of Army Ground Forces Study on Comparisons of General Officers and Colonels (Infantry), 1946).

Social historians verified the adage that Americans in World Wars I and II (as well as before) were great problem solvers. This was because the experiences that those generations had in life forced them to solve problems. This generation had more ED through life experiences (like rites of passage in cohesion and shared tough experiences), while today's Generations X and Y possess fine motor skills but have lower ED. They demonstrate these skills in sterile, non-threatening environments. Their input and receiving of information has been greater than ever; but on the other hand, because the United States has become so wealthy, parents protect their children from those harder real-life experiences.

As a nation, the United States is sorely lacking in the development of both breadth and especially depth in thinking, which comes about in learning "how to" rather than "what to" think. ED is of the most concern. It develops through "hard knocks." If Generations X and Y do not get this learning, then our pool of potential leaders may be smart but will likely lack both high CD and ED.

In a military context, developing CD without ED could result in creating a bunch of "war mongers." They could figure how to kill the greatest numbers without considering the moral implications of doing so! The problem does not lie with the Army, which is now examining war across the context of operations outside fighting, but with the pool from which the Army will draw its potential leaders. It is a substantial reason to teach adaptability in the context of a tough learning environment where people can and will fail without administrators worrying about making numbers or political correctness.

ED, or maturity, is slower in the larger U.S. culture. Citizens have been conditioned to shirk responsibility. Like the military, U.S. society suffers from "zero defects," which translates into perfect resumes and scores on entrance exams. Resumes are filled with endless achievements, while for college entrance exams high schools students take preparatory courses and are allowed to take the exam several times to get the best score. How is this a measure of character and ability to learn when environments are so structured with strict processes on how to achieve?

Conclusion: Applications Outside the Army

In the end, TDGs in the context of a learning organization of an adaptive leader's course provide an educational approach for building a cadet's strength of character. Past curricula dealing with leader development used process and task training to train potential officers "what to think." In most wars, with the United States coming in late, and after the Germans were bled down and almost beaten, it made it appear in the "glow of victory" that the U.S. system of officer production was the right one. The Army is beginning to realize that the foundation of an effective future officer corps must begin early and, to create leaders that are adaptable, know "how to think" and have intuition.

Beyond decision making in war, the use of nontactical TDGs has great applications to the corporate world as well as any organization that needs leaders who are decisive and adaptable. Establishing the blend of instructional technologies to use, particularly in the institutional setting, is critical to promoting synchronous growth in CD, ED, and, consequently, KD.

Current instructional approaches lack opportunities for experiencing the emotional trauma of failing within a safe environment that is needed to promote ED. TDG tools can teach adaptability, and instructors can use them to teach both critical and reflective thinking, or *how* to think. This should replace the now almost total emphasis on *what* to think (content) to permit building richer and deeper understandings of the self and alternative world views, an understanding of which will enrich one's own self-understanding (Collins, 2001).

The Army's highly technical environment demands that the emphasis from the outset be on *transformation*, on growing by learning to learn, not learning information alone. I have focused on the use of one important tool, the TDG.

Note

The author would also like to thank the following for their insights and assistance: Major Andrew Dziengeleski, MSG Rob Frye, Lieutenant Allan Gill, Bruce I. Gudmundsson, Mark

R. Lewis, MAJ Khoi Nygon, Franklin Spinney, Dr. Steven Stewart, John Tillson, and the cadets of the Hoya Battalion.

References

Ambrose, S.E. (1983). *Eisenhower: Soldier, general of the army, president-elect, 1890–1952.* New York: Simon and Schuster.

Bald, D. (1986). The picture of the war and military guidance in the empire. In Düffler, J., & Hull, K. (Eds.), *Ready for the war: War mentality in Wihelminschen Germany, 1890–1914.* Göttingen, Germany: Vandenhoeck & Rupprecht.

Basseches, M. (1984). *Dialectical thinking and adult development.* Norwood, NJ: Ablex.

Beihefte, H. (1877). Military education and science. Supplements to the military weekly paper *Militär-Wochenblatt, 1.*

Center for Army Leadership. (2005, May 3). *Developing agile leaders in captains' career courses.* Fort Leavenworth, KS: U.S. Army Combined Arms Center.

Coffman, E.M. (1986). *The old army: A portrait of the American army in peacetime 1784–1898.* New York: Oxford University Press.

Collins, J. (2001). *Good to great: Why some companies make the leap . . . and others don't.* New York: Harper Business.

Dastrup, B.L. (1982). *The U.S. Army command and general staff college: A centennial history.* Manhattan, KS: Sunflower University Press.

Doughty, R. (1986). *Seeds of disaster: The development of French Doctrine, 1919–1939.* New York: Archon Books.

Gatto, J.T. (1991). *"The Prussian connection": The underground history of American education: An intimate investigation into the problem of modern schooling.* New York: New Society Publishers.

Gill, A., Lt. Col. (November 8, 2004). *The Hoya battalion.* Unpublished brief, Georgetown University Army ROTC, Washington, DC.

Gray, W., Col. (1995). *Playing war: The applicability of commercial conflict simulations to military intelligence training and education.* Bolling Air Force Base, Washington, DC: DIA Joint Military Intelligence College.

Hays, J.H. (1978). *The evolution of military officer personnel management policies: A preliminary study with parallels from industry.* Santa Monica, CA: Rand.

Hays, S.P. (1971). Introduction. In Isrel, J. (Ed.), *Building the organizational society.* New York: The Free Press.

Higgins, G.A., Maj. (1985). German and US operational art: A contrast in maneuver. *Military Review 65*(10), 22–29.

Hughes, D.J. (1986). Abuses of German military history. *Military Review, 66*(12), 66–76.

Jacobs, T.O., & Jaques, E. (1987). Leadership in complex systems. In Zeidner, J. (Ed.), *Human productivity enhancements: Vol. 2. Organizations, personnel, and decision making.* New York: Praeger.

Kilpatrick, W.H. (1951). *Introduction to Heinrich Pestalozzi: The education of man—Aphorisms.* New York: Philosophical Library.

Kirkland, F. (1990). The gap between leadership policy and practice: A historical perspective. *Parameters, XXV*(9), 54–55.

Kline, P. (2002). *Why America's children can't think: Creating independent minds for the 21st century.* Maui, HI: Inner Ocean Publishing Inc.

Lane, J.C. (1973, June). The military profession's search for identity. *Marine Corps Gazette, XXXIV*(12), 40.

Lasky, O. (2001). Linking two lines of adult development: The developmental structure/process tool. *Bulletin of the Society for Research in Adult Development (SRAD), 10*(1), 8–11.

Lind, W.S. (1985). *Maneuver warfare handbook.* Boulder, CO: Westview Press.

Magee II, R.R. (Ed.). (1999). *Strategic leadership primer.* Carlisle Barracks, PA: U.S. Army War College.

Morsy, Z. (Ed.). (1994). *Thinkers on education* (Vol. 3). Paris: UNESCO Publishing.

Reed, G., Bullis, C., Collins, R., & Paparone, C. (2004, Autumn). Mapping the route of leadership education. *Parameters, XXXIV*(3), 46–60.

Rothenberg, G. (1986). Moltke, Schlieffen and the doctrine of strategic envelopment. In Paret, P. (Ed.), *Makers of modern strategy from Machiavelli to the nuclear age.* Princeton, NJ: Princeton University Press.

Scales, Jr., R., Maj. Gen. (2004). Culture-centric warfare. *U.S. Naval Institute Proceedings, 130,* 5–10.

Schein, E. (1997). *Organizational culture and leadership.* San Francisco: Jossey-Bass.

Senge, P. (1990). *The fifth discipline.* New York: Doubleday.

Stewart, S.R. (1987). *Leader development training assessment of U.S. Army TRADOC brigade commanders.* Washington, DC: U.S. ARI Research Report 1454.

Swift, E., Maj., U.S. Army. (1906). *Field orders, messages, and reports.* Washington, DC: Government Printing Office Document UB283.A45.

Tiberi, P., Lt. Col. (1985). German versus Soviet blitzkrieg. *Military Review, 65*(9), 63–71.

U.S. Department of the Army, Headquarters. (1999). *Field manual 22–100, army leadership.* Washington, DC: U.S. Government Printing Office.

U.S. Marine Corps. (1989). *Fleet marine field manual: Warfighting.* Quantico, VA: Author.

U.S. War Department General Staff. (1946). Memorandum for the Assistant Chief of Staff, G-1. Subject: Promotion of Officers, Regular Army, Encl 1. *Factors involved in plan for promotion, 1.* Source: National Archives: RG 165, War Dept. Filing no. 210.2.

Vandergriff, D.E., Maj. (2003, October). *Lessons learned with decision making.* Unpublished After Action Review, Georgetown University Army ROTC, Washington, DC.

Vandergriff, D.E. (2002). *Path to victory: America's army and the revolution in human affairs.* Novato, CA: Presidio Press.

Vandergriff, D.E. (1998, January–February). Without the proper culture: Why our army cannot practice maneuver warfare. *ARMOR Magazine,* 20–24.

Verdy du Vernois, J. von (1877). Military wargaming. *Journal of the Royal United Service Institution, 50.*

von Moltke, H.G. (1993). Moltke on the art of war. In Hughes, D.J. (Ed.), *Moltke on the art of war: Selected writings.* (Hughes, D.J. & Bell, H. Trans.) Novato, CA: Presidio.

Weigley, R.F. (1971). Elihu root reforms and the progressive era. In Geffen, W. (Ed.), *Command and commanders in modern warfare.* Washington, DC: Office of Air Force History.

White, C. (1988). *The enlightened soldier: Gerhard Scharnhorst and the Militarische Gesellschaft.* New York: Praeger.

Wilber, K. (Ed.) (2000). *Integral psychology.* Boston, MA: Shambhala.

Wong, L. (2004). *Developing adaptive leaders.* Carlisle, PA: Strategic Studies Institute, Yuma, Arizona.

Related Reading

Skelton, I. (December 8, 2004). Remarks for the Association of the United States Army Space & Missile Defense Symposium and Exhibition Dinner, Yuma, Arizona.

Major Donald E. Vandergriff retired from the U.S. Army during the summer of 2005. He has served in numerous troop, staff, and education assignments in the United States and overseas. Don is a recognized authority on the U.S. Army personnel system, the Army culture, leadership development, and soldier training in light of how war has evolved into the fourth-generation warfare.

Don has written numerous books—*Spirit, Blood and Treasure: The American Cost of Battle in the 21st Century* (Presidio 2001), *Path to Victory: America's Army and the Revolution in Human Affairs* (Presidio 2002), and *Raising the Bar: Creating and Nurturing Adaptive Leaders to Deal with the Changing Face of War* (Center of Defense Information (forthcoming)). He has also written 50 articles and held briefings for audiences that have ranged from the Secretary of the Army Thomas White, Chiefs of Staff such as General Dennis Reimer, Vice Chiefs of Staff such as General Jack Keane, Congressmen, and think tanks. Numerous Army task forces such as the Unit Manning Task Force (later Stabilization Task Force) that worked the details for moving the Army from an individual-centric to unit-centric personnel system have honored Don by asking him to participate in their work. He has also been on panels dealing with military personnel and education reform such as the U.S. Army Future Center Symposium "Defining War" (April 2004) and the American Enterprise Institute "The Future of the U.S. Army" (April 2005).

The U.S. Army Training and Doctrine Command's Future Center hired Don to contribute to the evolution of Army Leader development programs and recommend changes that will prepare the Army's leaders and soldiers for the future. He wrote this article in his final days at Georgetown University Army ROTC. Don and his wife, Lorraine, currently reside in Woodbridge, Virginia, with their six dogs and a cat. He may be reached at vandergriffdonald@usa.net.

Statement to Congress*

Franklin C. Spinney
Staff Analyst, Department of Defense
Before
The Subcommittee on National Security, Veterans Affairs and International Relations
Committee on Government Reform United States House of Representatives
June 4, 2002

Mr. Chairman and Members of the Committee:

Thank you for the opportunity to provide the Committee with my views on the financial management problems facing the Defense Department.

Although my appearance has been approved by my superiors, I am presenting personal views that do not reflect an official view of anyone in a position of authority in the Department of Defense or in the current Administration. They are, however, based on thirty-three years of experience, including over seven as an officer in the United States Air Force and twenty-six as a civilian in the Office of the Secretary of Defense.

In my view, the Defense Department's financial management problems cannot be divorced from the defense budget now before Congress. Moreover, this budget is really a point in a time continuum linking us to the past and to the future. Viewed from this perspective, the requirements of sound financial management become clear: Today's budget should reflect a sound appreciation of and account for the intended consequences of past decisions as well as the future consequences of current decisions.

The DoD's financial management problems can be summed up quite succinctly: Both links are broken. The historical books cannot pass the routine audits required by law and planning data systematically misrepresent the future consequences of current decisions. The double breakdown in these information links makes it impossible for decision makers to assemble the information needed to synthesize a coherent defense plan that is both accountable to the American people and responsive to the changing threats, opportunities, and constraints of an uncertain world.

My aim today is twofold: In Part I, I want establish a point of departure by describing the basic structure of the top-level financial management information

---

*Reprinted with the permission of the author.

system now used by the Pentagon's senior leadership to shape the Department's plans and control the evolution of our nation's defense policies. Then I will place the double breakdown in the context of this system, with emphasis on the breakdown in the link between the present and future. In Part II, I want to submit for the record the broad outlines of a proposal for a program to produce the kind of information needed to resolve this crisis.

Part I

The PPBS, the FYDP Database, and the Link Between Output and Input

The budget before Congress is actually the first year of a comprehensive five-year budget plan known as the FY 2003–2007 Future Years Defense Plan or FYDP (pronounced 'fiddup'). This plan was produced over the last year by the deliberative procedures of the Planning-Programming-Budgeting System or PPBS. The PPBS is a step-by-step strategic decision-making process and is designed to link the threat assessments and the policy intentions of our political leadership via a national defense strategy to the thousands of detailed force structure, modernization, and readiness decisions which are needed each year to keep the Defense Department running coherently in the desired direction.

Slide 1 (*see* http://www.d-n-i.net/fcs/spinney_testimony_060402.htm) places the current FYDP in a historical perspective. Specifically, it shows how the new five-year plan compares to the history of past appropriations reaching back to 1945. Note that the distorting effects of inflation have been removed and all budget numbers are expressed in FY 2003 constant dollars.

The FY 2003–2007 FYDP calls for enormous increases in future defense budgets out to FY 2007. These budget increases have been justified as being necessary to fight the global war against terrorism that was triggered by the criminal attack on the World Trade Center and Pentagon last September 11. Yet Slide 1 shows that most of the budget growth was put into place by the PPBS before September 11.

The dotted line projected backward from fiscal 2003 makes it easy to compare the current budget request to past budgets as well as the average budget level of the entire Cold War, which is represented by the heavy black line. The dotted line tells us that the FY 2003 budget would be higher than that averaged during the Cold War, when America faced the threat of a nuclear tipped Soviet superpower instead of a criminal network of terrorists funded by fanatical anti-American Saudi millionaire. Only the budgets that paid for the Korean and Vietnam Wars and those of the Reagan Administration exceeded the request now before Congress. Nevertheless, this spring, the leaders of the military services told Congress the FY 2003 budget shortchanged their funding requirements by roughly $25 billion, according to Congressman Curt Weldon.

Turning our attention to the future, the dark blue triangle topped by the red band shows how the defense budget is projected to rise to a level almost $98 billion higher in 2007 than the defense projection used by the Bush Administration in its so-called "placeholder" federal budget of April 2001 which, you will recall, was part of the package of financial calculations supporting the proposed tax cut (portrayed in Slide 1 by the light yellow bars). Note also that 82% of that $98 billion increase, or $81 billion, was produced during the summer program review in the Pentagon, between May and August of 2001. Nevertheless, this increase may not be enough. On May 3, Defense Secretary Rumsfeld ordered the services to study options for cutting back major modernization programs, because the Pentagon cannot afford all the weapons in the pipeline.

The only part of the defense increase that can be directly attributed to the changed conditions brought about by the attack on September 11 is the thin red ribbon on top of the dark gray triangle. By any measure, this add-on is a tiny part of the total defense budget, and this increase may also not be enough. In April, the senior military officials claimed they needed to increase personnel end strength by 50,000, because our forces have been stretched thin by the global war on terrorism.

Slide 1 may provide insight into the relative size of the FYDP and how it evolved, but it says nothing about what these expenditures will or will not buy. That requires a detailed analysis of its innards, yet there are already indications that these innards are unraveling.

Bear in mind, the goal of the PPBS was to link the threat assessments and the policy intentions of our political leadership to thousands of detailed force structure, modernization, and readiness decisions. Its end product—the FYDP—describes these decisions, and it does so with a huge table containing thousands of rows of accounting data. Each row of the FYDP table specifies a program element by laying out a five-year stream of detailed budget numbers for a specific function or activity.

The program elements are supposed to be the output-oriented building blocks of defense policy. The resource allocations (i.e., the tradeoffs) among them define their relative values or priorities. The entire table, therefore, is—or should be—a comprehensive statement of the priorities and tradeoffs used to shape our nation's defense strategy. Yet the ink was not dry on this table before pressures emerged to change the table.

The situation is complicated by the fact that these program elements do not correspond to the traditional input-oriented appropriation categories used by Congress to raise money for the armed forces. In fact, a single program element in the FYDP is likely to include more than one appropriation category in its money stream. For example, a program element for a component of force structure, like "F-15 Squadrons," could conceivably include the moneys from the R&D, Procurement, O&M, Milpers, and Milcon appropriations. Taken together, the data in this program element are the highest-level financial management information summarizing the past, present, and future states of the F-15 force (its size, its modernization, and its readiness).

The appropriations request the Pentagon sends to Congress re-tabulates the various components of the detailed program element data into the standard appropriations format. This transformation is conceptually straightforward and easy to do with computers, but it shifts the decision-maker's frame of reference to input categories. This shift can be a source of confusion which, in my opinion, is one reason why budget battles inside the Pentagon as well as between the Pentagon and Congress often degenerate into context-free food fights over appropriations inputs rather than policy-based deliberations over programmatic outputs—the ongoing fracas over the Crusader howitzer being an excellent case in point.

Viewed from the programmatic perspective, the four outyears of the current FYDP (i.e., FY 2004–2007) are the Defense Department's definitive output-oriented statement of the future consequences of a Congressional decision to appropriate the details of the FY 2003 budget. The accounting data in these outyears tell the Secretary of Defense, the President, the Congress, and the American people what they can expect to buy and how much they will spend over the long term if they make a current decision to fund the FY 2003 budget. Yet there are already signs that this FYDP understates the true cost of the entire defense program.

The mass of detailed program element decisions in FY 2003–2007 FYDP are also linked to the past decisions by a complimentary program-element table of the Pentagon's past expenditures. This historical table makes it possible to understand how the individual program elements in budget request evolved out their counterparts in past budgets. The historical database has various forms of program element data reaching back to 1962.

The historical data can be compared to data in past FYDPs to determine if the actual evolution of the defense program is the product of policy driven decisions. Such a comparison can provide valuable feedback to guide corrective action. It also would help us gage the reliability of the projections in the current FYDP. The past, present, and future times horizons of the FYDP database, therefore, should be able to provide the information needed to understand and control the evolution of defense policies over time.

Taken together, the PPBS and the FYDP database are the central tools of financial management in the Department of Defense at the highest policy level. All the expenditure and budget planning data produced by the Department's various subordinate or specialized financial management systems should be consistent with and reliably rolled up into the FYDP's financial management information system.

With this background in mind, I will now discuss the double breakdown of the Defense Department's financial management systems.

Slide 2 (*see* http://www.d-n-i.net/fcs/spinney_testimony_060402.htm) places the Defense Department's financial management problems in context of the FYDP's time continuum. The left box refers to the breakdown in the link between the present and the past, and the right box refers to the breakdown between the present and the future. The next two subsections describe the implications of each breakdown.

There can be no dispute over the contention that the link connecting the present with the past is broken. One needs only to glance at the pile of reports produced by the General Accounting Office and the Defense Department's Inspector General as well as the final report of Mr. Stephen Friedman's financial transformation panel (Transforming Department of Defense Financial Management A Strategy for Change, April 13, 2001) to appreciate the rich variety of detailed information about the incredibly complex nature of the Defense Department's bookkeeping shambles. Yet within that variety, these reports converge on two central conclusions.

First, the Defense Department's accounting systems do not provide the information needed to relate financial inputs to policy outputs. The Friedman report says, for example, these systems do not provide reliable information that "tells managers the costs of forces or activities that they manage and the relationship of funding levels to output, capability or performance of those forces or activities."

A logical consequence of this conclusion is that unreliable accounting information makes it impossible to link the intended consequences of past decisions to the defense budget now before Congress. Such a conclusion is tantamount to saying it is not possible to determine whether or not the internal activities of the Defense Department are matched to the external requirements of its environment. Second, these reports agree that the Pentagon's bookkeeping systems do not comply with legal requirements of the Chief Financial Officers (CFO) Act of 1990. This conclusion goes well beyond the principles of sound financial management and strikes at the soul of the Constitution. The CFO Act requires government agencies to pass annual audits of the links between an executive agency's expenditures and the legally enacted appropriations authorizing those expenditures. This audit requirement is intended to sharpen the teeth of the Appropriations and Accountability Clauses in the Constitution, Article 1, Section 9, Clause 7, which says, "No Money shall be drawn from the Treasury, but in Consequence of Appropriations made by Law; and a regular Statement and Account of the Receipts and Expenditures of all public Money shall be published from time to time." This clause, as we all know, assigns the power of the purse to Congress, and it does so with language that denotes (1) a clear and absolute prohibition on spending (i.e., "No Money") and (2) an all-encompassing requirement for accountability (i.e, "all public Money"). The sweeping construction allows no room for exception. Nor is this construction an outdated artifact of arcane 18th Century language. According to the eminent constitutional scholar Professor Edward S. Corwin, this clause is Congress's most important check on the actions of other branches of government in the Constitution's entire scheme of checks and balances. It is therefore clear that a finding of non-compliance with the CFO Act is a dagger aimed at the heart of American constitutional theory—namely, the idea of making the government accountable to be people via a legal system of checks and balances—a system, I might add, that everyone in the federal government has sworn freely and without reservation to uphold, protect, and defend.

In conclusion, the breakdown in the link between the past and present carries with it profound managerial, constitutional, and moral implications. The historical accounting shambles is a crisis, and it must be rectified as soon as possible, but this is only half the story: We face a double crisis, because the accounting systems that link the present budget to the future are also a shambles. I call this the Plans/Reality Mismatch.

The Breakdown in the Link Between the Present and the Future: The Plans/Reality Mismatch, the Defense Power Games, and the Boom and Bust Cycle of Decay.

The Pentagon has produced a new FYDP each year since the PPBS was introduced by Defense Secretary McNamara in 1961. Each of these FYDPs was derived in theory from a defense strategy based on an appreciation of threats to our security and the political leadership's policy intentions. Each FYDP, therefore, should be a comprehensive numerical portrait of the defense policy made by the Secretary of Defense and approved by the President at a given point in time. The data in each FYDP's predictions are also an historical record of what the Defense Department's said would happen over the long term if Congress appropriated the funds to pay for the first year of that plan. This historical record makes it possible to compare the pattern of intentions (i.e., the "Plans") to the pattern of the pattern of actual behavior as documented by the historical FYDP database (i.e., the "Reality"). For reasons that will become clear, I call this kind of comparison the Plans/Reality Mismatch.

Bear in mind, no one can predict the future with 100% accuracy, but if the PPBS is an unbiased decision-making process, the predictive errors in the succession of FYDPs should be randomly distributed, even if the historical record is not accurate. If, on the other hand, the distributions of predictive errors are systematically skewed, we can conclude that behavioral biases are shaping the real long-term decisions, and the first year of the FYDP is masquerading under false pretenses. Moreover, a repetition of these biases year after year would be evidence that this a product of habitual behavior.

State-of-the-art data processing technologies makes it possible, at least in theory, to perform this kind of comparison across many FYDPs for any program element or aggregation of elements in the defense budget. In practice, such an analysis is complicated by many intractable factors. On the one hand, there will never be unambiguous output metrics for parts of the program elements in the FYDP data base, like the contribution of the all important moral factors to measurements of a unit's readiness for combat or a global measurement of a weapon's effectiveness, which is always scenario dependent. On the other hand, it is easy to quantify the first order outputs of procurement decisions (i.e., the number of items procured) and the first order inputs of procurement decisions (i.e., the budgets and unit costs for each item). So a plans/reality mismatch analysis is quite straightforward for the procurement data in the FYDP's program elements.

To this end, we combined the last twenty-six procurement annexes of the FYDPs into a 90-megabyte database (FY 1976 thru FY 2001—the most recent data has not yet been included). This database permits a planner to examine how accurately the cost, quantity, and budget predictions of our modernization plans matched up to what really happened (in inflation adjusted dollars). The methodology underpinning these comparisons was validated by a GAO audit in 1996, made at the request of Senators Grassley and Roth. The next three slides are a typical case study of these comparisons and will be used to illustrate the biased nature of the information linking the present with the future.

In the mid-1970s, the Navy's tactical airpower (tacair) program faced an aircraft aging crisis not unlike that faced today. The only two airplanes in production—the F-14 and the A-6—were too expensive to buy in sufficient quantities to maintain the Navy's goal of an average age of 7.5 years for the tacair aircraft in its inventory. The Navy faced the possibility of not having enough airplanes in the long term to equip its aircraft carriers with modern full-strength tacair squadrons. The F-18 program became the centerpiece of a strategy to solve the crisis. The idea was to compliment the low production rates of the F-14s and A-6s with higher production rates of lower-cost F-18s. This plan became part of a larger modernization policy known as the "High-Low Mix," a snappy but meaningless sound byte that unfortunately remains with us to this day. The next three slides show how this policy came unglued with the passage of time.

The Plan/Reality Mismatch: Production

The Navy's F-18A/B/C/D tactical fighter began development in the mid 1970s and entered production in 1979. Slide 3 (*See* http://www.d-n-i.net/fcs/spinney_testimony_060402.htm), which compares planned purchases to actual purchases, shows the result.

Each "line" in Slide 3 depicts a separate FYDP's prediction of the number of F-18s that would be purchased in each of its future years, whereas the "bars" portray actual number of F-18 purchased each year. The Defense Department planned to increase the F-18's production rate to somewhere between 150 and 200 F-18s per year, but actual production never exceeded 84 per year, notwithstanding the largest peacetime defense budgets in history. Moreover, the Defense Department maintained its grossly biased vision of the future production until the FY 1987–1991 FYDP (i.e., the line ramping up from the 1986 "bar"), long after it should have been clear that the production plan was a pipedream.

The Plans/Reality Mismatch: The Program Budget. The conventional wisdom is that production cutbacks, like those in Slide 3, cause cost growth, but our data shows that this is generally not the case for programs in the early years of their production life cycle, as was the F-18 in the first half of the 1980s. Slide 4 (*see* http://www.d-n-i.net/fcs/spinney_testimony_060402.htm) continues the example with a Plans/Reality Mismatch diagram that compares the F-18's predicted budgets to its actual budgets. Like Slide 3, the "lines" represent the FYDPs while the "bars" portray the actual budgets. Bear in mind, the effects of predicted and actual inflation have been removed and all numbers are expressed in FY 2001 dollars.

Slide 4 reveals that the actual procurement budgets in the historical FYDP data base exceeded those predicted by the succession of FYDPs for the first six years its of F-18's production run—i.e., 1979 to 1984. So, money was being added to the F-18 production program while its production rates were cut back drastically from intended levels. This means cost growth must have caused the cutbacks not budget cuts. Slide 5 (*see* http://www.d-n-i.net/fcs/spinney_testimony_060402. htm) addresses this issue, and it gets to the heart of the biases creating the plans/reality mismatch and the breakdown in the financial management information linking the present to the future.

The Plans/Reality Mismatch: Unit Costs

The information in our database shows that the long-range cost predictions made during the development phase (i.e., pre-production) and the early production stages of a major weapon's life cycle almost always understate its eventual production costs by large amounts. The dangers posed by this phenomenon are particularly relevant today, because the current FYDP contains an unprecedented bow wave of programs in the development or the early production pipeline.

The F-18 is a typical albeit unusually clear example of the bias to grossly underestimate the unit costs of a weapons program in the early stages of its acquisition life cycle. The production data in Slide 3 can be divided into the budget data in Slide 4 to calculate the predicted and actual unit production costs. All this data can be placed on one chart, if cost is plotted as a function of cumulative production rather than by year. Slide 5 shows the result. It relates the average annual cost of an F-18 (on the vertical axis) to the total number produced (on the horizontal axis). The average annual costs can be thought of as an approximation of each additional F-18 produced or what an economist would refer to it as "marginal cost".

The heavy black line with the "ball" markers shows how the F-18's actual costs changed as the total number produced increased. This portrayal is known in the Pentagon and the defense industry as a learning curve. The thin lines show the planned learning curves contained in each of the five-year plans (FYDPs). All costs have the effects of inflation removed and are depicted in constant FY 2001 dollars.

Slide 5 should be read as follows: We know from slides 3 and 4 that the first year of F-18A's production was 1979; this is denoted by the leftmost "ball" in Slide 5. Moving to the right, each successive "ball" represents a successive year, and the horizontal distance from the preceding "ball" represents the annual purchases for that year.

Perhaps an example will make this clearer: The first seven years of production take us from FY 1979 to 1985 and are depicted by the left-most seven "balls." The horizontal distance covered by the heavy black line in Slide 5 indicates we bought a total of about 400 F-18s over these seven years. The downward slope of the heavy line shows that actual unit costs declined from about $113 to $41 million per copy during this period. So, as would be expected, marginal costs declined as production increased. But the important point to note is that these costs did not decline as fast and as far as predicted by a wide margin.

This can be seen if we compare the actual costs to the F-18's predicted costs (i.e. the thin lines). Note how the earliest plans (the thin lines furthest to the left) are far below the solid black line. Slide 5 tells us that the early plans predicted that the 400th F-18A would cost about $20 million, but it actually cost about $41 million. So, we have a mismatch between plans and reality, and even though actual costs declined from $113 to $41 million per copy between 1979 and 1985, the 400th F-18 still cost twice a much as predicted by the costs in the pre-production estimates that were used to justify the High-Low Mix modernization policy. Several points should be noted: First, most of the cost growth occurred in the first six years of production (i.e., between 1979 and 1984)— precisely when money was being added to the predicted budgets (Slide 4). Second, the cost growth in Slide 5 associated with the budget cutbacks made after 1986 (Slide 3) was far less disruptive than the cost growth that occurred in the pre-production stage of the F-18's acquisition life cycle, when money was being added to the program. Finally, the mismatches continued year after year, notwithstanding feedback that actual costs were exceed ing predicted costs; suggesting habitual behavior was driving the planning process.

The Defense Power Games

A repetitive bias to grossly understate future costs is typical of programs in the early stages of their acquisition life cycles. Our database contains a large number of programs exhibiting patterns similar to those of the F-18. In part, this bias is a natural result of uncertainty—as weapons get more complex, it becomes more difficult to predict what they will eventually cost. But more importantly, in my opinion, the bias reflects the first step in an ubiquitous two-step bureaucratic gaming strategy, known as Front Loading and Political Engineering. These strategies are explained in detail in a report that can be down loaded from the internet.

> Brutally stated, the aim of this gaming
> strategy is to turn on the money spigot and
> lock it open.

Front loading is the art of planting seed money today while downplaying the future consequences of a decision to spend that money. While it takes many forms, the most well known form is the so-called "Milestone II Buy-In," a deliberately "low-balled" estimate of future costs made to obtain a Milestone II approval in a weapons acquisition program. A Milestone II approval is crucially important, because it allows an acquisition program to move into concurrent engineering and manufacturing development (EMD). Once EMD is approved, the defense contractor can begin to "invest" contract dollars (i.e., tax dollars) in building a geographically distributed production base as well as a nationwide network of suppliers. The EMD decision, in effect, gives the contractor permission to use public money to build his political protection network by systematically spreading subcontracts and production facilities to as many congressional districts as possible. This spreading operation is the second step in the gaming strategy and is known as political engineering.

The goal is to raise the political stakes before the true costs of the front-loaded program become apparent. By the time these costs emerge, as they clearly did in the case of the F-18, the series of sequential adjustments in the succession FYDPs have bought enough time and desensitized decision makers to the effects of additional production cutbacks, while the political cost of a fundamental redirection (i.e., termination) has become prohibitive. So, decision-makers on both sides of the Potomac take the easy way out: they cut back production rates to reduce total costs in order to protect the jobs and profits of their constituents. Viewed in the context of the defense power games, production stretch-outs, like those in Side 3, were a predictable, indeed inevitable, consequence of a decision to front load the F-18 into the budget in the late 1970s and early 1980s.

While these power games may work to get programs started in the short term, they create a brain lock that produces a vicious cycle of decay over the long term.

The Boom and Bust Cycle of Decay

The "low-balled" cost projections made during the pre-production phase of a weapon's life cycle permit too many new programs to get stuffed into the out years of the FYDP. This sets the stage for repeated increments of cost growth and ever rising pressure to grow the entire defense budget.

But the budget cannot grow as fast as the unit costs of front-loaded programs increase and eventually a retrenchment sets in. At the same time, the effects of political engineering paralyze decision-makers and induce them to absorb the cost growth through inefficient expediencies, like repeated production stretch-outs in lieu of terminations. The lower rates of production naturally decrease the rate of inventory turnover, which increases the age of weapons and makes them more expensive to operate, thereby driving up the operating budget. But the increasing age of the equipment also increases the pressure to transfer money from the operating budget to the modernization budget, while the rising cost of operating the older weapons makes it more difficult to do so. Consequently, cost pressure builds up rapidly over time, and a kind of boom and bust cycle is born: Budget retrenchments like those in the 1970s and 1990s make problems worse, which are followed by budget expansions that naturally overreach when the front loaders and political engineers plant the seeds for anther round of outyear underfunding problems, as happened in 1980s. Over time, the cycle of decay takes the form of the so-called death spiral of shrinking combat forces, decreasing rates of modernization, aging weapons inventories, with the rising cost of operations creating continual pressure to reduce readiness.

Slide 6 (*see* http://www.d-n-i.net/fcs/spinney_testimony_060402.htm) portrays the outer manifestations of this boom and bust cycle. It compares the history of the defense budgets predicted by the FYDPs (the lines) to the history of actual budgets (the bars). Note that Slide 6, unlike the data in Slide 1, includes the effects of inflation; this is necessary because of data limitations.

The pattern of mismatches in Slide 6 suggests a dynamically unstable system capable of steadily increasing growth pressures ending with grotesque overreaching. A comparison of the 1970s to the 1990s sheds light on its underlying dynamics and places the current burst of growth in perspective.

The 1970s, like the 1990s were periods of post war budget retrenchments and reduced growth, producing a general pattern of low rates of weapons production, aging forces, and emerging readiness problems. But these periods were alike in another way: Each was characterized by the front loading of a substantial number of new high-cost modernization programs into the development pipeline. The programs, being in the early stages of the acquisition cycles, had uncertainties like the F-18 example discussed above. This created a growing bow wave of unspent balances in the modernization accounts during each decade.

Moreover, in each period, the growing readiness problems coupled with the rising cost of operations precluded a funding strategy that shifted substantial resources from the readiness accounts to the modernization accounts. Consequently, as each decade progressed, the pressure to increase the defense budget increased, and FYDPs were gradually ratcheted upward to accommodate the growing internal pressure (the effects of high inflation added to the pressure in the 1970s but not in the 1990s). The internal pressure built up in the 1970s exploded in the 1980s and the FYDP predictions leaped away from any resemblance to reality. The rapid growth of the most recent FYDP projections in Slide 6 suggest that the pressure is again building up rapidly and the internal dynamic may be poised for yet another round of explosive overreaching.

The exploding growth of internal pressure is also suggested by the data in the most recent Selected Acquisition Report (SAR) sent to Congress. The SAR describes the funding status of most of the major acquisition programs in the modernization pipeline. Its data includes information on each program's prior expenditures, its current budget, and the amount remaining to be spent (i.e., the unspent balance). The ratio of a program's unspent balance to its current budget tells us how many years it would take to buy out the program, if spending remained at the current level and there was no cost growth. A rising ratio would indicate a shift to new programs (and a preponderance of "low-balled" pre-production cost estimates) in the SAR mix, which implies greater uncertainty, and a growing bow wave, both of which would increase the internal pressure to grow the defense budget more rapidly over the long term. In September 1971, for example, that ratio equaled 4.6 years. By 1979, just prior the budget's liftoff in the

1980s, the ratio stood at 8.1 years. According to the data in the most recent SAR (December 2001), that ratio now stands at 18.1 years (and that does not include an estimate for the unspent balances in the National Missile Defense Program!), with the unspent balance being the largest on record.

Interim Summary

Let me now bring the entire discussion of Part I together. We can think of the Defense Department as a living goal-seeking organism. The procedures of PPBS are the tools used by the collective brain to set goals by matching the organism's inner workings to the threats, opportunities, and constraints in its external environment. The FYDP, being the end product of that brain's activities is therefore the essential source of financial management information that describes this matchup.

But the FYDP's description is fatally flawed. The information in the historical FYDP database cannot pass an audit and the data used in its planning projections are unreliable, arbitrary and, in important cases, systematically biased to grossly understate the future consequences of current decisions. These problems were avoided during the retrenchment of the 1990s, while the internal pressure built up rapidly in the latter half of the decade, and there are now signs that the PPBS may be about to go unstable like it did in the 1980s in reaction to the retrenchment of the 1970s.

Consider, please, the dire implications of this breakdown: Without reliable information, there can be no confidence that the required matchup between the Defense organism and its environment has been or will be achieved. When such a condition of uncertainty persists, the interaction of chance with necessity guarantees that it is only a matter of time before dangerous mismatches creep insensibly into the relationship between organism and its environment. When this occurs, the unreliable information in the database creates a kind of virtual reality that disorients decision makers, yet keeps them busy, thereby blocking corrective action, while the internal activities shaped by their decisions become progressively disconnected from and vulnerable to the threats and constraints in the real world.

Moreover, without decisive action to correct the source of the disorientation—i.e., the corrupted information—the disorientation will grow worse over time, leading inevitably to a growing sense of confusion and disorder that feeds back into and magnifies the disorientation even further. Eventually the breakdown in the goal seeking process will produce paralysis, and the activities of the organism will be directed more by inner workings of its constituent factions than by the requirements of the environment. Naturally, such a self-referencing process would become far more dysfunctional if the external environment changed suddenly and unexpectedly, as did the national security environment in the 1990s.

The bottom line: we face crisis that will take extraordinary action to resolve. The next section is a strawman proposal for building a strategy that works in the real world of uncertain threats, changing opportunities, and constrained resources.

Part II

Teach the Pentagon to Think Before It Spends

The FYDP is a strategic vision of the future, yet it does not account for the future consequences of current decisions. This kind of planning is by no means a new phenomenon in the Pentagon. Politicians and defense intellectuals have complained for years that the Pentagon cannot determine priorities because it has no strategy. The legislation passed by Congress in 1996 mandating a Quadrennial Defense Review was but one example of this long-standing frustration. Nevertheless, in one strategic review after another, the critics have recommended and defense planners have executed the same step-by-step procedure to solve the strategy conundrum:

- Identify national goals and the threats to these goals.
- Determine the strategy to counter the threats.
- Determine the forces needed to execute the strategy.
- Determine the budget needed to build and maintain these forces.

That this Cartesian procedure cannot solve the strategic puzzle ought to be clear from the recurrent calls for yet more strategy reviews. While this mode of thinking is not a direct cause of the readiness, modernization, and bookkeeping problems discussed above, I believe the formulaic determinism of this procedure shackles our minds and prevents us from realizing a solution to these problems. This becomes clear when one examines how the logic underpinning this chain of dependencies prevents an interaction with the environment.

In theory, each step of the four-step procedure depends on the preceding step but is independent of the subsequent step. Strategy is the key link in this chain; it ties our relations to the outside world (goals and threats) to our internal conditions (forces and budgets). But it is wrong to think that strategy depends only on external factors, like goals and threats and is independent of internal conditions.

The fatal flaw in the logic of the PPBS procedure becomes apparent if one applies the four-step formula to a simple military problem. Let's assume a battalion commander receives a "mission order" to counter a threat on the flank of his division. Under the concept of mission orders he is told what to do but not how to do it. He therefore needs to formulate a strategy for accomplishing his mission. If he used the PPBS method to solve his "strategic" problem, he would define his strategy before he examined how personnel or materiel limitations might shape or limit his maneuver and fire options. His operational plan, for example, would not be affected by the fact that one-third of his battalion had been wounded in a previous engagement and the other two thirds were short of ammo. This is nonsense.

In the real world, strategy is the art of the possible, and any strategic decision-making procedure that ignores how one's internal constraints might limit or shape what is possible is a contradiction in terms.

A decision-making strategy should link our relations with the external world (goals and threats) to our internal conditions (the constraints of forces and resources). A biologist would view strategic planning as a selection process that harmonizes the internal structure of the organism with the demands of its environment. One side of the link does not uniquely determine the other, but each simultaneously feeds back on and shapes the other. The environment shapes the organism while the organism shapes the environment. Like evolution, a strategic decision-making process should be a creative process of combination and selection in an ever-changing, co-evolving domain consisting of external threats and opportunities on the one hand and changing internal structures and limitations on the other. The shaping effects of positive feedback in this interaction make strategic planning a nonlinear, non-sequential mental activity. That is one reason why intuitive behavior is so important on the battlefield.

Viewed from this perspective, strategic decision-making is a synthetic activity and is by its nature simultaneous, constructive, creative, and adaptive.

Compare this richness of this view to the sterility exhibited by the four-step process used in the PPBS. Its rigid procedure is an analytical recipe for a dissection that follows a predictable, sequential, non-adaptive path. By its nature, it is not creative, which is the main reason why repeated strategic reviews always produce a plan that protects the status quo. The analytical elegance of the recipe may appeal to intellectuals housed in Cartesian towers, but the primitive assumption that strategy uniquely determines forces and budgets, in effect, presumes resources (money) are unlimited.

In the real world, where messy bureaucratic conflicts bubble up out of a clash of competing agendas, this kind of unconstrained thinking provides no incentive for making the hard decisions needed to discover a harmonious set of priorities among incommensurable but nevertheless competing options. Unconstrained thinking simply adds things together into unaffordable wish lists.

Furthermore, by ignoring internal constraints like resource limitations, our strategists have abdicated their responsibility for hard decisions. That puts the onus on others to make the real decisions—the bean counters, budgeteers, and porkbarrelers. These people have different agendas—as evidenced by the fact that recent votes in Congress suggest that preservation of jobs is now the real goal of our nation's defense "strategy."

A strategic planning process should discover priorities by systematically exploring the interplay among the uncertainties surrounding the external threats and opportunities, on the one hand, and those uncertainties surrounding our internal structures and constraints, on the other. The following proposal sketches out a combination-and-selection process that explicitly addresses the co-evolving essence of strategic planning. Rather than viewing priorities as an input, which is another way of saying we start with answer, the following proposal views priorities as an output, or more precisely, it views priorities as an emergent property of a complex adaptive tradeoff process.

Strategic Planning as a Complex Adaptive Process—Theory

By far, the most important internal constraint shaping the evolution of our military capabilities is the perpetual budget squeeze. Since this squeeze is a consequence of habitual behavior patterns that produce an economic relationship wherein costs always grow faster than budgets, a necessary condition for a competent decision-making activity is to make the long-term consequences of this asymmetry evident before decision-makers lock themselves into a given course of action. But a requirement to make the long term consequences of current decisions visible before the fact embodies a necessary pre-condition: Reliable information.

> Job 1, therefore, is to fix the Pentagon's accounting problems, or at least reduce them to a acceptable level.

Fixing the books is not sufficient to produce a sound strategy, but it is self-evident that a more reliable description of our internal conditions, as well as the future consequences of changes to those conditions, would give planners the wherewithal to better understand the strengths and weaknesses of a given defense program in terms of its perceived matchup, or mismatch, with external reality.

The greater knowledge accompanying a more accurate description of our readiness and modernization problems, combined with state-of-the-art computer software technology, would make it possible for planners to understand how internal structures and capabilities of our military forces would change over a range of long-term budget scenarios—from optimistic to pessimistic. Under the different constraints imposed by each scenario, planners could determine the marginal effects of different force structure combinations in terms of achieving goals and neutralizing threats. By using a trial-and-error process of combination (which unleashes creativity and imagination) and evaluation (which uses testing and logic to discipline the imagination), planners could maximize strengths and minimize weaknesses of alternative combinations in order to gradually select (i.e., evolve) the most capable force structure option within the constraints of each given budget scenario. In so doing, planners would use their judgment to discover priorities (which are a reflection of the opportunity costs of incommensurable capabilities) by evolving the least painful program cuts as they move from higher to lower budget levels. The iterative process of combination and evaluation would also identify the best way to add programs, should the budget come in at higher levels. By disciplining the selection process in this way, priorities—or core values—would emerge naturally out of a free competition in a marketplace of ideas.

Contingency planning and sensitivity analyses are common enough in war planning and business planning; there is no reason why they can not be done for defense program planning. Three phases of operation are needed to translate this abstract idea into concrete action. The first phase cleans up the books, the second phase constructs service level contingency plans, and the third phase synthesizes the service-level plans into a comprehensive Defense Department contingency plan.

Phase I: A Crash Program to Clean the Books

* Fund the War on Terrorism on a "Pay as You Go" Basis
* Freeze the Core Program to Clean Up the Books

We have seen that DoD's annual budget, as submitted to Congress, is the linchpin of an accounting continuum (the FYDP database) reaching backward in time to record actual expenditures and forward for five or six years to record future expenditures. Looking backward, the coherency of a defense strategy (and its supporting force structure, modernization and readiness levels) depends in part on the consequences of past expenditures. But the auditing problems revealed by the General Accounting Office and the Defense Department's Inspector General and the Friedman Report prove we cannot link past expenditures to today's budget/policy decisions.

The Plans/Reality Mismatch shows that future years of the FYDP database are also disconnected from the budget. The case study of the F-18 (Slides 3, 4, and 5) is but one example of hundreds of FYDP/reality mismatches evident over the last twenty-six years. At the macroscopic level (Slide 6), these mismatches have created a boiling programmatic soup in which "low balled" cost estimates breed like metastasizing cancer cells throughout the entire defense program. Biased numbers hide the future consequences of current policy decisions, permitting too many programs to get stuffed into the "outyears" of the long-range budget plan. This sets the stage for unaffordable budget bow waves, repeating cycles of cost growth and procurement stretch-outs, decreasing rates of modernization and older weapons, shrinking forces, and continual pressure to bail out the self destructing modernization program by robbing the readiness accounts.

The end of the Cold War in 1990 provided a unique opportunity to take decisive action without jeopardizing our national security, but that opportunity was squandered over the next decade. And now the open-ended war on terrorism makes the required fix far more difficult.

But the war should not be used as an excuse to live with the status quo. To be sure, a decisive correction will be more painful today than it otherwise might have been, yet the readiness and modernization problems that emerged in the late

1990s, together with the exploding bow wave, cry more urgently for action to put the Defense Department on a more sustainable pathway into the future. Moreover, the crisis in intensified by the fact that we must get our house in order before the demographic time bomb of retiring baby boomers starts sucking money out of the federal tax base early in the next decade. To be decisive, the military services must first produce better decision-making information. It will take at least a year to begin the necessary book-cleaning operation, yet during that time, we must provide the military with resources to fight the war on terrorism.

The President, the Secretary of Defense, and the leaders of Congress should announce that, henceforth, the war on terrorism will be financed on a pay-as-you-go basis, with special requests made to Congress at appropriate intervals using the instrumentalities of supplemental budget requests. While this policy may seem unorthodox at first glance, the red ribbon in Slide 1 and the ongoing use of war supplementals suggest that the cost of the war is simply being added to the core defense program. War financing is already evolving on a pay-as-you-go basis as a practical matter of fact. This recommendation would simply extend a formal recognition to this fact. Moreover, the comptroller organizations in Office of the Secretary of Defense and the military services should set up special war financing branches to prepare the supplemental requests on a standardized basis. The pay-as-you-go procedure would have the added benefit of facilitating informed debate over the course the war on terrorism by making its costs more evident to the President, the Secretary of Defense, the Congress, and the American people.

In parallel, with questions of war financing now off the table, the President and the Secretary of Defense should immediately stop the ongoing FY 2004 2009 budgeting cycle and order a one-year PPBS freeze at the FY 2003 spending level or whatever budget level Congress appropriates for the FY 2003.

The purpose of the PPBS freeze is to buy the time needed to begin scrubbing the books. During this period, decision-makers in the Defense Department should strive continually to maintain or increase their flexibility to make future decisions (which will be needed in Phases II and III). To this end, they would make no new long-term contractual commitments during the program freeze. All acquisition milestones would be postponed, but existing programs, like the F-22, would continue at their current level on a "work-in-process" basis. On the other hand, decision makers would proceed with any actions that would increase the Defense Department's flexibility or adaptability into the future, like planned terminations, cutbacks, or base closings. Finally, they should remove special-access clearances for all programs, except those intelligence programs requiring protection of sources and methods. Black clearances stifle accountability, they increase costs, and they hide unprincipled behavior. Doubters should study the Navy's A-12 debacle, in which the contractors used the government's illegal behavior as an excuse for their failure to perform.

Obviously, a program freeze will be disruptive and create economic inefficiencies in the short term, but unfortunately, that is the price leaders must pay now to obtain greater efficiency and strategic coherence in the long term.

While programs are frozen, the audit agencies of the Defense Department will undertake a maximum effort to do comprehensive financial audits of the expenditure control system, the FYDP database, and the assets assigned to each organization. One of their main goals would be to build a solid foundation for assembling a DoD-wide double-entry accounting system for tracking transactions, matching transactions to appropriations, and building an effective management accounting system so decision makers have the wherewithal to know what is going on inside their own organization. At the same time, war planners would commence a comprehensive readiness audit of current condition in each military service (including the real factors affecting morale, retention, training, doctrine development, and material condition). Using the more realistic cost numbers produced by the financial audits, each military service would then build a new FY 2004 to 2009 high-readiness baseline program by re-pricing the procurement and O&M programs in the approved program (i.e., the existing FY 2003 to 2007 program, adding in any un-funded requirements—see below) that was submitted to Congress in February 2002.

Taken together, these re-priced budget estimates would become the new DoD baseline budget scenario, which will require substantially larger budgets than the FY 2003–2007 FYDP approved by the President sent to Congress. The stage is now set for Phase II.

Phase II—The Construction of Component Planning Options

In Phase II, Planners in each military service and independent defense agency would use the more reliable information produced by Phase I to as a basis for examining how the internal capabilities and structures of their service would change over a range of optimistic to pessimistic budget scenarios (notional scenarios are defined at the end of this section), assuming each service's historic share of the total defense budget remained constant in each scenario. These shares will be subject to change in Phase III, but they are necessary in Phase II to get the process started.

The objective of Phase II is to discover the parochial priorities of each military service in the context of that service's capabilities and worldview, according to the theory of combination and selection outlined above.

To this end, military planners in each service would be free to construct their most effective force package within each given budget scenario by maximizing its strengths and minimizing its weaknesses, while conforming to that scenario's overall resource constraints. Service planners would be free to use their parochial perspectives to define the threats they will face. The only restriction on that definition would be a requirement to classify each threat guiding their planning options according to the taxonomies of Second, Third, and Fourth Generation Warfare. A general introduction describing these taxonomies can be found on the web. This generational classification in necessary to establish a common doctrinal frame of reference for evolving and evaluating the global syntheses of Phase III and ensuring proper resource allocations.

Subject to this restriction, planners in each service would be free to use their own perspectives and judgment to shape and identify preferred force structures (together with the supporting modernization strategies and readiness states) in a way they think best addresses the threat uncertainty. By constraining their planning options to each budget level, service planners would have to evolve a selection process that naturally identifies opportunity costs and their own service's parochial priorities by identifying the least painful programmatic adjustments as one moves from higher to lower budget levels and the most beneficial adjustments as one moves from lower to higher budget levels. Each military service would conclude the sensitivity analyses of Phase II by producing a comprehensive written net assessment of the force package selected for each budget level. Such a net assessment would identify the long-term military consequences (i.e., the preferred strategy, strengths, weaknesses, risks, and opportunities) of the force structures, together with the supporting readiness states and modernization strategies for each package. The final product at each budget level, together with the net assessments and the common taxonomy under which each net assessment is structured, become a Component Planning Option, or CPO. The selected set of CPOs evolved by each service in Phase II for each budget scenario become the basic building blocks for the defense-wide or global selection process in Phase III.

A crucial decision for Phases II and III is identifying a realistic and appropriate range of future budget scenarios. The remainder of this sub-section discusses this choice.

Tighter budget constraints are necessary to discipline the selection process at the microscopic and the macroscopic level of organization. It is therefore absolutely imperative that these budgets scenarios span a realistic range of the future possibilities. The choice, therefore, boils down to a question of how much is enough over the long term. Like most normative questions, the question of how much we should spend is a matter of judgment for which there will never be a clear answer.

While many factors combine to shape this judgment, two general ones stand out and must be explicitly accounted for in any strategic planning process. The first is external. This relates to the threats facing our forces and what our nation wants to do in the world. The second is internal. This relates to the constraints that limit our action. Internal constraints define what is possible over the long term. They require an explicit consideration of internal limitations, like available technology, evolving demographic conditions, and competing non-defense priorities, as well as general economic restrictions.

How Much Spending Is Enough?—Accounting for the External Threat

The conventional Second and Third Generation threats posed by competing nation states are enormously diminished compared to the Soviet threat of the Cold War.

Using data in compiled by the International Institute for Strategic Studies (IISS), Slide 7 (*see* http://www.d-n-i.net/fcs/spinney_testimony_060402.htm)

shows how the US now stands alone in the world, like a colossus, planning to spend as much on defense in FY 2003 as the next 20 largest nations combined.

According to the ISS, the combined defense budgets of the three nations cited most often as threats—the so-called axis of evil made up of Iran, Iraq, and N. Korea—are less than $12 billion, or only about three per cent of the US proposed defense budget for 2003.

To be sure, the spread of non-state Fourth Generation threats, like al-Qa'ida, around the globe represent increasingly dangerous threats, but the forces needed to counter these threats do not require the large numbers of high cost, hi-tech weapons or the large standing armies needed to fight the industrial wars characterized by Second and Third Generation Warfare among nations. Nevertheless the overwhelming bulk of the defense budget, together with the current combat force structure and supporting modernization programs, continues to be devoted to conventional and nuclear forces designed to fight Second and Third Generation threats. Only a small portion of the defense budget is allocated to developing, building, and training forces for the irregular requirements of Fourth Generation Warfare, like the war on terrorism.

Clearly, current levels of defense spending are driven more by the legacy of the Cold War and the internal dynamics described in Part 1 than by the external threats we face.

How Might We Begin to Better Rationalize This Situation in Terms of Real Needs?

Perhaps a couple of examples will help place this question into perspective. The first relates to the Royal Navy and the second relates to Israel. In the late Nineteenth Century, the Royal Navy also bestrode the world's oceans like a colossus when compared to other Navies, but, it should be noted, to a lesser extent than the U.S. military relates to the rest of world's conventional forces today. Strategic planners in the Royal Navy adopted what came to be known as the Two Power Standard to maintain their superiority. They used this standard to plan for the Royal Navy's budgets, particularly its battleship modernization program. The Two Power Standard simply meant that the Royal Navy should maintain a battleship fleet that was at least as powerful as the next two biggest fleets combined, which were those of United States and Germany. Note that this standard was applied to friend as well as foe. If we applied the logic of this standard to the current U.S. defense budget, the next two biggest spenders would be Russia and China (about $102B total). So, a Two Power Standard applied to the United States defense budget would reduce the current budget by over 70 percent.

A second example illustrating the judgment of how much spending is enough is the case of Israel. Israel faces direct strategic threats from Iraq and Syria but also has to consider the potential threats posed by organized military capabilities of Jordan, Egypt, Iran, Libya, and Saudi Arabia in its strategic planning (for the purpose of illustrating this point, we can neglect the additional capabilities of any other Arab Counties, like Kuwait or the UAE, etc.). If Israel applied the Royal

Navy's standard to the defense budgets of the above listed adversaries, we could say that Israel maintains a One-Quarter Power Standard. Nevertheless, few doubt Israel's capability to defend itself with its conventional forces in a Second/Third Generation war (like that of 1967 or 1973) against these nations. On the other hand, Intifada I, the debacle in Lebanon, and the ongoing Intifada II, all raise serious questions about the capability of Israel's military to defeat the threats posed by a Fourth Generation adversary. But these Fourth Generation threats, serious as they may be, are hardly related to relative size of the defense budgets of Israel, let alone the United States.

Some might be tempted to argue that a One Quarter Power Standard by Israel is misleading, because Israeli spending is far more efficient than its adversaries. This is true, no doubt. But this argument is a double edged sword, because it would also apply to the Twenty Power Standard of the United States, in effect making the overwhelming nature of that comparison even larger, particularly when applied against the likes of Iraq, Iran, or North Korea.

Our military exists to cope with the real threats to our nation's security. But the bulk of U.S. spending is directed toward maintaining and modernizing its second and third generation military capabilities left over from the Cold War with a modern equivalent of a twenty-power standard.

On the other hand the U.S. is paying the budgetary equivalent of lip service to Fourth Generation threats which are clearly becoming more prevalent and dangerous, as the al-Aqsa Intifada and the war against terrorism show.

Taken together, (1) the low level of defense spending by other nations states suggests that the likely range of possible budget scenarios ought to include lower spending options for the long term as planning scenarios, and (2) the growing importance of Fourth Generation Warfare (4GW) suggests that planners ought to begin allocating more effort to building a force and training people to meet these threats. The 4GW requirement makes it necessary for the services to provide information on how the Component Planning Options produced under the different budget scenarios in Phase II would conform to a taxonomy of second, third, and fourth generation warfare. The notional options described below will provide budget scenarios covering a range of power standards.

How Much Is Enough?—Accounting for Internal Constraints

The second factor shaping the selection of a range of relevant budget scenarios relates to what can be realistically afforded and justified over the long term. This factor is internal, and it derives from the long-term pressure to balance the budget while financing the increasing burden of Medicare and Social Security as well as other domestic needs, like education and infrastructure.

There are signs that these constraints may be increasing in the near term, and they are certain to increase sharply over the long term.

The projections of large budget surpluses over the long term are evaporating rapidly. In January 2002, the Congressional Budget Office (CBO) projected that if the tax and spending policies remained the same, the government would run surpluses totaling about $1.6 trillion over the 10 years between 2002 and 2011, a reduction of $4 trillion, or 71 per cent, from the $5.6 trillion surplus over the same period it had projected only a year earlier.

The Congressional Budget Office (CBO) released a report on October, 2000 analyzing the federal government's long term budget outlook. CBO concluded policy changes to Social Security and Medicare (read changes to reduce expenditures per capita) would be needed, because under current policies " . . . federal deficits are likely to reappear and eventually drive federal debt to unsustainable levels," once the baby boomers start collecting social security and Medicare. If those programs are not changed, CBO concluded in January 2002, decision makers will face the prospect of approving steep tax increases, big cuts in other government spending, or large budget deficits.

Let us now bring the threads of discussion together to identify a range of budget scenarios to guide the conduct of Phases II and III. The absurdity of maintaining a 20 Standard in a world made up mostly of friends, the vastly diminished nature of second and third generation national threats, the rise non-state threats practicing Fourth Generation Warfare, the vanishing surplus, and the looming financial crisis in supporting an aging population all combine to suggest it would be prudent for defense planners to examine the future consequences of alternative courses of action in the context of decreasing defense budgets as well as increasing budgets.

How Much Is Enough? Hypothetical Budget Scenarios

Decision makers, therefore, need to anticipate the possibility that the budget projections in Slide 1 will unravel like those in the mid-1980s (Slide 6).

The only way to break out of the destructive boom and bust cycle is to think through the problem before it occurs.

This requires planners to examine the impact of budget uncertainties (and cost uncertainties) before the fact. This can be done through a contingency analysis of the alternative programmatic changes flowing from a range of pessimistic budget scenarios as well as those attending the optimistic scenarios. Once the effects of these changes are understood, planners can synthesize the mix of force options best able to cope with or adjust to the effects of the uncertainty. In so doing, planners can discover a priority system that identifies what is truly important and what is nice to have. Under this approach, priorities are not set arbitrarily before the fact but are viewed as emergent properties discovered via an iterative trial-and-error process of combination and selection.

Bearing in mind that the war on terrorism will be funded on a pay-as-you-go basis, Slide 8 (*see* http://www.d-n-i.net/fcs/spinney_testimony_060402.htm) introduces a range of three alternative spending scenarios to the core Defense program that was put into place in August 2001 (see discussion Slide 1). These four notional scenarios are examples of the kind of constraints that could be used to guide the trade offs in Phases II and III. During the service-controlled deliberations of Phase II, the budget share allocated to each military service and defense agency would be determined by the average proportion of the total budget it received during the first decade of the post-Cold War era (1991–2000). These shares equate to 26% for the Army, 31% for the Navy and Marine Corps, and 30% for the Air Force, with the remainder being allocated to the various defense agencies.

Slide 8 should be read as follows. Using the more reliable pricing information produced by the book cleaning operation of Phase I, planners in each service would assemble and price out four budget scenarios based on the overall constraints portrayed in Slide 8. These options include–

1. The Core Program, which would an extend the program put into place in August 2001 (see Slide 1) for two year and build to a 23 Power Standard by 2009, assuming other countries maintain a budget freeze. Under this this option, the defense budget in 2009 would be 14% higher than that averaged during the 40 years of Cold War.
2. The second scenario (0% real growth per year) would freeze the budget in constant dollars at 98% of the cold-war average, resulting in a 13 Power Standard in 2009.
3. The third scenario would would decrease the core program by 1.5% per year, declining to a 10 Power Standard by 2009 or 90% of the cold-war average.
4. The fourth scenario would decrease the core program by 3% per year, dropping to a 9 Power Standard by 2009, or 82% of the budget averaged during the Cold War.

Phase III—The Construction of Strategic Planning Options

Phase III operates according to the following principle: What is best for the individual military service may not be best for the Defense Department or the nation.

The aim of Phase III is to synthesize the parochial priorities of Component Planning Options (CPOs) produced by each service in Phase II into a coherent system of national defense priorities that reflects and exploits the changed conditions of the post-Cold War era. This task should be the responsibility of the Joint Chiefs of Staff (JCS) and the Office of the Secretary of Defense (OSD). In Phase III, JCS and OSD would combine the CPOs produced by the military services in Phase II into a comprehensive set of DoD-level Strategic Planning Options (SPOs) covering the four budget scenarios portrayed above.

The force options in the 12 CPOs (4 from each service) produced in Phase II, plus those of the defense agencies, including their net assessments, provide the building blocks of a true policy-level decision-making process. Like their service counterparts in Phase II, planners in JCS and OSD would use a combination-and-selection process to continuously maximize the strengths and minimize the weaknesses of the total force while conforming to the macroscopic budget constraints of each scenario. In this way, they would systematically explore the marginal effects of different macroscopic combinations. Creative tradeoffs among the variety of individual force packages might reveal interesting new macroscopic possibilities. The most effective Option #2 DoD SPO, for example, might combine a Option #4 Air Force package with a Option #1 Navy/Marine Corps package and a Option #3 Army package.

Perhaps a hypothetical example of this JCS/OSD SPO will make the idea more concrete: Option #2 would freeze the DoD budget at its current level out to FY 2009, resulting in a 13 Power Standard in FY 2009, implying a reduction of $57 billion from the level projected for FY 2009 by the Core Program. Under the tighter restrictions of this constraint, strategic planners might choose to spend far less on the Air Force (an Option #4 CPO). They might do this by transferring a very large percentage of its forces to the reserves, which are noted for their excellence, and closing a large number of bases, thus preserving its combat power for a mobilization/reinforcement scenario. They might also choose to reduce the Army's budget to an Option #3 CPO by eliminating some active forces and transforming its active/reserve divisional structure into a much smaller and leaner force structure based on heavy, light, and medium weight battlegroups, made more flexible in expeditionary 4GW scenarios by a de-centralized command and control system. Such a force would be more deployable in the short term, but would preserve the balance of a large continental army, should we need to expand it sometime in the distant future. These reductions could permit planners to fund the more expensive, re-priced Navy/Marine Option #1 CPO while conforming to the tighter constraints of the Option #2 budget projection.

Senior planners might argue that this hypothetical Option #2 SPO better adapts the military to the realities of the post-Cold War era. It returns the United States to its traditional military posture, based on intervention, as opposed to forward basing of large forces, because it:

- Reduces the budget;
- Maintains the expeditionary capabilities needed to protect our historical interests in the world's littorals, with the Navy and Marine Corps being the rapid deployment option, reinforced by the more mobile Army battlegroups and mobilized Air Force reserves, if necessary.
- Retains a capability to field the heavy air/ground combat power needed to offset any major power imbalances in Europe or East Asia, should the need re-emerge sometime in the distant future. The supporting modernization programs, nuclear forces, and programs in the independent defense agencies would also be tailored to fit the world conditions that are implied by this strategic choice.

The information produced in Phase II would permit the exploration of such tradeoffs by JCS and OSD planners as they search for and evolve truly national priorities out of the parochial priorities of each service. JCS and OSD would conclude their efforts by producing a macroscopic net assessment for each preferred DoD SPO. This net assessment would include the assumptions and tradeoffs made, an analysis of its deficiencies and limitations, its impact on national security in terms of achieving goals and neutralizing threats (categorized by the taxonomy described earlier), and the best military strategy for working around its limitations. The final report, when approved by the President, would be a comprehensive strategy coupled to the skeleton of a new FYDP, complete with global priorities and pre planned hedging options to cope with uncertainty.

The systematic combination and selection process at the different levels of organization would provide the ingredients of a seamless information system that permits decision-makers to shift their focus back and forth among the microscopic and macroscopic levels of organization. This kind of decision-making information would reveal the true cost of a microscopic decision by forcing an examination of its macroscopic consequences prior to making commitments. If, for example, AF planners insisted on buying more B 2s in each CPO or SPO, they would have to eliminate more and more other programs—such as F-22 fighters, carrier battlegroups or army divisions—as they moved toward lower budget levels. These tradeoffs, coupled with excursions into the consequences of cost growth, would reveal when the cost of the B 2 becomes prohibitive in terms of the incommensurable sacrifices made elsewhere. In this way, the reciprocal explorations of these microscopic and macroscopic uncertainties would enable planners to anticipate problems, tease out options, evolve priorities, and perhaps do things differently.

Faultfinders will be tempted to argue that the Phase I program freeze will create chaos in the middle of a war. This criticism is patently absurd for three reasons: First, it formally acknowledges the fact that the war is being funded on a pay-as-you-go basis, and by doing so, will make the costs of this war more transparent to the American people. Second, the defense program is already in chaos and the recently completed QDR and PPBS cycles did nothing to diminish it. Third, and most important, the Defense Department's bookkeeping mess makes a mockery of the principle of accountability and, by extension, the Constitution we have sworn to defend. Fixing the books eliminates a threat to constitutional governance by making our decisions transparent and understandable to the Congress and the American people. Moreover, it is a moral duty, given our oath to preserve and protect the Constitution.

Others may argue that threats should drive strategy, but this proposal has budgets driving strategy. This linear babble ignores the nonlinear nature of strategy, not to mention the changed conditions of the post-Cold War era. In the real world, actions to neutralize threats and the constraints limiting those actions continuously interact with and fold back on each other. This proposal enables planners to shape a real strategy precisely because it is designed to explore the co evolving interplay of threats, events, opportunities, internal structures and constraints.

It might be feared that even thinking about lower defense budgets will create a self fulfilling prophecy, because it will open the door to opportunistic budget-cutting by an irresponsible OSD or Congress. This argument plays well in the mendacious atmosphere of Washington. But it must be rejected for logical as well as moral reasons: To say that the Pentagon should continue producing irresponsible plans, because acting responsibly will provoke OSD or Congress into acting irresponsibly leads to the conclusion that we should deliberately misrepresent our needs; in other words, we are justified in committing a crime—lying to Congress—because we are morally superior.

Strategy is not a game; it is the art of the possible in a world where changing threats and constraints force us to choose between unpleasant or imperfect alternatives. The aim of any strategy should be to continuously improve our capacity to shape and adapt to these changes. To do this, we must continually strive to improve the "fit" of our plans to the reality we face today while preserving or increasing our fitness to cope with unpredictable changes in the future. If we want meaningful strategic priorities, we must understand the tradeoffs they imply before we make rigid commitments that lock us into a long-term, non-adaptive course of action. Who knows, with a little accountability, perhaps the Pentagon can learn to think before it spends. That might help the President and Congress adapt our military forces to the end of the Cold War, balance the budget, avoid a budget war with Social Security and Medicare, and preserve the integrity of the Constitution.

Franklin Spinney, a former Air Force officer, has worked in the Office of the Secretary of Defense since 1977.

Genghis John*

Franklin C. Spinney

Proceedings of the U.S. Naval Institute

July 1997, pp. 42–47

One hardly expects the Commandant of the Marine Corps to agree with a dovish former Rhodes Scholar, or an up-from-the-ranks, brass-bashing retired Army colonel, or a pig farmer from Iowa who wants to cut the defense budget. Yet, within days of each other in mid-March 1997, all four men wrote amazingly similar testimonials to the intellect and moral character of John Boyd, a retired Air Force colonel, who died of cancer on 9 March at the age of 70.

General Charles Krulak, our nation's top Marine, called Boyd an architect of victory in the Persian Gulf War. General Krulak was "awed" by Boyd's intellect, character, integrity, and his selfless devotion to our nation's welfare. James Fallows, Editor of U.S. News and World Report, claimed that Boyd's "ideas about weapons, leadership, and the very purpose of national security changed the modern military." Retired Army Colonel David Hackworth, one of our nation's most decorated combat soldiers, wrote that Boyd's "legacy will be that integrity—doing the hard right over the easy wrong—is more important than all the stars, all the plush executive suites and all the bucks." And in a 20 March speech, Senator Charles Grassley (R-IA) declared that John Boyd, "the leader of the Military Reform Movement," was a man who "always set the example of excellence—both morally and professionally."

What kind of man could unite the emotions of such disparate men?

I met Colonel John Boyd in 1973, when I went to work for him in the Pentagon as a 27-year-old captain in the Air Force. He already was a legend, yet his most important work lay before him. Over the next 23 years, my life became intertwined with this maddening mix of eccentricity, intellect, creativity, and moral courage—a mix that did not fit into neat compartments. Over a career that spanned 50 years, he evolved from "40-Second Boyd," to the "Mad Major," to the "Ghetto Colonel," to "Genghis John."

Boyd opened his military career as a 19-year-old draftee in the U.S. Army occupying Japan during the cold, wet winter of 1945–46. Morale was terrible. The

---

*Reprinted with permission of Naval Institute Press, www.usni.org. © 1997.

soldiers froze in damp tents, often eating uncooked K-rations, while their officers indulged themselves with hot food in warm quarters. Boyd led the inevitable revolt—the mud soldiers chopped down a wooden hangar and burned it to keep warm. The Army, being the Army, court-martialed Boyd for destroying government property, but Boyd, being Boyd, converted the trial into a referendum on leadership and responsibility. The officers lost, the troops got hot chow, and the military got its first look at John Boyd.

40-Second Boyd

He left the Army and went to college on the G.I. Bill, where he met his wife, Mary, a woman best described as a saint. He graduated with a degree in economics, was commissioned in the Air Force, and became a fighter pilot. He flew about 20 combat missions in F-86s at the tail end of the Korean War—enough to warrant his selection as one of the first instructors at the fledgling Fighter Weapons School at Nellis Air Force Base in Nevada. He designed the dogfight tactics curriculum and earned the nickname "40-Second Boyd" as a result of a standing bet that he could maneuver from a position of disadvantage (challenger on his tail) to advantage (positions reversed) in 40 seconds—or pay the challenger 40 dollars. One of Boyd's lifelong friends, Ron Catton, a retired fighter pilot, and one of the few ever to graduate from the Fighter Weapons School with a perfect score, told me that Boyd usually needed only 20 seconds to win, but liked a little insurance in case something went wrong.

Boyd never lost. By the late 1950s, he was widely regarded as the finest fighter pilot in the Air Force.

He personified the romantic image of a fighter jock—tall, lanky, wildly gesticulating, loud, and irrepressible, an in-your-face type of guy, who smoked long thin stogies and blew smoke in your face, while he shouted and sprayed saliva at you in a head-on attack, from two inches, nose to nose. But 40-Second Boyd's flamboyant exterior hid an incisive mind, and he was about to blossom into a warrior-scientist—the "Mad Major."

The Mad Major

In the late 1950s, he began this improbable mutation by teaching himself enough calculus to work out the formulas describing his view of the maneuver-countermaneuver aerial duel. He published his results in a book-length technical report, the Aerial Attack Study, a secret document that eventually spread throughout the Free World and became the international bible of air combat.

His next stop was Georgia Tech in Atlanta. The Air Force sent him there to learn industrial engineering, a standardized curriculum that forced him to take a survey course in thermodynamics—the science of heat and energy. On the way to class one day, he had a flash of insight: the laws of thermodynamics, particularly those governing the conservation and dissipation of energy, were like the tactical give-and-take of an air-to-air duel. It was the kind of insight that characterized his genius for using analogies to combine seemingly unrelated pieces of information, gleaned serendipitously from very different disciplines, into a new world view.

As any logician will tell you, reasoning by analogy is a very dangerous game for most mortals. False similarities can capture our imagination, restrict our vision, and seduce us into seeing things that do not exist. To the orderly, Cartesian thinkers of the self-styled defense intelligentsia, Boyd had a very spooky way of thinking. To make matters worse, he had an IQ of only 90, which he claimed was an advantage because it forced him to be more efficient.

Nevertheless, Boyd always seemed to end up with the winning answer when the bureaucracy begrudgingly permitted the free market of ideas to work its painful magic. Most people attributed his success to luck, but he had a secret weapon: his uninhibited imagination was tightly coupled to a maniacal discipline to follow the truth wherever it might lead—even if it meant trashing his own creations. Boyd subjected each new synthetic analogy to rigorous analysis and testing, rolling it over and over in his mind, checking it obsessively for internal consistency as well as its matchup to reality, tearing it to pieces on paper, or during interminable phone calls at two in the morning, or, in the case of the analogy between thermodynamics and tactics—inside a computer.

Boyd hypothesized that a fighter's performance at any combination of altitude and airspeed could be expressed as the sum of its potential and kinetic energies and its ability to change these energy states by maneuvering. With this idea as a point of departure, he thought he could describe how well a fighter could perform at any point in its flight envelope. If the hypothesis were true, the next step would be to compare the performance of different fighters and determine which one was superior to the other at each point in the envelope. Establishing such a global standard of comparison promised two enormous payoffs:

- First, he could compare the flying characteristics of an existing fighter to those of another, say an American F-4 to a Soviet MiG-17, and thereby identify what tactical regions of the flight envelope were most advantageous or dangerous to the friendly pilot.
- Second, he could evolve a design for a truly superior fighter by developing a comprehensive tradeoff process that systematically compared the performance of successive, marginally different designs.

While elegant in its simplicity, and computationally straightforward, Boyd's energy-maneuverability theory was a gargantuan number-cruncher that required millions of calculations. The only way to do these calculations was with a computer, but in the early 1960s computer calculations were slow, computer time was expensive—and Boyd had no budget. Furthermore, the aeronautical engineers were not interested in the inspiration of a dumb fighter pilot with a yukky industrial engineering degree. To make matters even worse, Boyd had no right to design airplanes—he worked at Eglin Air Force Base, Florida, where rednecks tested bombs designed by others, whereas the airplane designers worked at Wright-Patterson Air Force Base in Dayton Ohio, the home of the Wright brothers and the mecca for aeronautical engineering. For a man like Boyd, there was only one thing to do. He concocted a daring plan to steal thousands of hours of computer time by making it appear that the computer was being used for something else.

Much to the dismay of the autocrats at Wright-Pat, the Mad Major's theory of energy-maneuverability (E-M) turned out to be a stunning success. It provided a universal language for translating tactics into engineering specifications and vice versa and revolutionized the way we look at tactics and design fighter airplanes.

Boyd used it to explain why the modern F-4 Phantom performed so poorly when fighting obsolete MiG-17s in Vietnam and went on to devise new tactics for the Phantom—whereupon Air Force pilots began to shoot down more MiGs.

He used it to re-design the F-15, changing it from an 80,000-pound, swing-wing, sluggish behemoth, to a 40,000-pound fixed-wing, high-performance, maneuvering fighter. His crowning glory was his use of the theory to evolve the lightweight fighters that eventually became the YF-16 and YF-17 prototypes—and then to insist that the winner be chosen in the competitive market of a free-play flyoff.

The YF-16, which won, is still the most maneuverable fighter ever designed. The production successors, the not-so-lightweight F-16 (Air Force) and the F/A-18 (the Navy-Marine Corps aircraft that evolved from the YF-17), together with the F-15, dominate the skies today. Naturally, Boyd believed they could have been much better war machines if the bureaucrats had not corrupted their thoroughbred design with so many bells and whistles. Nevertheless, more than any other single person, the Mad Major is responsible for our nation's unsurpassed air superiority, which began in the mid-1970s and continues to this day.

Boyd received the accolades, if not the acceptance, of the aeronautical engineering aristocracy for his pioneering work, and the thanks of the combat pilots who now understood how to fight an F-4 against the more maneuverable MiGs.

The Air Force, being the Air Force, tried to court-martial Boyd for stealing the computer time but it could not come up with the evidence; in the end, investigators found only four hours of stolen time. When confronted, the Mad Major blew cigar smoke in the chief inspector's face and explained calmly how he had stolen the rest. He then showed the inspectors a thick file of letters, which documented how his requests for computer time had been refused repeatedly by the bean counters at Eglin and the autocrats at Wright Patterson. He suggested they call Headquarters, Tactical Air Command, and tell the Commanding General that Boyd was about to be hosed for uncovering better combat tactics.

The inspectors, being inspectors, sensed a debacle and retreated. The bureaucracy, being a bureaucracy, said it had always liked Energy-Maneuverability and awarded Boyd a scientific achievement award and the Legion of Merit.

The Ghetto Colonel

All this was the stuff of legend in 1973 when I met Boyd, who was living modestly with Mary the Saint and their five children in a run-down apartment complex in Northern Virginia. He was well into his third mutation: the Ghetto Colonel. Like Immanuel Kant, he was an austere man of intense rectitude, whose life had become devoted to the study of science, philosophy, and the humanities in a small room. Like Kant, Boyd was obsessed with understanding how the mind creates knowledge, or in modern parlance, how it creates theoretical models of the real world—how new observations make existing theories obsolete, and how the mind replaces old theories with new theories in a never-ending cycle of destruction and creation.

To this end, he devoured books on physics, mathematics, logic, information theory, evolutionary biology, genetics, cognitive psychology, cultural anthropology, sociology, political science, economics. Between 1973 and 1976, he poured his intellectual energy into producing a 16-page double-spaced, type-written paper describing his theory. Entitled "Destruction and Creation," this abstract treatise describes how a dialectical interplay of analysis and synthesis destroys and creates our mental images of the external world. It describes what pressures drive this mental process, and how internal phenomena naturally regulate it in a never-ending dialectic cycle, which takes on the outward manifestations of disorder turning into order, and order turning into disorder.

At the heart of Boyd's theory of knowledge was a natural regulation mechanism that he discovered by unifying for the first time certain aspects of the Incompleteness Theorem of Mathematics and Logic discovered by Kurt Godel, an Austrian mathematician; physicist Werner Heisenberg's Uncertainty Principle; and the Second Law of Thermodynamics. Typically, he did not even try to publish his paper, although he did vet it through many distinguished scientists and mathematicians—none of whom was able to poke any holes in it.

"Destruction and Creation" became the intellectual foundation of his monumental study of competition and conflict—although at the time, he had no idea where his philosophical musings might take him.

Looking back at those four years between 1973 and 1976, I now understand that they were a period of intellectual refueling for the next campaign in Boyd's war against a bureaucratic establishment that had lost sight of its goal. For unlike Immanuel Kant, Boyd worked in the Pentagon, a moral sewer dedicated to using other people's money to feed the predators in the Hobbsean jungle known as the military-industrial-congressional complex.

Viewed from this perspective, the Ghetto Colonel's lifestyle was much more than an aesthetic philosopher's quirk. It was a deliberate choice reflecting that bureaucratic warfare in the Hobbsean jungle had replaced the aerial dogfight as his first love.

Boyd loved a good skunk fight and he played for keeps—instinctively applying Napoleon's dictum of preparing a circumspect defense before unleashing an audacious attack. He built up his defenses by eschewing careerism and materialism, which left the generals and bureaucrats nothing to work on, no opportunity to gain leverage on him, no bait to tempt him into corruption. The Ghetto Colonel became an impenetrable fortress, a bastion of moral power in a way that Mohandas Gandhi would have easily understood. From the perspective of the bureaucracy's authoritarian mentality, however, the man was certifiably insane; even worse, he was completely out of control.

I once asked him why he lived this way. He got in my face, the ever-present cigarillo clenched between his teeth, its hot tip popping up and down a quarter of an inch from my nose, and amidst a gush of suffocating smoke, he explained: "The most important thing in life is to be free to do things. There are only two ways to insure that freedom—you can be rich or you can you reduce your needs to zero. I will never be rich, so I have chosen to crank down my desires. The bureaucracy cannot take anything from me, because there is nothing to take."

This statement went to the core of a puritanical ethos. For the Ghetto Colonel, life revolved around a simple choice: To be or to do? He could be somebody, with all the shallow accoutrements of power and small achievements—high rank, a big office in the Pentagon's E-ring, and a big post-retirement job with a defense contractor—or he could do important things and make a real contribution to society. The Ghetto Colonel was more interested in doing things than in being somebody, so he cranked down his needs. His choice really was very simple and logical, if somewhat bizarre and indecipherable to the inhabitants of Sodom on the Potomac.

I resigned from the Air Force in 1975. Boyd retired a few months later. He stopped smoking cigars, but not before accidentally burning a hole in a general's tie while using one as a pointer. By 1975, his work on Energy-Maneuverability, the F-15, and the Lightweight Fighters had made him the pre-eminent designer on new fighter concepts in America, if not the world. Most people with his kind of resume would have sold out to industry for a high six-figure income. The airplane contractors, in particular, wanted his talents desperately. One even offered me a fat job if I could convince Boyd to come with me. But the Ghetto Colonel had other things on his mind. His refueling operation was over, and he was ready for action. He was about to mutate into "Genghis John," the creator, chief strategist, and spiritual leader of the Military Reform Movement.

Genghis John

The transformation began quite modestly. After he retired, his old friend and partner in crime from the E-M days at Eglin, Thomas Christie, now a senior civilian in the Pentagon, arranged to hire Boyd as a consultant to the Program Analysis and Evaluation Directorate in the Office of the Secretary of Defense. Housed in a small cubicle of room 2C281, the infamous TacAir shop, Boyd worked 50-hour weeks, although he would accept payment for only one day per two-week pay period. He wanted to work for free, and the Ghetto-Colonel lifestyle enabled him to live on his retirement salary, but a minimal stipend was necessary to keep his security clearance current, and more important, to give him unfettered access to telephones and Xerox machines, which in the primitive days before e-mail were the weapons of choice among the small fraternity of reform guerrillas.

Operating out of this tiny cubicle, a man who held no official position used the force of his intellect and character to become, in the words of the Commandant of the Marine Corps, an architect of victory in the War with Iraq. The transformation of the Ghetto Colonel into Genghis John, however, had its origins in an unrelated anomaly.

The paradoxical results of the flyoff between the YF-16 and YF-17 continued to bother Boyd after he retired. The energy-maneuverability calculations predicted a much closer outcome, with the YF-17 theoretically superior in some portions of the flight envelope. But the pilots were unanimous—the F-16 won hands down. To a man of Boyd's mental discipline, test results in the real world had to be the final authority. So something was missing from his theory, but he did not know what.

He questioned the pilots closely, and with their help, he gradually determined that the decisive advantage of the YF-16 rested in flying characteristics like its "buttonhook" turn. When a YF-16 pilot pulled into an increasingly tight turn, the aircraft lost energy faster than did the YF-17. Normally, this would have been a disadvantage. Since the dawn of fighter aviation in 1914, power limitations made this kind of energy-dumping maneuver a desperation tactic. Once the energy was lost, it was difficult, if not impossible, to regain energy quickly enough to continue the dogfight if one was facing a competent adversary. But the high thrust-to-weight ratios of the new fighters changed the tactical nature of energy dumping in a very fundamental way.

The high-powered YF-16 could regain energy very quickly, and although the E-M calculations had led to the high thrust-to-weight designs of the lightweight fighters, the tactical effects of the added power were not fully appreciated during the design stage. During the flyoff, however, the pilots learned by trial and error to take advantage of this power by evolving quick energy-dumping as well as quick energy-pumping tactics. The energy-maneuverability theory could not predict the tactical advantages accruing from such fast-transient maneuvers, and it is a tribute to Boyd's iron discipline and integrity that he uncovered the limitations of the very theory that made him a world-renowned designer.

The discovery of the importance of fast-transient maneuvers, together with his research and writing of "Destruction and Creation" triggered the transformation of the Ghetto Colonel into Genghis John. Strangely, the evolution began with a return to his roots and a new look at F-86 performance in the Korean War.

American fighter pilots achieved roughly a 10:1 kill ratio over their North Korean and Chinese adversaries. Nevertheless, it had long been recognized that the enemy's principal fighter, the MiG-15, could out-turn and out-climb the F-86 in most parts of the flight envelope. Why had American pilots done so well?

The conventional wisdom was that our advantage lay in better-trained pilots, a significant and undeniable fact. Boyd was the first to agree that people always are far more important than hardware in war. He often said "Machines don't fight wars, people do—and they use their minds." Nevertheless, his new appreciation of the tactical benefits of fast-transient maneuvers enabled him to understand how two technical advantages of the F-86 gave the pilot a powerful tactical advantage in a mind-time-space frame of reference.

The first related to visibility. The MiG-15 and F-86 were roughly the same size (the MiG was slightly smaller) and therefore about equally visible at a given distance with perhaps a slight edge going to the MiG. The pilot of the F-86, however, had a high-visibility bubble canopy and could see out of the F-86 much better than his counterpart in the MiG, whose head was confined by a more compact, aerodynamically streamlined canopy. So, in terms of one's ability to observe his adversary, the F-86 had a distinct advantage over the MiG.

In addition, the F-86 had a fully-powered hydraulic flight control system, whereas the MiG had a hydraulically-boosted mechanical system. An F-86 pilot could move the control stick with one finger, but the greater resistance of the control stick in the MiG meant that its pilot had to exert himself physically every time he turned. This difference in control power enabled the pilot of the F-86 to flip from maneuver to another more easily and quickly than his adversary. Moreover, this advantage grew more important as a dogfight continued, because the higher workload on the MiG pilot increased his mental and physical fatigue at an ever-increasing rate.

Putting these two advantages together, Boyd reasoned that a competent pilot in an F-86 could observe more effectively and decide and act more quickly than an equally competent pilot flying a MiG-15. Put simply, an F-86 that was losing the fight—with a MiG about 40 degrees of his tail—could start a turn in one direction, then, as the MiG followed, reverse the turn using the F-86's superior maneuverability. The maneuver might gain the F-86 pilot 10 degrees almost immediately, putting the MiG 50 degrees off. Repeating this maneuver-counter maneuver sequence—often called a scissors—would put the MiG pilot farther and farther out of sequence: relatively quickly, the F-86 pilot would be able to work himself into an advantageous firing position. Add in the decision-making effects of better-trained pilots, and our cumulative advantage in the observation-decision-action cycle permitted the F-86 pilot to operate inside his adversary's mind-time-space frame of reference.

Grasping another of his analogies, Boyd reasoned that the Germans had used their blitzkrieg to penetrate the French mind-time-space frame of reference in

1940. Perhaps his insight applied to ground warfare as well as air combat. Over the 15 years between 1977 and 1992, Boyd became obsessed with expanding his insight in to a general theory of competition and conflict. To this end, he absorbed the writings of great military theorists, like Sun Tzu, Clausewitz, and Jomini. He analyzed campaigns of the master practitioners, like Genghis Khan, Tamerlane, Belisarius, Frederick the Great, Napoleon, Grant, Manstein, T. E. Lawrence, Lettow-Vorbeck, Mao, and Giap. Beginning with the Peleponnesian War, he studied conventional battles and guerrilla warfare.

Boyd did not read books, he devoured them—marking them up, cross-correlating information in the front with information in the back, seeking out contradictions with every turn of the page, gleefully tearing each author's argument to pieces. After only six months, his copy of Clausewitz looked as if it were 100 years old. He never attempted to publish his work, but assembled all his research into a 13-hour briefing called a "Discourse on Winning and Losing." He gave the briefing to enlisted men and generals, congressmen, newspaper reporters, scientists, futurists, academics, anyone who would listen.

He thought that any conflict could be viewed as a duel wherein each adversary observes (O) his opponent's actions, orients (O) himself to the unfolding situation, decides (D) on the most appropriate response or counter-move, then acts (A). The competitor who moves through this OODA-loop cycle the fastest gains an inestimable advantage by disrupting his enemy's ability to respond effectively. He showed in excruciating detail how these cycles create continuous and unpredictable change, and argued that our tactics, strategy, and supporting weapons' technologies should be based on the idea of shaping and adapting to this change—and doing so faster than one's adversary.

While the concept of disrupting an opponent's decision cycle is an old idea in military affairs, Boyd's theory of operating inside an adversary's decision cycle—or OODA loop—and its relationship to conflict is a bold new conception. His strategic aim was to isolate his adversary—physically, mentally, and morally—from his external environment by destroying his view of the world: his orientation. The key to appreciating the power of Boyd's idea is to understand why the orientation function is the door through which a competitor can penetrate his opponent's decision cycle.

Each of us bases our decisions and actions on observations of the outside world that are filtered through mental models that orient us to the opportunities and threats posed by these observations. As Konrad Lonrenz and others have shown, these mental models, which the philosopher of science Thomas Kuhn called paradigms, shape and are shaped by the evolving relationship between the individual organism and its external environment.

In conflict, each participant, from the individual soldier trying to survive to the commander trying to shape strategy, must make decisions based on his orientation to reality—his appreciation of the external circumstances which he must act on. Boyd argued that one's orientation to the external world changes and evolves, because it is formed by a continuous interaction between his observations of unfolding external circumstances and his interior orientation processes that make sense of these circumstances. These interior process take two forms activity: analysis (understanding the observations in the context of pre-existing patterns of knowledge) and synthesis (creating new patterns of knowledge when existing patterns do not permit the understanding needed to cope with novel circumstances).

The synthetic side of the dialectic is crucially important to one's orientation, because it is the process by which the individual (or group) evolves a new world view, if and when one is needed to cope with novel circumstances. But as Kuhn and others have shown, the synthetic process can be extremely painful, because its nature is to build a new paradigm by destroying the existing one. Boyd strove to use multiple, quick-changing destructive thrusts to isolate his adversary from reality by destroying his existing paradigm, and at the same time, deny his adversary the opportunity to synthesize a new paradigm. The combination of menacing pressure and an inability to cope with external circumstances cause the adversary to experience various combinations of uncertainty, doubt, confusion, self-deception, indecision, fear, panic, discouragement, and despair—which, in turn, overload his capacity to adapt or endure.

John Boyd is dead, but his ideas live on. They are cropping up in books, often without proper citation, in subjects ranging from warfare to economic competition to political strategy. Representative Newt Gingrich (R-GA) used them to plot the Republican takeover of Congress. Secretary of Defense Dick Cheney used Boyd's ideas when he overrode the Army's plan and insisted on the famous left hook into Kuwait. But the Marines have paid the retired Colonel the highest compliment. They will dedicate a section of their library at the Marine Corps University at Quantico, Virginia, to a collection of his unpublished papers and research materials.

His intellectual achievements pale beside the moral example he set. He asked for nothing other than the opportunity to contribute. I saw first hand how he passed up riches and status to make his contribution. He put service to truth and country ahead of everything else. He set an example of integrity and morality that is rare in a Washington where the Lincoln bedroom is for sale, the Speaker of the House flunks the ethics test, and the special interests of the defense contractors carry more weight that the needs of our soldiers and the rights of taxpayers—which is why men as different as General Charles Krulak, James Fallows, Colonel David Hackworth, and Senator Charles Grassley went out of their way to pay homage to a great man's passing.

John Boyd always said the choice facing us all is "To Be or To Do." Paradoxically, Genghis John did things—and still ended up being somebody.

Colonel Boyd is survived by his wife, five children, two grandchildren, and—much to the chagrin of the card-carrying members of the military-industrial-congressional complex—a growing number of disciples who are carrying forward his good work.

Franklin Spinney, a former Air Force officer, has worked in the Office of the Secretary of Defense since 1977. He worked closely with Colonel Boyd for more than 23 years.

Fourth Generation War*

William S. Lind

The following is a manual for fighting "4th Generation Warfare" written by a seminar convened by military reformer William S. Lind. The also manual can be found at http://www.d-n-i.net/lind/lind_7_06_05.htm.

DRAFT

FMFM 1-A

Fourth Generation War

Imperial and Royal Austro-Hungarian Marine Corps

August 2005

Introduction

> *"Just as Alexander's exploits only reached the Middle Ages as a dim, fantastic tale, so in the future people will probably look back upon the twentieth century as a period of mighty empires, vast armies and incredible fighting machines that have crumbled into dust. . . . "*
>
> Martin van Creveld, *The Transformation of War*

War Is Changing

War always changes. Our enemies learn and adapt, and we must do the same or lose. But today, war is changing faster and on a larger scale than at any time in

*Reprinted with the permission of the author.

the last 350 years. Not only are we, as Marines, facing rapid change in *how* war is fought, we are facing radical changes in *who* fights and what they are fighting *for*.

All over the world, state militaries, including our own, find themselves fighting *non-state* opponents. This kind of war, which we call Fourth Generation war, is a very difficult challenge. Almost always, state militaries have vast superiority over their non-state opponents in most of what we call "combat power:" technology, weapons, techniques, training, etc. Despite these superiorities, more often than not, state militaries end up losing.

America's greatest military theorist, Air Force Colonel John Boyd, used to say:

> "When I was a young officer, I was taught that if you have air superiority, land superiority and sea superiority, you win. Well, in Vietnam we had air superiority, land superiority and sea superiority, but we lost. So I realized there is something more to it."

This FMFM is about that "something more." In order to fight Fourth Generation war and win, Marines need to understand what that "something more" is. That in turn requires an intellectual framework—a construct that helps us make sense of facts and events, both current and historical.

The intellectual framework put forward in this FMFM is called "The Four Generations of Modern War."[1] It was first laid out in an article in the *Marine Corps Gazette* in October, 1989.[2] In this framework, modern war began with the Peace of Westphalia in 1648 which ended the Thirty Years War. Why? Because with that treaty, the state—which was itself relatively new[3]—established a monopoly on war.

After 1648, first in Europe and then worldwide, war became something waged by states against other states, using state armies and navies (and later air forces). To us, the assumption that war is something waged by states is so automatic that we have difficulty thinking of war in any other way. We sometimes (misleadingly) call war against non-state opponents "Operations Other Than War" (OOTW) or "Stability and Support Operations" (SASO).

In fact, before the Peace of Westphalia, many different entities waged wars. Families waged wars, as did clans and tribes. Ethnic groups and races waged war. Religions and cultures waged war. So did business enterprises and gangs. These wars were often *many-sided*, not two-sided, and alliances shifted constantly.

Not only did many different entities wage war, they used many different means. Few possessed anything we would recognize as a formal army, navy or Marine Corps (Marines were often present, as the fighting men on galleys). Often, when war came, whoever was fighting would hire mercenaries, both on land and at sea. In other cases, such as tribal war, the "army" was any male old enough, but not too old, to carry a weapon. In addition to campaigns and battles, war was waged by bribery, assassination, treachery, betrayal, even dynastic marriage. The lines between "civilian" and "military," and between crime and war, were hazy or non-existent. Many societies knew little internal order or peace; bands of men with weapons, when not hired out for wars, simply took whatever they wanted from anyone too weak to resist them.

Here, the past is prologue. Much of what Marines now face in Fourth Generation wars is simply war as it was fought before the rise of the state and the Peace of Westphalia. Once again, clans, tribes, ethnic groups, cultures, religions and gangs are fighting wars, in more and more parts of the world. They fight using many different means, not just engagements and battles. Once again, conflicts are often many-sided, not just two-sided. Marines who find themselves caught up in such conflicts quickly discover they are difficult to understand and harder still to prevail in.

The Root of the Problem

At the heart of this phenomenon, Fourth Generation war,[4] is not a military but a political, social and moral revolution: a crisis of legitimacy of the state. All over the world, citizens of states are transferring their primary allegiance away from the state to other things: to tribes, ethnic groups, religions, gangs, ideologies and so on. Many people who will no longer fight for their state will fight for their new primary loyalty. In America's two wars with Iraq, the Iraqi state armed forces showed little fight, but Iraqi insurgents whose loyalties are to non-state elements are now waging a hard-fought and effective guerilla war.

The fact that the root of Fourth Generation war is a political, social and moral phenomenon, the decline of the state, *means that there can be no purely military solution to Fourth Generation threats.* Military force is incapable, by itself, of restoring legitimacy to a state. This is especially the case when the military force is foreign; usually, its mere presence will further undermine the legitimacy of the state it is attempting to support. At the same time, Marines will be tasked with fighting Fourth Generation wars. This is not just a problem, it is a dilemma—one of several dilemmas Marines will face in the Fourth Generation.

With this dilemma constantly in view, FMFM 1-A lays out how to fight Fourth Generation war.

Chapter I: Understanding Fourth Generation War

> "*The first, the supreme, the most far-reaching act of judgment that the statesman and commander have to make is to establish ... the kind of war on which they are embarking; neither mistaking it for, nor trying to turn it into something that is alien to its nature.*"
>
> Carl von Clausewitz, *On War*

Before you can fight Fourth Generation war successfully, you have to understand it. Because it is something new (at least in our time), no one understands it completely. It is still evolving, which means our understanding must continue to evolve as well. This chapter lays out *our best current understanding* of the Fourth Generation of Modern War.

Three Levels of War

The three classical levels of war—strategic, operational and tactical—still exist in Fourth Generation war. But all three are affected and to some extent changed by the Fourth Generation. One important change is that while in the first three generations, strategy was the province of generals, the Fourth Generation gives us the "strategic corporal." Especially when video cameras are rolling, a single enlisted Marine may take an action that has strategic effect.

An example comes from the first phase of Operation Iraqi Freedom. U.S. Marines had occupied a Shiite town in southern Iraq. A Marine corporal was leading a patrol through the town when it encountered a funeral procession coming the other way. The corporal ordered his men to stand aside and take their helmets off as a sign of respect. Word of that action quickly spread around town, and it helped the Marines' effort to be welcomed as liberators. That in turn had a strategic impact, because American strategy required keeping Shiite southern Iraq, through which American supply lines had to pass, quiet.[5]

Another change is that all three levels may be local. A Marine unit may have a "beat," much as police do – an area where they are responsible for maintaining order and perhaps delivering other vital services as well. The unit must harmonize its local, tactical actions with higher strategic and operational goals, both of which must be pursued consistently on the local level. (When a unit is assigned a "beat," it is important that the beat's boundaries reflect real local boundaries, such as those between tribes and clans, and not be arbitrary lines drawn on a map at some higher headquarters.)

These changes point to another of the dilemmas that typify Fourth Generation war: what succeeds on the tactical level can easily be counter–productive at the operational and, especially, strategic levels. For example, by using their overwhelming firepower at the tactical level, Marines may in some cases intimidate the local population into fearing them and leaving them alone. But fear and hate are closely related, and if the local population ends up hating us, that works toward our strategic defeat. That is why in Northern Ireland, British troops are not allowed to return fire unless they are actually taking casualties. The Israeli military historian Martin van Creveld argues that one reason the British have not lost in Northern Ireland is that they have taken more casualties than they have inflicted.

Fourth Generation war poses an especially difficult problem to operational art: put simply, it is difficult to operationalize. Often, Fourth Generation opponents' strategic centers of gravity are intangible. They may be things like proving their manhood to their comrades and local women, obeying the commandments of their religion or demonstrating their tribe's bravery to other tribes. Because operational art is the art of focusing tactical actions on enemy strategic centers of gravity, operational art becomes difficult or even impossible in such situations. This was the essence of the Soviet failure in Afghanistan.[6]

The Soviet Army, which focused on operational art, could not operationalize a conflict where the enemy's strategic center of gravity was God. The Soviets were reduced to fighting at the tactical level only, where their army was not very capable, despite its vast technological superiority over the Afghan Mujaheddin.

Fourth Generation war sometimes cuts across all three classical levels of war. An example comes from Colonel John Boyd' s definition of grand strategy, the highest level of war. He defined grand strategy as the art of connecting yourself to as many other independent power centers as possible while isolating your enemies from as many other power centers as possible.

A Fourth Generation conflict will usually have many different independent power centers not only at the grand strategic level but down all the way to the tactical level. The game of connection and isolation will be central to tactics and operational art as well as to strategy and grand strategy. It will be important to ensure that what you are doing at the tactical level does not alienate independent power centers you need to connect with at the operational or strategic levels. Similarly, you will need to be careful not to isolate yourself today from independent power centers you will need to connect to tomorrow.

Again, while the classical three levels of war carry over into the Fourth Generation, they change. We do not yet know all the ways in which they will change when Marines face Fourth Generation opponents. As Marines' experience in Fourth Generation conflicts grows, so must our understanding. It is vital that we remain open to new lessons and not attempt to fit new ways of war into outdated notions.

Three New Levels of War

While the classical three levels of war carry over into the Fourth Generation, they are joined there by three new levels which may be more important. Colonel Boyd identified these three new levels as the physical, the mental and the moral. Further, he argued that the physical level—killing people and breaking things—is the *least* powerful, the moral level is the most powerful and the mental level lies between the other two. Colonel Boyd argued that this is especially true in guerilla warfare, which is more closely related to Fourth Generation war than is formal warfare between state militaries. The history of guerilla warfare, from the Spanish guerilla war against Napoleon through Israel's experience in southern Lebanon, supports Colonel Boyd's observation.

This leads to the *central dilemma* of Fourth Generation war: *what works for you on the physical (and sometimes mental) level often works against you at the moral level.* It is therefore very easy in a Fourth Generation conflict to win all the tactical engagements yet lose the war. To the degree you win at the physical level by pouring on firepower that causes casualties and property damage to the local population, every physical victory may move you closer to moral defeat. And the moral level is decisive.

Some examples from the American experience in Iraq help illustrate the contradiction between the physical and moral levels:

- The U.S. Army conducted many raids on civilian homes in areas it occupied. In these raids, the troops physically dominated the civilians. Mentally, they terrified them. But at the moral level, breaking into private homes in the middle of the night, terrifying women and children and sometimes treating detainees in ways that publicly humiliated them (like stepping on their heads) worked powerfully against the Americans. An enraged population responded by providing the Iraqi resistance with more support at every level of war, physical, mental and moral.
- At Baghdad's Abu Ghraib prison, MPs and interrogators dominated prisoners physically and mentally – as too many photographs attest. But when that domination was publicly exposed, the United States suffered an enormous defeat at the moral level. Some American commanders recognized the power of the moral level when they referred to the soldiers responsible for the abuse as, "the jerks who lost us the war."
- In Iraq and elsewhere, American troops (other than Special Forces) quickly establish base camps that mirror American conditions: air conditioning, good medical care, plenty of food and pure water, etc. The local people are not allowed into the bases except in service roles. Physically, the American superiority over the lives the locals lead is overwhelming. Mentally, it projects the power and success of American society. But morally, the constant message of "we're better than you" works against the Americans. Traditional cultures tend to put high values on pride and honor, and when foreigners seem to sneer at local ways, the locals may respond by defending their honor in a traditional manner— by fighting. In response to the American presence, Fourth Generation war spreads rather than contracts.

The practice of a successful Fourth Generation entity, al Qaeda, offers an interesting contrast. Osama bin Laden, who comes from a wealthy family, lives in a cave. In part, it is for security. But it also reflects a keen understanding of the power of the moral level of war. By sharing the hardships and dangers of his followers, Osama bin Laden draws a sharp contrast at the moral level with the leaders of local states, and also with senior officers in most state armies.

The contradiction between the physical and moral levels of war in Fourth Generation conflicts is similar to the contradiction between the tactical and strategic levels, but the two are not identical. The physical, mental and moral levels all play at each of the other levels—tactical, operational and strategic. Any disharmony among levels creates openings which Fourth Generation opponents will be quick to exploit.

Of course, we can also exploit our opponents' disharmonies. For example, let us say that one of our opponents is a religious grouping. In a town where we have a presence, a local feud results in the killing of a clergyman by members of the same grouping. In itself, this is a minor tactical event. But if we use our own information warfare to focus the public's attention on it, pointing out how the tenets of the religion are not being observed by those who claim to speak for it, we might create a "moral bomb." A physical action would play on the moral level, just as a tactical action would play on a strategic level. Here we see how the classical and new levels of war intersect.

* * *

Fighting Fourth Generation War

"Without changing our patterns of thought, we will not be able to solve the problems we created with our current patterns of thought." Albert Einstein

At this point, you should have some understanding of Fourth Generation war – perhaps as much as anyone, since there is still much to be learned. In this chapter, we will discuss how Marines should fight in Fourth Generation conflicts.

Some Preconditions

In Book Two, chapter two of *On War*, Clausewitz draws an important distinction between preparing for war and the conduct of war. Most of this chapter will be devoted to the conduct of Fourth Generation war. But there are some preconditions that fall under "preparing for war" we must address first. If these preconditions are not met, success is unlikely.

The first precondition is reforming the personnel system. Entire books have been written on how to do this.[7] In general, we need a new personnel system that creates and preserves unit cohesion by stabilizing assignments, eliminates "up or out" promotion (and the careerism it mandates) and significantly reduces the size of the officer corps above the company grades. The latter reform is of central importance for "flattening" our organizations both by reducing the number of headquarters and making those that remain much smaller. Calls for decentralization that do not reduce the number and size of headquarters are empty rhetoric.[8]

The second precondition is that we must have a workable strategy. Field manuals usually do not discuss strategy, but the matter is too important not to discuss briefly. We have already noted that our strategic goals must be realistic; we cannot remake other societies and cultures in our own image. Here, we offer another caution, one related directly to fighting Fourth Generation war: our strategy must not be so misconceived that it provides a primary reason for others to fight us.

Unlike state armed forces, most Fourth Generation entities cannot simply order their men to fight. Most Fourth Generation fighting forces are, in effect, militias. Like other militias throughout history, motivating them to fight is a major challenge. We must ensure that we do not solve that problem for Fourth Generation opponents by adopting a strategy that makes their militiamen *want* to fight us.

What that means to specific situations varies case-to-case. And, the rule of not providing the enemy's motivation applies to operational art and tactics as well as strategy. We emphasize the strategic level here in part because errors at the strategic level cannot be undone by successes at the operational and tactical levels (that is the primary lesson from Germany's defeats in both World Wars), and because states often violate this rule in Fourth Generation conflicts. When they do so, they are defeated.

Fighting Fourth Generation War: Two Models

In fighting Fourth Generation war, there are two basic approaches or models. The first may broadly be called the "de-escalation model," and it is the focus of this FMFM. But there are times where Marines may employ the other model. Reflecting a case where this second model was applied successfully, we refer to it as the "Hama model." The Hama model refers to what Syrian President Hafez al— Assad did to the city of Hama in Syria when a non-state entity there, the Moslem Brotherhood, rebelled against his rule.

In 1982, in Hama, Syria, the Sunni Moslem Brotherhood was gaining strength and was planning on intervening in Syrian politics through violence. The dictator of Syria, Hafez El-Assad, was alerted by his intelligence sources that the Moslem Brotherhood was looking to assassinate various members of the ruling Ba'ath Party. In fact, there is credible evidence that the Moslem Brotherhood was planning on overthrowing the Shiite/Allawite-dominated Ba'ath.

On Feb. 2, 1982, the Syrian Army was deployed into the area surrounding Hama. Within three weeks, the Syrian Army had completely devastated the city of Hama, resulting in the deaths of between 10,000 and 25,000 people, depending on the source. The use of heavy artillery, armored forces and possibly poison gas resulted in large-scale destruction and an end to the Moslem Brotherhood's desires to overthrow the Ba'ath Party and Hafez El-Assad. After the operation was finished, one surviving citizen of Hama stated, "We don't do politics here anymore, we just do religion."

The results of the destruction of Hama were clear to the survivors. As an article in the June 20, 2000 edition of *The Christian Science Monitor* wrote, "Syria has been vilified in the West for the atrocities at Hama. But many Syrians—including a Sunni merchant class that has thrived under Alawite rule—also note that the result has been years of stability."

What distinguishes the Hama model is overwhelming firepower and force, deliberately used to create massive casualties and destruction, *in an action that is over fast.* Speed is of the essence to the Hama model. If a Hama-type operation is allowed to drag out, it will turn into a disaster on the moral level. The objective is to get it over with so fast that the effect desired locally is achieved before anyone else has time to react or, ideally, even to notice what is going on.

This FMFM will devote little attention to the Hama model because situations where Marines will be allowed to employ it will probably be few. Domestic and 'international political considerations will normally rule it out. It might become an option if a Weapon of Mass Destruction were used against us on our own soil.

The main reason we need to identify the Hama model is to note a serious danger facing state armed forces in Fourth Generation situations. It is easy, *but fatal*, to choose a course that lies between the Hama model and the de-escalation model. Such a course inevitably results in defeat, because of the power of weakness.

Historian Martin van Creveld compares a state military that, with its vast superiority in lethality, continually turns its firepower on poorly-equipped Fourth Generation opponents to an adult who administers a prolonged, violent beating to a child in a public place. Regardless of how bad the child has been, every observer sympathizes with the child. Soon, outsiders intervene, and the adult is arrested. The mismatch is so great that the adult's action is judged a crime.[9]

This is what happens to state armed forces that attempt to split the difference between the Hama and de-escalation models. The seemingly endless spectacle of weak opponents and, inevitably, local civilians being killed by the state military's overwhelming power defeats the state at the moral level. That is why the rule for the Hama model is that the violence must be over fast.

Any attempt at a compromise between the two models results in prolonged violence by the state's armed forces, and it is the duration of the mismatch that is fatal. To the degree the state armed forces are also foreign invaders, the state's defeat occurs all the sooner. It occurs both locally and on a world scale. In the 3,000 years that the story of David and Goliath has been told, how many listeners have identified with Goliath?

Generally, the only promising option for Marines will be the de-escalation model. What this means is that when situations threaten to turn violent or actually do so, Marines in Fourth Generation situations will usually focus their efforts on lowering the level of confrontation until it is no longer violent. They will do so on the tactical, operational and strategic levels.

The remainder of this FMFM is devoted to the de-escalation model.

Fighting Fourth Generation War: Less Is More

When the Marine Corps is given a mission to intervene in a Fourth Generation conflict, its first objective must be to keep its own "footprint" as small as possible. This is an important way to minimize the contradiction between the physical and moral levels of war. The smaller our physical presence, the fewer negative effects our presence will have at the moral level. This is true not only for us but for the state we are attempting to buttress against Fourth Generation opponents.

If the situation is such that Marines' presence must be obvious—that is, we cannot limit it in *extent*—another way to minimize our footprint is to limit its *duration*. Therefore, Marines will often attempt to deal with Fourth Generation enemies not by occupying an area, but by conducting punitive expeditions, or raids. These raids will usually be sea-based.

If all else fails, and only then, Marines will invade and occupy another country, usually as part of a joint or combined force. This is the *least desirable* option, because as foreign invaders and occupiers, we are at a severe disadvantage from the outset at the moral level of war.

Preserving the Enemy State

In situations where Marines and the joint or combined force of which they are a part do invade and occupy another country, they will often find it relatively easy to defeat the opposing state and its armed forces. While this is a decisive advantage in wars between states, in Fourth Generation situations it brings with it a serious danger. In a world where the state is growing weaker, our victory can easily destroy the enemy state itself, not merely bring about "regime change."

If this happens, it may prove difficult or impossible for us or for anyone to re-create a state. The result will then be the emergence of another stateless region, which is greatly to the advantage of Fourth Generation entities. As is so easy in the Fourth Generation, we will have lost by winning.

Therefore, we *must learn how to preserve enemy states at the same time that we defeat them*. The specifics will vary according to the situation. But in many situations, the key to preserving the enemy state will be to preserve its armed forces. Here, the revival of an 18th century practice may be helpful: rendering the opposing armed forces the "honors of war." Instead of humiliating them, destroying them physically or, after our victory, disbanding them, we should do them no more damage than the situation requires.

Prisoners should be treated with respect. If they are senior officers, they should be treated as "honored guests," invited to dine with our generals, given the best available quarters (perhaps better than our own), etc. After a truce or armistice, we should praise how well they fought, give them every public mark of respect, and perhaps, through the next government, increase their pay. Throughout the conflict, all our actions should be guided by the goal of enabling and encouraging the armed forces we are fighting to work with us when it is over to preserve the state.

The same is true for civil servants of the enemy state. It is critical that the state bureaucracy continue to function. Again, a quick pay raise may be helpful. When we have to remove senior leaders of the state, the number should be as small as possible. We must be careful not to leave any segments of the enemy's society unrepresented in a new government. And, that government should be headed by local figures, not by someone from another country.

These matters will usually be decided at a level higher than the Marine Corps. But it is essential that senior Marine officers speak forcefully to the political level about the need to preserve the enemy state after it is defeated. If that state disappears, the inevitable strengthening of Fourth Generation forces that will result will fall directly on Marines at the tactical level. Strong words from senior officers early can save many Marine lives later. Offering such advice is part of the moral burden of command.

Fighting Fourth Generation Opponents: Light Infantry Warfare

As Fourth Generation war spreads, it will be inevitable that, even if all the advice offered above is followed, Marines will find themselves fighting Fourth Generation enemies. It is important both for the preparation for war and the conduct of war that Marines know that *Fourth Generation war is above all light infantry warfare.*

As a practical matter, the forces of most of our non-state, Fourth Generation adversaries will be all or mostly irregular light infantry. Few Fourth Generation non-state actors can afford anything else, and irregulars do enjoy some important advantages over conventional forces. They can be difficult to target, especially with air power and artillery. They can avoid stronger but more heavily equipped opponents by using concealment and dispersal (often within the civil population). They can fight an endless war of mines and ambushes. Because irregulars operate within the population and are usually drawn from it, they can solicit popular support or, if unsuccessful, compel popular submission.

Light infantry is the best counter to irregulars because it offers three critical capabilities. First, good light infantry (unless badly outnumbered) can usually defeat almost any force of irregulars it is likely to meet. It can do this in a "man to man" fight that avoids the "Goliath" image. If the light infantry does not load itself too heavily with arms and equipment, it can enjoy the same mobility as the irregulars (enhanced, as necessary by helicopters or attached motor vehicles).

Second, when it uses force, light infantry can be far more discriminating than other combat arms and better avoid collateral damage. This is critically important at both the mental and moral levels.

Third, unlike soldiers who encase themselves in tanks or other armored boxes, fly overhead in tactical aircraft or man far-away artillery pieces or monitoring stations, light infantrymen can show the local population a "human face." They can be courteous and even apologize for their mistakes. They can protect the local people from retaliation by the irregulars, assist with public works projects or help form and train a local defense force.

Marines reading this FMFM may think at this point that we are ahead of the game because we have light infantry in our force structure already. Unfortunately, what we call light infantry is really mechanized and motorized infantry without armored fighting vehicles. It possesses neither the tactical repertoire nor the foot mobility of true light (or Jaeger) infantry. A detailed discussion of the changes required to create a genuine Marine light infantry may be found in appendix B. Here, we will note only that without true light infantry, we will seldom be able to come to grips with the elusive irregulars who will be our opponents in most Fourth Generation conflicts.

"Out-G'ing the G": Lessons from Vietnam

Fourth Generation war is guerilla warfare more than "terrorism." Terrorism is an enemy special operation, a single tactical action designed to have direct operational or strategic effect. Because targets that have such direct operational or strategic effect are few and are usually well-protected, terrorism normally plays a minor role in Fourth Generation conflicts—though when it does occur the effects can be wide-ranging.

Most of what Marines will face in Fourth Generation situations is guerilla warfare. Here, lessons from past guerilla wars, especially Vietnam, remain relevant on the tactical level. Perhaps the most important lesson is that to defeat guerillas, we have to become better at their own game than they are. When Colonel David Hackworth commanded a battalion in the Vietnam War, he called this "out-guerilla'ing the guerilla," or "out-g'ing the G." In his memoirs, *About Face*, he wrote,

"We would no longer be the counterinsurgents who, like actors on a well-lit stage, gave all their secrets away to an unseen, silent and ever-watchful (insurgent) audience in a darkened theater. Instead we would approach the battlefield and the war as our enemy approached it, and in so doing begin to outguerilla the guerilla—"out-G the G,", as I hammered it again and again into the men of the Hardcore (battalion)—and *win*."

"The basic concepts behind my changes were that men, not helicopters or mechanical gimmicks, won battles, and that the only way to defeat the present enemy in the present war at a low cost in friendly casualties was through adopting the enemy's own tactics, i.e., 'out G-ing the G' through surprise, deception, cunning, mobility . . . imagination, and familiarity with the terrain . . . .[10]"

In training a Marine unit for Fourth Generation war, commanders should make use of the extensive literature on guerilla warfare, from the Spanish guerilla war against Napoleon through the present. Field training should be free-play exercises against guerilla opponents (Marine enlisted "aggressors" usually make excellent guerillas) who are allowed to make full use of such typical guerilla tools as mines, booby traps and infiltration of their enemy's rear areas. Guerillas don't do jousts.

Integrating with the Local Population

American-style "Force Protection" is highly disadvantageous in Fourth Generation war, because it seeks security by isolating American troops from the surrounding population. Effectiveness against Fourth Generation opponents demands the opposite: integration with the local populace. Far from making our Marines less secure, integration will improve their security over the long run. The reason is that just as Marines protect the local people, so the local people will protect them.

Perhaps the best example of this symbiotic protection is the traditional British "bobby." The bobby was, until recently, unarmed. The reason he did not need a weapon was that just as he protected the neighborhood, the neighborhood protected him. The bobby had a regular beat, which he patrolled on foot. He came to know every house and its inhabitants, and they came to know him. He became part of the neighborhood. Just as his familiarity with his beat enabled him to see very quickly if anything was out of the ordinary, so the fact that the local people knew him as an individual meant they told him what he needed to know. They did not want any harm to come to "their" bobby.

Marines will not be able to go about unarmed in most Fourth Generation situations. But they can become part of a neighborhood. To do so, they must live in that neighborhood, get to know the people who inhabit it and become known by them in turn. They will usually do so in small groups, squads or even fire teams. To be effective, they must reside in the same neighborhood or village for some time. Results in Fourth Generation war usually come slowly.

American Marines had a program of integration with the local population during the Vietnam War, the CAP program. By all accounts, it was highly effective. Again, Marine commanders should attempt to learn from such past successes as the CAP program and not have to "reinvent the wheel" in each new conflict. The more lessons we can learn from history, the fewer we will have to learn by suffering casualties or failures or both in Fourth Generation situations.

Do Not Escalate: De-escalate

Unless Marines are employing the "Hama model," it will of decisive importance that they manage most confrontations by de–escalating, not by escalating. What does this require?

First, Marines must understand that *much of their training for combat is inappropriate.* In most training, Marines are taught that if they are not getting the result the situation requires, they should escalate. What this means is that Marines' *natural instincts will often be wrong* in Fourth Generation conflicts. They must be conscious of this fact, or those instincts will drive them to escalate, and lose at the moral level.

Second, Marines need to learn from police. There are many police in Marine Reserve units, and it may be advisable to give them leading roles both in training for Fourth Generation war and in dealing with actual Fourth Generation situations.

The most common and most effective tool police use to de-escalate situations is talk. Here, Marines in Fourth Generation wars immediately find themselves at a disadvantage: they do not speak the local language. Nonetheless, they *must develop ways to talk with the local population, including opponents.*

Specific techniques are beyond the scope of a doctrine manual. However, examples include:

- Hiring locals as interpreters. Always remember that locals who work with Marines must survive after we leave, which means they may have to work for both sides. A program where we could offer them a "Green Card" in return for loyal service could prove useful.
- Bringing American citizens who are fluent into the Marine Corps on a lateral-entry, no-boot-camp basis, to provide interpreters whose loyalty we could count on.

- Giving Marines "flash cards" with key words. The cards should include phonetic pronunciations; not all locals will be literate. Also, learn local gestures.

In general, the key to successful communication is patience. Even with no common language, people can often communicate in a variety of ways. What is not useful is resorting to four-letter words screamed in English. Marines have the self-discipline to do better than that.

Perhaps the most important key to de-escalation is simply *not wanting to fight*. In April of 2004, when U.S. Marines ended their first attempt to storm Fallujah in Iraq, the 1st Marine Division's commander, General Mattis, said, "We did not come here to fight." In Fourth Generation situations, that will be true in most encounters Marines have with local people, including many armed Fourth Generation entities. Given the mismatch between Marines and local armed elements, any fighting works to our disadvantage on the all-important moral level. In addition, the disorder fighting inevitably brings works to the advantage of non-state elements.

Marines need to educate and train themselves to develop a mental "switch." When the switch is set for combat with state armed forces, Marines must want to fight. When instead it is set for Fourth Generation situations, Marines must be equally keen not to fight. The second involves risks, as does the first. But the second is just as important as the first, because not wanting to fight is as important to victory in the Fourth Generation as wanting to fight is in the Third. The key, as elsewhere, is Marines' well-known self-discipline.

One part of "not wanting to fight" may prove especially difficult for Marines: in the Fourth Generation, victory may require taking more casualties than you inflict. In most Fourth Generation situations, it is more important not to kill the wrong people that it is to kill armed opponents. This means that even when Marines are under fire, they must discipline themselves to return fire only when they are certain they are firing on armed enemies and on them only. Anytime an innocent person is wounded or killed by Marines, his family and clan members are likely to be required by the local culture to take revenge. When that happens, Marines' opponents get a stream of new recruits.

If Marines are fired on in a situation where it is not clear who is firing or those attacking the Marines are intermixed with the civilian population, the best solution may be to withdraw. Later, we can attempt to engage the enemy on our own terms. We need not "win" every firefight by leaving behind a pile of dead local people. In Fourth Generation conflicts, such "victories" are likely to add up to strategic defeat.

Finally, despite a policy of de-escalation, there will be some situations where Marines do need to escalate. When that happens, we again stress that it must be *over fast*. To return to Martin van Creveld's analogy, an adult can get away with giving a kid one good whack in public. He cannot administer a prolonged beating. Once the escalation terminates, Marines must make every effort to demonstrate that de-escalation remains Marine Corps policy.

Politics Is War, and All Politics Is Local

Clausewitz, writing of war between states, said that "War is the extension of politics by other means." In Fourth Generation situations, the opposite is more likely to be true: politics can be a useful extension of war, one that gives us power but also is consistent with de-escalation.

Nowhere more than in a post-state, Fourth Generation situation is the old saying true, "All politics is local." When the state vanishes, everything becomes local. By understanding and leveraging local political balances, we may be able to attain many objectives without fighting.

A useful model here is the old British Northwest Frontier Agent. The Northwest Frontier was the lawless tribal area between British India and Afghanistan. In this area, the British government was represented by Frontier Agents. These were Englishmen, but they were also men who had lived in the area for a long time and knew the local players and politics well. Their actual power was small— some cash and usually a company of Sepoys, Indian troops. But that small power was often enough to tilt the local political and military balance for or against a local chieftain. The local leaders were aware of this, and they usually found it worth their while to maintain good relations with the British so as to keep them on their side, or at least not actively intervening against them.

Here again, the key is good local intelligence, especially political intelligence. By integrating with the local population, Marines can learn what the local political divisions and alignments are so that they can play on them. Just as with the Northwest Frontier Agents, Marines can leverage relationships to achieve their ends while avoiding fighting.

Your Most Important Supporting Arm: Cash

What artillery and air power are in Third Generation war, cash is in the Fourth Generation: your most useful supporting arm. *Local Marine commanders must have a bottomless "slush fund" of cash to use at their discretion.* Obviously, this cash cannot be subject to normal accounting procedures; most will, necessarily and properly, be used for bribes. Regulations which currently make this difficult or impossible must be changed.

One way to do this might be to establish the billet of "Combat Contracting Officer." The Combat Contracting Officer would have legal authority to pay money as he sees fit in order to support the Marine commander's objectives. This would include payments to get local services operating quickly, support local political leaders who are working with Marines and obtain local resources Marines could use. Again, it would include authority to pay bribes. That is simply how much of the world works, and if Marines are to obtain results they must be able to adjust to the world they find themselves in rather than expecting the world to operate as we would like it to.

The Fourth Generation's Geneva Conventions: Chivalric Codes

While Marines will remain bound by the Geneva Conventions in Fourth Generation conflicts, their opponents will not be. Non-state forces are not party to law between states.

However, in some cases it may be possible to agree with Marines' Fourth Generation opponents on a "chivalric code" that sets rules both sides will follow. Some (not all) Fourth Generation entities have self-images that make honor, generosity, and lineage tracing to "knightly" forebears important to them. Just as chivalry was important before the state, it may again become important after the state. Where these attributes are present, it may be to our advantage (especially on the moral level) to propose a "chivalric code."

The specifics of such a code would vary place-to-place. It might include agreements such as that we will not use air bombardment and they will not set off bombs in areas where civilians are likely to be present. Regardless of the specifics, such codes will generally work to our advantage. They will diminish our "Goliath" image, demonstrate that we respect the local people and their culture, and generally help de-escalate the conflict. They will also assist in improving public order, which in turn helps in preserving or re-creating a local state. Disadvantages such codes may bring to us at the physical level will generally be more than compensated by advantages at the mental and moral levels.

The "Mafia Model": Everyone Gets Their Cut

Just as the Northwest Frontier Agent offers us some useful ideas for Fourth Generation conflicts, so does the "Mafia Model." How would the mafia do an occupation?

One key to a mafia's success is the concealed use of force as well as money as weapons. If an individual needs to be "whacked," then it is usually done with little fanfare and in the shadows. The rule is, "No fingerprints." Unless there is a specific message to be sent out to a larger audience, people who are killed by the Mafia are almost never found. This usually requires patience. It often takes a long time for the right situation to present itself.

If there is a message to be made to a larger audience, then a public display of violence can be used. But this is usually avoided, as it can backfire against the aims and goals of the organization due to public opinion.

The mafia also operates on the principle that "everybody gets his cut." If you are willing to work with the mafia, you get part of the profits. Money is a powerful motivator, especially in the poorer parts of the world where most Fourth Generation conflicts occur. In working with the local population, Marines should carefully design their approach so that everyone who cooperates with them gets a financial reward. The rewards should grow as the "business" expands, that is, as Marines get closer to achieving their objectives. This is also important for leaving a stable situation behind when Marines finally withdraw. If everyone is profiting from the new situation Marines have created, they will be less eager to overturn it and return to instability.

Techniques in Fourth Generation War

In general, techniques have no place in a doctrinal manual because techniques should never be doctrine. Defining techniques as doctrine is a mark of a Second Generation military. In the Third and Fourth Generations, techniques are entirely at the discretion of whoever, regardless of rank, has to get a result. He is responsible only for getting the result, never for employing a set method. That *is* doctrine!

Third Generation militaries also recognize that any technique usually has a short "shelf life" in combat. As soon as the enemy comes to expect it, he turns it against you. This, in turn, means that the ability to invent new techniques is highly important. Units that develop a successful new technique should communicate their discovery laterally to other Marine units. Fourth Generation war makes this all the more important, because Fourth Generation opponents will often use techniques very different from our own. Their "way of war" will reflect their culture, not ours.

Here, we will nonetheless offer a few techniques for Fourth Generation war, *as examples only*. The purpose of doing so is to illustrate the creative thinking that is required for techniques for Fourth Generation conflicts:

- Equip every patrol with a camera. If the patrol is fired on, it attempts to get a picture of those doing the firing. Then, a "contract" is put out on those who can be identified.
- Sponsor a local television program where captured enemies who have killed civilians are interrogated by the local police. This has been highly effective in Iraq.
- Distinguish between captured opponents on the basis of motivation, tribe, religion or some other basis that local people will recognize. Then, treat some as "honored guests" and send them home, while continuing to detain others. This can cause suspicions and divisions among our opponents.

Intelligence in Fourth Generation Warfare

In conventional warfare, intelligence specialists employ an elaborate system of information collection, processing and dissemination called the Intelligence Cycle. Intelligence officers draft complex, multi-level collection plans. They develop and manage detailed enemy force orders of battle, focusing on unit types, sizes, equipment, activities and locations. They "template" enemy forces based primarily on detailed terrain analyses, doctrine and prescribed, generic unit relationships. Personal identities don't matter; except at the highest levels (anonymous) commanders and their units are viewed interchangeably as things to be represented on a map with rectangular symbols. The conventional enemy is viewed as a large, elaborate, depersonalized system of people, equipment and military functions.

As in other areas, intelligence planning, collection, processing and dissemination is hierarchal, driven from the top down. The nature of intelligence is such that it is the most stove-piped and compartmentalized functional area of a military organization. As a result, non-intelligence professionals participate merely as "intelligence customers," to whom the intelligence itself is carefully rationed.

In Fourth Generation warfare, intelligence is fundamentally different. The starting point is the local culture, history and sociology. In a failed or failing state, the "battlefield" is a shifting patchwork quilt of social organizations and power relationships. The social organizations may be based on personalities, family ties, ideologies, religions or commercial enterprises. Trying to mold irregular forces into order of battle "templates" is misleading and minimizes the most important element of understanding your enemy—the human dimension.

Fourth Generation intelligence works exactly opposite of conventional warfare intelligence; its starting point is bottom up. In Fourth Generation war, *every Marine* is an "intelligence professional," operating in an open architecture that shares information freely up and down and laterally. Instead of specialists operating in some elaborate, rule-based, insular system, every Marine is learning from the local population, building networks and using his knowledge of the local situation and culture to plan and execute intelligence collection schemes.

Local information is usually the only information that matters; "intelligence" from higher headquarters is usually too late or too general to be of use. The model is a good beat cop who knows how to effectively interact with the locals, and also recognizes when things are abnormal in the area his beat covers.

The Role of the Reservists in Fourth Generation Warfare

Reservists and National Guardsmen may be better suited to Fourth Generation situations than many regulars. They are, on average, older and better educated than the Active Component Marine. Most are skilled in trades other than warfighting.

Police officers and prison guards are often found in Reserve and National Guard units. The police officer who has walked a beat in any major American city has dealt with gang warfare, illicit drug dealing, gun running and other criminal enterprises. Fourth Generation war does not look much different than the streets of an American ghetto. The level of violence may be more extreme, but many police who serve on SWAT teams in major cities have dealt with more violence in a month than most Marines do in a year.

Reservists often have many skills that can help local people who are looking for American protection. When an Army National Guard infantry captain returned from Iraq in late 2004, he said that "what we needed weren't grunts. There were plenty of them around. We looked for plumbers, carpenters, electricians, masons and anyone who was handy with construction material. When we fixed the plumbing in someone's house in Iraq or rebuilt a wall for them, we knew that we would be safe in their neighborhood, as the Iraqis did not have the knowledge and capabilities themselves and were looking for any help they could get."

The skills needed are not limited to simple tasks. Many Reservists are engineers, doctors, city planners, lawyers or professionals. The skills of each Marine and Army Reservist and National Guardsman should be identified at the battalion level. As a Fourth Generation situation develops, the battalion commander can then assign his Reservists and Guardsmen to tasks that take advantage of their civilian skills.

Fourth Generation War and the Press

Marines can take two different general approaches to the press, defensive or offensive. In the defensive approach, the objective is to minimize bad press by controlling the flow of news. This was typical of how militaries approached the press in Second and Third Generation wars.

The offensive approach seeks to use the press more than to control it, though some control measures may still be in place. Many Fourth Generation entities are highly effective in using the press, including the informal internet press, for their own ends. If Marines do not also undertake a press offensive, they are likely to find themselves ceding to the enemy a battlefield that is important at the mental and moral levels.

In turn, the key to an offensive press strategy is openness. Few members of the press or media such as the internet will allow themselves to be so controlled as to present only the good news about Marines' activities. Unless Marines are open about mistakes and failures, the press will devote most of their effort to ferreting them out. Worse, Marines will lack credibility when they have real good news to present.

Paradoxically, openness is the key to controlling negative information in the few situations where that is really necessary. Sometimes, openness builds such a cooperative relationship with the media that they become part of your team and don't want to report something that will really hurt you. At other times, you can expend the credibility you have built through a general policy of openness to deceive when deception is absolutely necessary. Just remember that when you do so, you may be using your only silver bullet.

Winning at the Mental and Moral Levels

At the mental level, Fourth Generation war turns Clausewitz on his head. Clausewitz wrote

> ... that war is the extension of politics by other means. At the mental level of Fourth Generation war, politics is the extension of war by other means. Not only are all politics local, but everything local is politics.

To win, Marines must learn how to make the local politics work toward the ends they are seeking. If they fail, no military gains will last once Marines depart, as at some point they must. Much of this manual has been devoted to what Marines must do to succeed in the local political environment, including understanding the local culture, integrating with the local population and developing an effective bottom-up intelligence system.

At the most powerful level of war, the moral level, the key to victory is to convince the local people to identify with us, or at least to acquiesce to us, rather than identifying with our enemies. Because we are foreign invaders representing a different culture (and sometimes a different religion), this is a difficult challenge.

Meeting this challenge will depend to a significant degree not on what we do, but on what we do *not* do. We cannot insult and brutalize the local population and simultaneously convince them to identify with us. We cannot represent a threat to their historic culture, religion or way of life. We cannot come across as Goliath, because no one identifies with Goliath. Nor do people identify with Paris, the Trojan champion in the *Iliad*, who fought from a distance (he was an archer) and was therefore a coward.

This does not mean we should be weak, or project an image of weakness. That is also fatal, because in most other cultures, men do not identify with the weak. History is seldom determined by majorities. It is determined by minorities who are willing to fight. In most Fourth Generation situations, the critical "constituency" we must convince to identify with or acquiesce to us is young men of fighting age. To them, we must appear to be strong without offering a challenge to fight that honor requires them to accept. They may identify with an outsider who is strong. They will fight any outsider who humiliates them

In terms of ordinary, day-to-day actions, there is a Golden Rule for winning at the moral level, and it is this: Don't do anything to someone else that, if it were done to you, would make you fight. If you find yourself wondering whether an action will lead more of the local people to fight you, ask yourself if you would fight if someone did the same thing to you. This Golden Rule has a corollary: when you make a mistake and hurt or kill someone you shouldn't or damage or destroy something you shouldn't—and you will—apologize and pay up, fast. Repair and rebuild, quickly, if you can, but never promise to repair or rebuild and then not follow through

This brings us to the bottom line for winning at the moral level: your words and your actions must be consistent. We have deliberately not talked about Psychological Operations (PsyOps) in this manual, because in Fourth Generation war, everything you do is a PsyOp—whether you want it to be or not. No matter what the local population hears you say, they will decide whether to identify with you, acquiesce to you or fight you depending on what you do. Any inconsistency between the two creates gaps your enemies will be quick to exploit.

Keep in mind that Fourth Generation war is also fought on the home front. Our Fourth Generation opponents will attempt to win strategically by pulling our own country apart at the moral level. Contradictions between what Marines say and what they do in the local theater of war will become known at home. There, they will work to fracture public support for the war and generate sympathy for the Fourth Generation forces opposing us. No matter how successful Marines are in the field, if our opponents succeed in pulling us apart at home, we will lose the war.

Conclusion

With the adoption of this manual, the Imperial and Royal Austro-Hungarian Marine Corps officially accepts the Fourth Generation of Modern War as part of our doctrine. This marks progress on the road to ensuring we are preparing for war as it is, not as we might like it to be.

In the 1930s, the U.S. Marine Corps, which was then just beginning to develop amphibious warfare, issued a "Tentative Manual for Landing Operations." In similar fashion, this manual is also tentative. It must be so, because state militaries are only beginning to understand Fourth Generation war. Experience in such conflicts will undoubtedly bring many revisions, some possibly quite large.

Regardless of how our doctrine for Fourth Generation war changes in the future, one characteristic of the Fourth Generation is likely to remain: it will still be very challenging for state armed forces to defeat Fourth Generation enemies. Nothing could be more incorrect than to believe that if Marines just follow what is laid out in this manual—in present or future editions—they will win. The complexities and subtleties of the moral level of war are far too great to permit any such confidence.

It therefore logically follows that we should avoid Fourth Generation wars whenever that is possible. This brings us back to a point we made in our discussion of strategy: senior Marine leaders must be prepared to discuss the risks and uncertainties of Fourth Generation war with civilian decision-makers, *whether their advice is desired or not.*

Another moral burden lies on all Marines, regardless of rank. To assist the Marine Corps and our country to defend effectively against Fourth Generation threats, *we must study war!* A useful way to begin that study is with the "canon," a list of seven books which, read in the correct order, will take the reader from the First Generation of Modern War through the Second and Third Generations and into the Fourth. A short annotated bibliography describing the canon is included in this FMFM as appendix C. Any Marine who is unfamiliar with these works should remedy that deficiency as soon as his other duties permit.

While the canon offers a necessary framework, Marines' study of war ought not end there. Important new works on Fourth Generation war, both books and articles, appear regularly. Marines have a duty to study these as well. And, Marines should contribute their own ideas and observations, based both on study and on personal experiences and observations, to this growing literature.

A prominent American political figure recently wrote, "The real cause of the great upheavals which precede changes of civilizations, such as the fall of the

Roman Empire and the rise of the Arabian Empire, is a profound modification of the ideas of the peoples." That well describes what is now happening in the world Marines must confront. Marines may choose either to be driven by those profound modifications of ideas, or to be agents of change by developing ideas of their own. His Imperial and Royal Majesty, Kaiser Otto, expects his Marines to select the second option.

Viribus Unitis!

Appendix A: The First Three Generations of Modern War

The Chinese military philosopher Sun Tzu said, "He who understands himself and understands his enemy will prevail in one hundred battles." In order to understand both ourselves and our enemies in Fourth Generation conflicts, it is helpful to use the full framework of the Four Generations of modern war. What are the first three generations?

First Generation war was fought with *line and column* tactics. It lasted from the Peace of Westphalia until around the time of the American Civil War. Its importance for us today is that the First Generation battlefield was usually a battlefield of order, and the battlefield of order created a *culture of order* in state militaries. Most of the things that define the difference between "military" and "civilian"—saluting, uniforms, careful gradations of rank, etc.—are products of the First Generation and exist to reinforce a military culture of order. Just as most state militaries are still designed fight other state militaries, so they also continue to embody the First Generation culture of order.

The problem is that, starting around the middle of the 19th century, the order of the battlefield began to break down. In the face of mass armies, nationalism that made soldiers want to fight and technological developments such as the rifled musket, the breechloader, barbed wire and machine guns, the old line and column tactics became suicidal. But as the battlefield became more and more disorderly, state militaries remained locked into a culture of order. The military culture that in the First Generation had been consistent with the battlefield became increasingly contradictory to it. That contradiction is one of the reasons state militaries have so much difficulty in Fourth Generation war, where not only is the battlefield disordered, so is the entire society in which the conflict is taking place.

Second Generation war was developed by the French Army during and after World War I. It dealt with the increasing disorder of the battlefield by attempting to impose order on it. Second Generation war, also sometimes called firepower/attrition warfare, relied on centrally controlled indirect artillery fire, carefully synchronized with infantry, cavalry and aviation, to destroy the enemy by killing his soldiers and blowing up his equipment. The French summarized Second Generation war with the phrase, "The artillery conquers, the infantry occupies."

Second Generation war also preserved the military culture of order. Second Generation militaries *focus inward* on orders, rules, processes and procedures.

There is a "school solution" for every problem. Battles are fought methodically, so prescribed methods drive training and education, where the goal is perfection of detail in execution. The Second Generation military culture, like the First, *values obedience over initiative* (initiative is feared because it disrupts synchronization) and relies on *imposed discipline.*

The United States Army and the U.S. Marine Corps both learned Second Generation war from the French Army during the First World War, and it largely remains the "American way of war" today.

Third Generation war, also called maneuver warfare, was developed by the German Army during World War I. Third Generation war dealt with the disorderly battlefield not by trying to impose order on it but by adapting to disorder and taking advantage of it. Third Generation war relied less on firepower than on speed and tempo. It sought to present the enemy with unexpected and dangerous situations faster than he could cope with them, pulling him apart mentally as well as physically.

The German Army's new Third Generation infantry tactics were the first non-linear tactics. Instead of trying to hold a line in the defense, the object was to draw the enemy in, then cut him off, putting whole enemy units "in the bag." On the offensive, the German "storm-troop tactics" of 1918 flowed like water around enemy strong points, reaching deep into the enemy's rear area and also rolling his forward units up from the flanks and rear. These World War I infantry tactics, when used by armored and mechanized formations in World War II, became known as "Blitzkrieg."

Just as Third Generation war broke with linear tactics, it also broke with the First and Second Generation culture of order. Third Generation militaries *focus outward* on the situation, the enemy, and the result the situation requires. Leaders at every level are expected to get that result, regardless of orders. Military education is designed to develop military judgment, not teach processes or methods, and most training is force-on-force free play because only free play approximates the disorder of combat. Third Generation military culture also *values initiative over obedience,* tolerating mistakes so long as they do not result from timidity, and it relies on *self-discipline* rather than imposed discipline, because only self–discipline is compatible with initiative.

When Second and Third Generation war met in combat in the German campaign against France in 1940, the Second Generation French Army was defeated completely and quickly; the campaign was over in six weeks. Both armies had similar technology, and the French actually had more (and better) tanks. Ideas, not weapons, dictated the outcome.

Despite the fact that Third Generation war proved its decisive superiority more than 60 years ago, most of the world's state armed forces remain Second Generation. The reason is cultural: they cannot make the break with the culture of order that the Third Generation requires. This is another reason why, around the world, state armed forces are not doing well against non-state enemies. Second Generation militaries fight by putting firepower on targets, and Fourth

Generation fighters are very good at making themselves untargetable. Virtually all Fourth Generation forces are free of the First Generation culture of order; they focus outward, they prize initiative and, because they are highly decentralized, they rely on self-discipline. Second Generation state armed forces are largely helpless against them.

Appendix B: The Canon

There are seven books which, read in the order given, will take the reader from the First Generation through the Second, the Third and on into the Fourth. We call them "the canon."

The first book in the canon is C.E. White, *The Enlightened Soldier*. This book explains why you are reading all the other books. It is the story of Scharnhorst, the leader of the Prussian military reform movement of the early 1800s, as a military educator. With other young officers, Scharnhorst realized that if the Prussian army, which had changed little since the time of Frederick the Great, fought Napoleon, it would lose and lose badly. Instead of just waiting for it to happen, he put together a group of officers who thought as he did, the *Militaerische Gesellschaft*, and they worked out a program of reforms for the Prussian army (and state). Prussia's defeat at the battle of Jena opened the door to these reforms, which in turn laid the basis for the German army's development of Third Generation war in the early 20th century.

The next book is Robert Doughty, *The Seeds of Disaster*. This is the definitive history of the development of Second Generation warfare in the French army during and after World War I. This book is in the canon because the U.S. Army and Marine Corps learned modern war from the French, absorbing Second Generation war wholesale (as late as 1930, when the U.S. Army wanted a manual on operational art, it just took the French manual on Grand Tactics, translated it and issued it as its own). *The Seeds of Disaster* is the only book in the canon that is something of a dull read, but it is essential to understanding why the American armed forces act as they do.

The third book, Bruce Gudmundsson's *Stormtroop Tactics*, is the story of the development of Third Generation war in the German army in World War I. It is also a book on how to change an army. Twice during World War I, the Germans pulled their army out of the Western Front unit-by-unit and retrained it in radically new tactics. Those new tactics broke the deadlock of the trenches, even if Germany had to wait for the development of the Panzer divisions to turn tactical success into operational victory.

Book four, Martin Samuels's *Command or Control?*, compares British and German tactical development from the late 19th century through World War I. Its value is the clear distinctions it draws between the Second and Third Generations, distinctions the reader will find useful when looking at the U.S. armed forces today. The British were so firmly attached to the Second Generation—at times, even the First—that German officers who had served on both fronts in World War I often said British troop handling was even worse than Russian. Bruce Gudmundsson argues that in each generation, one Brit is allowed really to understand the Germans. In our generation, Martin Samuels is that Brit.

The fifth book in the canon is again by Robert Doughty, the head of the History Department at West Point and the best American historian of the modern French army: *The Breaking Point*. This is the story of the battle of Sedan in 1940, where Guderian's Panzers crossed the Meuse and then turned and headed for the English Channel in a brilliant example of operational art. Here, the reader sees the Second and Third Generations clash head-on. Why does the Third Generation prevail? Because over and over, at decisive moments the Third Generation Wehrmacht takes initiative (often led by NCOs in doing so) while the French wait for orders. What the French did was often right, but it was always too late.

The sixth book in the canon is Martin van Creveld's *Fighting Power*. While *The Breaking Point* contrasts the Second and Third Generations in combat, *Fighting Power* compares them as institutions. It does so by contrasting the U.S. Army in World War II with the German Wehrmacht. What emerges is a picture of two radically different institutions, each consistent with its doctrine. This book is important because it illustrates why you cannot combine Third Generation, maneuver warfare doctrine with a Second Generation, inward-focused, process-ridden, centralized institution.

The seventh and final book in the canon is Martin van Creveld's, *The Transformation of War*. Easily the most important book on war written in the last quarter-century, *Transformation* lays out the basis of Fourth Generation war, the state's loss of its monopoly on war and on social organization. In the 21st century, as in all centuries up to the rise of the state, many different entities will fight war, for many different reasons, not just *raison d'etat*. Clausewitz's "trinity" of people, government and army vanishes, as the elements disappear or become indistinguishable from one another. Van Creveld subsequently wrote another book, *The Rise and Decline of the State*, which lays out the historical basis of the theory in *Transformation*.

Editor's Note: Send comments on the proposed FMFM 1-A to Bill Lind at pe-hughes@freecongress.org.

This manual was compiled under the direction of SFTT Contributing Editor William S. Lind, a veteran defense policy analyst, who is Director of the Center for Cultural Conservatism at the Free Congress Foundation. He can be reached through the foundation's mailform.

Notes

1. For a description of the first three generations, see Appendix A.
2. Republished with two follow-up pieces in the November, 2001 *Marine Corps Gazette*.
3. Martin van Creveld, *The Rise and Decline of the State* (Cambridge University Press, Cambridge, U.K.; 1999).

4. The Israeli military historian Martin van Creveld calls this kind of war "non-trinitarian warfare," because it does not fit within Clausewitz's trinity of government, army and people where each of those elements is related but distinct.

5. *San Francisco Chronicle*, "Special unit wants to win hearts, minds" by John Koopman (no date available).

6. See Col. Thomas Hammes, The Sling and the Stone

7. See especially *The Path to Victory* by Donald Vandergriff (Presidio Press; Novato, CA; 2002).

8. Another needed personnel reform is changing the way we develop junior officers. The current system is a "sausage factory" based on numbers; officer schools' "missions" are defined in terms of the number of people they graduate, not whether those newly-minted officers are qualified to lead in combat.

Officer education and training for Fourth Generation war must be based on quality, not quantity, at every grade level. The rule should be, "Better no officer than a bad officer." Schools must constantly put students in difficult, unexpected situations, then require them to decide and act under time pressure. Schooling must take students out of their "comfort zones." Stress—mental and moral as well as physical—must be constant. War games, map exercises, and free-play field exercises must constitute bulk of the curriculum. Drill and ceremonies are not important. Higher command levels overseeing officers' schools must look for high drop-out and expulsion rates as signs that the job is being done right. Those officers who successfully pass through the schools must continue to be developed by their commanders; learning cannot stop at the schoolhouse door.

Our Marine Corps takes in high quality people at both the enlisted and officer levels. The problem is what the system then does with them. That system must be changed to give us the imaginative, adaptable, responsibility-seeking officers and Marines Fourth Generation war requires. The current process-focused military education system is an inappropriate holdover from the Second Generation; reforming it must be a top priority.

9. Conversation between Martin van Creveld and William S. Lind, May 2004, Bergen, Norway.

10. Colonel David H. Hackworth, *About Face* (Simon and Schuster, New York, 1989) pp. 679-680.

Suggested Readings

(Note: The suggested readings listed here are not intended to give the reader an overview of military affairs or of military history; they are restricted to the subset of suggested readings on military reform. The comments below for these various entries are the views of coauthor Wheeler.)

Amlie, Thomas S. "Radar: Shield or Target." Special Report, *IEEE Spectrum*, April 1982. A radar expert who also helped to create the non-radar "Sidewinder" heat seeking air-to-air missile, very probably the most effective air to air missile in America's weapon inventory (and that of many others who copied it), Amlie points out in this seminal article that what many think to be a key to effectiveness in military technology (radar) also has many limitations and negative trade-offs. The concept of understanding trade-offs and assessing weapons based strictly on actual combat evidence is a hallmark of the reformers' approach to military technology.

Boyd, John R. *Discourse on Winning and Losing*, unpublished briefing charts, is available in five parts at the www.d-n-i.net Web site. The parts include (1) an introduction and abstract at http://www.d-n-i.net/boyd/pdf/intro.pdf; (2) the central "Patterns of Conflict" briefing at http://www.d-n-i.net/boyd/patterns_ppt.pdf; (3) the "Organic Design for Command and Control" at http://www.d-n-i.net/boyd/pdf/c&c.pdf; (4) a treatise on strategy at http://www.d-n-i.net/boyd/pdf/strategy.pdf; and (5) the "essence of Winning and Losing" at http://www.belisarius.com/modern_business_strategy/boyd/essence/eowl_frameset.htm.

———. *Destruction and Creation*, available at http://www.belisarius.com/modern_business_strategy/boyd/destruction/destruction_and_creation.htm. Col. Boyd steadfastly refused to publish his works, despite multiple offers to do so. The briefing slides to his extraordinary two-day set of briefings (*Discourse on Winning and Losing*) are available at the Web addresses cited above. Much can be gleaned from study of these usually dense, unglamorized slides, but much will also be missing. The Defense and the National Interest and Belisarius Web sites listed for the entries above contain much additional material useful for understanding Boyd's ideas, which some who today use do not understand.

The "Destruction and Creation" essay is the only material generally available today that Boyd wrote after his retirement from the Air Force. It is a good example of the simple lay out and yet profound nature of his thinking.

Burton, James G. *The Pentagon Wars: Reformers Challenge the Old Guard.* Annapolis, MD:Naval Institute Press, Annapolis 1993. Col. Burton describes in extraordinarily painful, sometimes profoundly depressing, detail the lengths to which the Army went on its mission to avoid and subvert rigorous testing of its own Bradley Fighting Vehicle. Burton did succeed in uncovering the vehicle's vulnerabilities to permit him to recommend appropriate modifications, and the Bradley was modified, thus saving uncounted soldiers' lives in the Persian Gulf wars. For this "crime" in the eyes of senior Army commanders, Burton was forced to retire.   '

The book concludes with a penetrating epilogue that explains the Army's failure to end the First Persian Gulf War on terms that obviated the second war against Iraq.

Christie, Thomas. "What Has 35 Years of Acquisition Reform Accomplished?" U.S. Naval Institute Proceedings, February 2006. Based on forty years of experience in the system, Christie explains why the Defense Department's acquisition system has become such a pervasive failure. His observations help to explain why so many "reforms" have changed nothing.

Cockburn, Andrew. *The Threat: Inside the Soviet Military Machine.* Random House, New York 1983. Cockburn's analysis of how the U.S. intelligence community ignored readily available data to assess actual Soviet military capabilities—choosing instead to cooperate with politically directed "threat inflation"—pertains to the bygone era of the cold war. However, the book remains most relevant today for understanding how contemporary threats can remain so poorly understood (and in many cases highly inflated beyond their likely actual capabilities).

———. *Rumsfeld: His Rise, Fall, and Catastrophic Legacy.* Scribner, New York 2007. Cockburn's biography traces not only Rumsfeld's personal career but also thirty-five years of Pentagon history. The author reveals a manager who can only be described as incompetent and focused not on the substance of issues but their politics and their impact on his own career. This is an important volume to understand the nature of the decline of American military prowess—a decline that many deny has occurred.

Coram, Robert. *Boyd: The Fighter Pilot Who Changed the Art of War.* Little, Brown & Co., New York 2002. To those who knew Col. Boyd and understand his ideas, Coram's book is both extraordinarily accurate and the definitive explanation for the layman of Boyd's thinking. Understanding military reform is impossible without understanding Col. Boyd, and understanding Col. Boyd is made possible by Coram's extraordinary book.

There are many today who ape Boyd's ideas without understanding him, even at a superficial level. Coram's eminently readable book should be mandatory reading for all today who talk about "decision cycles," "observation loops," "maneuver warfare," and especially "military reform."

Dupuy, Trevor N. *A Genius for War: The German Army and General Staff, 1807–1945.* Military Book Club, Garden City, NY 1977. There are many books that competently address the organizational concepts and the "styles of warfare" that the Germans adopted beginning in the nineteenth century and that were refined late in World War I and shortly thereafter—thereby laying the basis for the extraordinarily successful "blitzkrieg" form of warfare that Germany's World War II opponents had to attempt to emulate and adapt to in order to win that war. Dupuy's book listed here is one of many that are available.

Fallows, James. *National Defense*. Random House, New York 1981. With this book, the military reformers received their first major national exposure. By simply talking and listening carefully to the core reformers, Fallows produced a volume that accurately articulated their primary concerns and concepts. Now twenty-five years old, it still stands up as a description of the fundamental problems that beset the Pentagon and how to address them.

Fitzgerald, Ernest. *The High Priests of Waste*. Norton, Washington 1972.

————. *The Pentagonists: An Insider's View of Waste, Mismanagement and Fraud in Defense Spending*. Houghton Mifflin, 1989. These two volumes are "Ernie" Fitzgerald's descriptions of the extraordinary obstacles he met when trying to expose waste and fraud in the Pentagon to the Pentagon. As was the case with Col. Burton, for the pains Fitzgerald took to try to fix things, he had to pay with his career—in Fitzgerald's case several times and several ways.

Government Accountability Office (GAO), *Operation Desert Storm: Evaluation of the Air Campaign*. June 1997, U.S. General Accounting Office, GA)/NSIAD-97-134. Not easy-to-read and poorly organized, the appendices to this 200-page analysis of the air campaign of the first Persian Gulf War uses Air Force and Navy data to assess the actual—not hyped—performance of high and low-tech systems in that war. Virtually all of the impressive claims in favor of extraordinary performance of "precision," high-tech systems—and especially of a "revolution in warfare" occurring—were not just unsupported by the facts but refuted. The study found no correlation between high system cost and greater effectiveness. In many cases the lower cost, "low tech" systems were the more effective and the more appropriate.

Hammes, Thomas X. *The Sling and the Stone*. Zenith Press, St. Paul, MN 2004. One of the several quality analyses available on insurgent warfare.

Hammond, Grant T. *The Mind of War: John Boyd and American Security*. Smithsonian Institution Press, Washington 2001. Another biography of John Boyd. Hammond focuses on probing and explaining Boyd's thinking. As the first book length biography of Boyd, it will continue to be important reading to understand his concepts.

Korb, Lawrence J., et al. "Restoring American Military Power: A Progressive Quadrennial Defense Review," Center for American Progress 2006. This alternative to Secretary of Defense Donald Rumsfeld's 2006 "Quadrennial Defense Review" cites various defense programs to both increase and decrease. It aptly represents the thinking of many contemporary mainstream Democrats and other critics of current defense programs and policies.

Lawrence, T.E. *Seven Pillars of Wisdom: A Triumph*. Anchor, New York 1991. A classic description of insurgent warfare. Advocates of "fourth generation warfare" as something entirely new are well advised to review T. E. Lawrence's descriptions of it in the First World War. It is, of course, a form of warfare as old as warfare itself.

Lind, William S. *The Maneuver Warfare Handbook*. Westview Special Studies in Military Affairs, 1985.

Lind, William S., Keith Nightengale, John F. Schmitt, Joseph W. Sutton, and Gary I. Wilson. "The Changing Face of War: Into the Fourth Generation." *The Marines Corps Gazette*, October 1989.

Lind, William S. Unpublished discourse on military doctrine, FMFM 1-A Fourth Generation War, August 2005, available at http://www.d-n-i.net/lind/lind_7_06_05.htm.

Lind, William S. and Gary Hart. *America Can Win: The Case for Military Reform*. Alder & Alder, Bethesda, MD 1986. Over the years, Lind has written on an extraordinary breath of military reform issues. He is a truly original thinker, and reading his work is essential to understanding "military reform." As with any thinkers of his quality, his ideas are sometimes seen as "out there," only to become accepted as conventional wisdom later on—at which point he has moved on to new ideas. Didactic without being boring, his work is very readable.

Macgregor, Douglas. *Breaking the Phalanx: A New Design for Landpower in the Twenty-first Century.* Praeger, Westport, CT 1987.

———. *Transformation Under Fire: Revolutionizing How America Fights.* Praeger, Westport, CT 2003. Another original thinker who paid with his military career for not being a plodder, a yes man, and a careerist, Macgregor is an outspoken critic of low professionalism and poor ethics at the highest levels in the Army. More importantly, he has regularly made constructive change and adapting to changing developments in warfare the major focus of his work.. The abrasiveness of his criticism notwithstanding, many in the Army at senior and lower levels have attempted to adopt important elements of his ideas, but only rarely are they embraced completely or successfully.

Myers, Charles E. "Air Support for Army Maneuver Forces." *Armed Forces Journal*, March 1987.

———. "Littoral Warfare: Back to the Future." *Naval Institute Proceedings*, November 1990. "Chuck" Myers, another of the original "fighter mafia," conducted seminars on what he and the other reformers considered to be the core, if not only meaningful, mission of air forces in warfare: "close air support," or direct support to ground forces in contact with the enemy, the classic mission of the German "Stuka" in World War II and of the USAF A-10 in the wars in the Persian Gulf and Afghanistan. His 1990 article on littoral warfare presages the conflicts we are fighting today.

Rasor, Dina. *More Bucks Less Bang: How the Pentagon Buys Ineffective Weapons.* Bookpeople, New York 1983.

———. *Pentagon Underground.* Crown, New York 1985. With help from some of the core reformers, especially Ernie Fitzgerald and Pierre Sprey, Rasor uncovered horror story after horror story about prodigious Pentagon waste and unbelievably inept, and sometimes corrupt, management. Many of her anecdotes are so horrifying they are difficult to believe, but—sadly—they are all documented and too true.

Riccioni, Everest E. "The B-1B: In Memoriam: There are lessons to be learned from the B-1B." *U.S. Naval Institute Proceedings*, January 1996. One of the original "fighter mafia" that started the reform movement, Col. Riccioni rivals John Boyd as a brilliant and innovative aircraft designer. This article points out the many lessons to be learned from the B-1B bomber program, all of them negative.

Richards, Chester W. *A Swift Elusive Sword: What if Sun Tzu and John Boyd Did a National Defense Review?* Center for Defense Information, Washington, DC 2001.

———. *Certain to Win: The Strategy of John Boyd Applied to Business.* Center for Defense Information, Washington, DC 2004.

———. *Neither Shall the Sword: Conflict in the Years Ahead.* Center for Defense Information, Washington, DC 2006.

———. "Conflict in the Years Ahead." Unpublished briefing slides, 2006, available at http://www.defense-and-society.org/richards/conflict_years_ahead.htm. Col. Richards applies his thorough understanding of John Boyd to various disciplines, including missile defense, fourth generation warfare, and business operations. The briefing, "Conflict in the Years Ahead" is especially noteworthy as it summaries and explains Boyd's various concepts and presentations in the context of "4th Generation Warfare" much as many believe Boyd would explained them himself.

Shay, Jonathan. *Achilles in Vietnam: Combat Trauma and the Undoing of Character.* Scribner, New York 1985.

—. *Odysseus in America: Combat Trauma and the Trials of Homing Home.* Scribner, New York 2003.

Shay explains the human dimension of combat, using examples from the Homeric classics to understand the role and effects of stress. He considers the ways old and new societies deal with stress before, during, and after combat. Given the central role of human factors in understanding—and achieving—winning and losing, Shay's work is especially important.

Spinney, Franklin C. *Defense Facts of Life; The Plans/Reality Mismatch.* Westview Press, Boulder, Co 1985.

—. *Defense Power Games*, available at http://www.d-n-i.net/fcs/def_power_games_98. htm. In addition to the piece Spinney authored in Appendix C, these two publications represent major elements of his ground breaking research, findings, and conclusions. While few have given him credit, many have borrowed extremely heavily from Spinney's research on the problems—so much so that certain elements of Spinney's work from the 1980s constitutes contemporary conventional wisdom. However, virtually none of these borrowers have embraced the recommendations Spinney has made. While Spinney's ideas for reform are firmly grounded in the nature of the problems and are clearly appropriate steps to take, they would also require forceful, uncompromising action in areas, such as spending for hardware and bureaucratic ethics, that would clearly be career limiting to the political animals that dominate in the halls of the Pentagon, the White House, and, of course, Congress. As a result, while so much of Spinney's research on the problems has found many contemporary "fathers," his ideas for taking action remain today "orphans."

Sprey, Pierre M. "The Case for More Effective, Less Expensive Weapon Systems: What 'Quality Versus Quantity' Issue?" In *The Military Reform Debate: Directions for the Defense Establishment for the Remainder of the Century.* United States Military Academy, West Point, NY, June 3–5, 1982, Background Pamphlet.

—. "Land-Based Tactical Aviation." In *Critical Issues: Reforming the Military,* edited by Jeffery G. Barlow. The Heritage Foundation, 1981. Much of Sprey's written work is unpublished but exists in the form of remaining hard copies of briefing slides, with titles such as "What 'Quality vs Quantity' Issue?," "Comparing the Effectiveness of Current Tanks," "Combat Lessons from Lebanon and the Falklands: Is There a Little Wheat under All That Chaff?," and "Letting Combat Results Shape the Next Air-to-Air Missile." Like many of the other core reformers, Sprey has published very little, not from lack of opportunity but from little apparent desire to do so. The articles cited above, his briefing slides, and other materials are now available at www. d-n-i.net, the "Defense and the National Interest" Web site that carries many of the reformers' work.

Stevenson, James. *The Pentagon Paradox: The Development of the F-18 Hornet.* U.S. Naval Institute Press, Annapolis 1993.

—. *The $5 Billion Misunderstanding: The Collapse of the Navy's A-12 Stealth Bomber Program.* U.S. Naval Institute Press, Annapolis 2001. Stevenson's two lengthy treatises address much more than just the history of the aircraft in the titles. He also addresses the concepts behind the reformers' fighter designs and how the aviation bureaucracy in the Pentagon is willing to embrace, instead, poorly conceived fighter and bomber aircraft and then spend untold billions of dollars to bring those bureaucratically and politically driven aircraft concepts to fruition.

Tzu, Sun. *The Art of War.* Edited, translated, and with an Introduction by John Minford. Penguin Books, London 2002. Much more so than Clausewitz's "On War," Sun Tzu's classic, "The Art of War," articulates ideas about strategy and conflict that many of the reformers embraced and expanded upon.

van Creveld, Martin. *Fighting Power: German and U.S. Army Performance, 1939–1945.* Greenwood Press, Westport, CT 1982.

———. *Technology and War: From 2000 BC to the Present.* The Free Press, New York 1989.

———. *The Transformation of War.* The Free Press, New York, 1991. From his specific analysis of what made German ground combat units more effective, man for man, than American units in World War II to his more generalized discussions of weapons and warfare itself, van Creveld argues a uniquely well informed and perceptive point of view.

Vandergriff, Donald. *Spirit, Blood and Treasure.* Presidio Press, 2001.

———. *The Path to Victory: America's Army and the Revolution in Human Affairs.* Presidio Press, Novato, CA 2002. Yet another officer who paid with his career for offering data and analysis that made it painfully obvious the U.S. armed forces—in his case, the Army—must radically alter themselves to succeed in warfare in the modern age, Vandergriff seeks to move personnel policy, and especially military training and education, out of sterile, industrial age concepts into an understanding of the human dynamics that translate directly to success in many forms of conflict.

Wheeler, Winslow T. *The Wastrels of Defense: How Congress Sabotages US Security.* U.S. Naval Institute Press, Annapolis 2004. Coauthor Wheeler describes the high- and low-lights of his thirty-year career on Capitol Hill to assess what makes Congress tick on national security issues.

Wilson, George. *This War Really Matters: Inside the Fight for Defense Dollars.* Congressional Quarterly Press, Washington 2000.

———. *Mud Soldiers; Life Inside the New American Army.* Collier Books, New York 1991.

———. *Supercarrier: An Inside Account of Life Aboard the World's Most Powerful Ship, the US John F. Kennedy.* Berkeley Publishing Group Reissue, 1992. A veteran defense journalist of at least forty years, Wilson takes the reader inside the armed forces and the Pentagon for an unvarnished look at military affairs from the literal ground level up to the heights (rather depths) of Pentagon politics.

Index

About the Authors

WINSLOW T. WHEELER worked on national security issues for thirty-one years for members of the U.S. Senate and for the U.S. General Accounting Office (GAO). In the Senate, Wheeler worked for Jacob K. Javits (R, NY), Nancy L. Kassebaum (R, KS), David Pryor (D, AR), and Pete V. Domenici (R, NM). He was the first, and according to Senate records, the last Senate staffer to work simultaneously on the personal staffs of a Republican and a Democrat (Senators Pryor and Kassebaum). In the Senate, Wheeler worked on congressional measures, such as the War Powers Act, Pentagon reform bills, foreign air and arms control legislation, and the defense budget. At GAO, Wheeler directed comprehensive studies of the U.S. strategic triad and the air campaign of Operation Desert Storm. After Wheeler left Capitol Hill in 2002, he joined the Center for Defense Information as the Director of its Straus Military Reform Project. There, he wrote a book on Congress and national security (*The Wastrels of Defense*) and essays, articles, and commentaries on various defense issues.

LAWRENCE J. KORB is a Senior Fellow at the Center for American Progress and a Senior Adviser to the Center for Defense Information. Prior to joining the Center, he was a Senior Fellow and Director of National Security Studies at the Council on Foreign Relations. From July 1998 to October 2002, he was Council Vice President, Director of Studies, and holder of the Maurice Greenberg Chair. Prior to joining the Council, Mr. Korb served as Director of the Center for Public Policy Education and Senior Fellow in the Foreign Policy Studies Program at the Brookings Institution, Dean of the Graduate School of Public and International Affairs at the University of Pittsburgh, and Vice President of Corporate Operations at the Raytheon Company.

Printed and bound by CPI Group (UK) Ltd, Croydon, CR0 4YY

13/04/2025

14656449-0002